Osborne Gordon.

A MEMOIR:

WITH

A SELECTION OF HIS WRITINGS.

EDITED BY

GEO. MARSHALL, M.A.

RECTOR OF MILTON, BERKS, AND RURAL DEAN OF ABINGDON;
SOMETIME STUDENT OF CHRIST CHURCH.

WITH MEDALLION PORTRAIT.

Parker and Co

OXFORD, AND 6 SOUTHAMPTON-STREET,
STRAND, LONDON.

1885.

Printing Statement:

Due to the very old age and scarcity of this book,
many of the pages may be hard to read due to the
blurring of the original text, possible missing pages,
missing text, dark backgrounds and other issues
beyond our control.

Because this is such an important and rare work, we
believe it is best to reproduce this book regardless of
its original condition.

Thank you for your understanding.

INTRODUCTORY NOTICE.

THE family of the late Osborne Gordon avail themselves of this opportunity to express their grateful sense of the respect shewn to his memory.

The monument erected to him in the Cathedral
Cloister of Christ Church, executed by Mr. Conrad
Dressler, admirable in itself, has a further value, as
indicating the wide-spread sympathy, extending to
Royalty itself, in which it originated. His friends
are under especial obligations to the Dean and Chapter of Christ Church, to whose hearty co-operation
the successful completion of the memorial is mainly
due.

But they have also to offer their warmest acknow-
ledgments to the Lord Bishop of the Diocese, the
Lord Bishop of Manchester, the very Rev. the Dean
of Winchester, the Archdeacons of Berks and Maid-
stone; to the Rt. Hon. Sir J. R. Mowbray, the Rt.
Hon. Sir Michael Hicks-Beach, Sir R. Harington,
Col. H. B. N. Lane, J. Ruskin, J. G. Talbot, M.P.,
H. W. Fisher, Esqrs., the Revs. Canon Hill, R. Godfrey Faussett, T. Vere Bayne, H. L. Thompson, E.
F. Sampson, R. St. John Tyrwhitt, and to all those
noblemen and gentlemen who so cordially seconded
the proposed scheme.

As regards the account of Mr. Gordon's life, the
sources from which it is derived will be in many

cases sufficiently apparent. But his family desire to place upon record their further obligations on this head to the Rt. Hon. G. O. Trevelyan, late Chief Secretary for Ireland, Sir R. R. W. Lingen, K.C.B.; to the Rev. Dr. Liddon, for much valuable advice and suggestion; to his life-long friends the Rev. Prebendary Pulling, J. M. Lakin, and Joshua Bennett; to his friends of later date, the Rev. Geo. Gaisford, T. C. Barker, R. G. Whynyates, Professor H. B. Leech; and to C. F. Hawker, Esq., and Mr. Dougal of East Hampstead, for information upon many interesting particulars. His family would not have so many debts of gratitude to acknowledge had not so many been forward to help.

The Memorial at East Hampstead, with an inscription by Mr. Ruskin, has been carried out with no less success, and upon no smaller a scale, than that at Christ Church: to be followed, it is hoped, at no distant day, by a work for the benefit of the rapidly increasing population of the parish, which the late Rector had greatly at heart, and for which his successor, the Rev. Herbert Salwey, is equally solicitous.

For all the good offices and kindly sympathy which have abounded to do honour to a name so dear to them, the friends of Osborne Gordon beg once more to tender their respectful thanks.

Subjoined are the Inscriptions upon the two Monuments.

(*a.*) At Christ Church :—

M. S.

Osborne Gordon, S. T. B. hac in Æde
primum Alumni, deinde Tutoris ac Censoris,
Postea Easthampstediæ in agro Berch. Rectoris;
In Conc. Hebdomadale denuo constitutum
Inter primos electi,
Et VIIviris rei Academicæ ordinandæ
Quinto ante obitum anno adscripti.
Natus Aprilis 21, 1813, obiit Maij 25, 1883.
Ingenium illi acre subtile facetum facile,
Singularis itidem morum benignitas,
Adeo ut quicquid susciperet agendum,
Sive studia Academica,
Sive Parochiæ agrestis curam,
Omnia prospere cesserint,
Omnesque sibi cum æquales tum discipulos
Amicitia devinxerit.

———

Vivas in Christo, desideratissime!

———

Hoc monimentum P. C. amici moerentes.

(*b.*) At East Hampstead :—

THIS WINDOW AND MOSAIC PAVEMENT ARE DEDICATED
TO GOD'S PRAISE
IN LOVING MEMORY OF HIS SERVANT
OSBORNE GORDON, B.D.
STUDENT AND CENSOR OF CH. CH., OXFORD,
RECTOR OF THIS PARISH
FROM 1860 TO 1883.
AN ENGLISHMAN OF THE OLDEN TIME,
HUMANE WITHOUT WEAKNESS,
LEARNED WITHOUT OSTENTATION,
WITTY WITHOUT MALICE, WISE WITHOUT PRIDE,
HONEST OF HEART, LOFTY OF THOUGHT.
DEAR TO HIS FELLOW MEN AND DUTIFUL TO HIS GOD.
WHEN HIS FRIENDS SHALL ALSO BE DEPARTED,
AND CAN NO MORE CHERISH HIS MEMORY,
BE IT REVERED BY THE STRANGER.

J. RUSKIN.

SOME NOTICE OF THE LIFE

OF THE LATE

REV. OSBORNE GORDON, B.D.

RECTOR OF EAST HAMPSTEAD, BERKS.

OSBORNE GORDON was born April 21, 1813, at
Broseley, Salop, of George Osborne Gordon and
Elizabeth, his wife. His early education was at
Bridgnorth School, then enjoying a high and deserved reputation under the late Dr. Rowley. From
Bridgnorth he was elected as a Careswell Exhi-
bitioner to Christ Church, Oxford, in the summer of
1832, and came into residence Lent Term, 1833. In
1835 he gained the Ireland University Scholarship,
and in Easter Term, 1836, he was placed in the First
Class, both in Classics and Mathematics; the late
Professor Donkin sharing with him that enviable
distinction.

The following sketch of his School and College life
is from the pen of Sir R. R. Lingen, and will be read
with interest and delight by a wide circle beyond
Mr. Gordon's personal friends, from the vivid picture
which it presents of Oxford, as it was more than
a generation ago.

"Osborne Gordon passed the examination for his
B.A. degree at Easter, 1836, in the First Class both
of Classics and Mathematics. He obtained the Ire-

B

land Scholarship in 1835, and must have left the
Bridgnorth Grammar School towards the end of
1831 or early in 1832. I went to Bridgnorth at
the beginning of 1831, just before completing the
twelfth year of my age. He was at that time head
of the school, and I do not remember ever to have
spoken to him before he left. I have, however, a distinct recollection of his appearance at that time, and
I never knew any one whose appearance altered so
little in the course of half a century—the long, thick,
soft, and dark hair, the refined features, and the
large expressive eyes, the look rather absent[a] and
dreamy when at rest, but always with a lurking
mockery about it, instantly called by occasion into
characteristic and witty comments, — the rather
sauntering gait, the head somewhat on one side, and

---

[a] In illustration of this remark it may perhaps be allowable to
refer to an incident not otherwise worth recording, than as it
recalls the genial and kindly humour of a Prelate whom we have
lately lost, and whom those that had the honour of his acquaintance will never cease to remember with affection and respect.
Before the restoration of the Chapter-house of Christ Church under
the present Dean, which has added so much to the beauty and
harmony of the Cathedral Precincts, it was the custom for
the Dean and Chapter to entertain Students and other members
of Christ Church in the Chapter-house, especially before an ad-
journment to Hall to hear the Censors deliver their annual speeches.
It was usual before the company separated to drink the health of
the "Absent Canons;" and on a particular occasion the toast was
duly proposed, but Gordon, who was in the clouds and utterly ob-
livious of all sublunary things, took no notice; upon which
Dr. Jacobson, then Regius Professor of Divinity, who was sitting
near, turned to his next neighbour with his good-natured laugh—
"It should be the Absent Students."

the hand somewhat raised,—these traits, which I have retained from long knowledge of him, pass back also into my earliest memories.

"His reputation in my then part of the school was that of a genius who could dispense with work, and who occupied an unapproachable position of his own.

"This impression was immensely confirmed when he obtained the Ireland Scholarship, the news of which, something strange in those days for a country Grammar School, produced an effect among masters and boys which even now makes me smile to think of, and which was only possible in that remote quarter and in those unsophisticated times [b].

"Then, stroke on stroke, came the double-first, which, according to the local tradition, he obtained after being idle for the greater part of his under-graduate's career, and then working for a fabulous number of hours daily in the last year, especially towards the end of it, when the less critical spirits spoke of sixteen hours out of the twenty-four.

"Whatever be the historic worth of such details, they are proofs of the judgment of contemporaries. Meanwhile, as his home was not far from Bridgnorth, he was occasionally at the school during vacations; in the course of which visits I naturally, as now an

---

[b] Some future chronicler may perhaps describe the sensation created at Bridgnorth subsequently by Sir R. Lingen's own success, in obtaining not only the Ireland, but also the Latin University Scholarship, founded since Mr. Gordon's time, a First Class in Classics, and a Fellowship of Balliol, in addition to the Scholarship at Trinity alluded to in the text. His later distinctions are known to the world.

older boy, became better acquainted with him, having already learnt, from his exercises in the old 'ex' books, into which the more approved specimens were allowed to be copied, *honoris causá*, by the authors, how strong and admirable a scholar he was, both in matter and form.

"I went up to Oxford myself to try for one of the Trinity Scholarships in May, 1837—how different an Oxford from the present—the old 'Tantivy,' with its appropriate air on the guard's key-bugle, its perfect team, and the travellers all white with the dust of Long Compton and Enstone, trotting rapidly along the beautiful avenue that then led up St. Giles's. To this day, though I have travelled a good deal since, I hardly retain an impression of such beauty.

"I was booked to Osborne Gordon's rooms at Christ Church, and great was my comfort at being thus able to connect the surprisingly new world about me with an old experience, which his genuine kindness made all the more real. The youngsters of these days would hardly believe how little the generality of boys, who did not belong to rich families, had travelled fifty years ago. All changes of place, therefore, were much stranger than they are now. I remember exactly my reception by Osborne Gordon, and his anxiety lest a violent bleeding of the nose, with which I was seized almost as soon as I entered his room, should interfere with my chances at the examination which began next day.

"At critical moments of life, the impressions received of kindness or the reverse never fade: and this scene is as present to me now as when it happened.

"Being myself obliged to work very hard at Oxford, and Osborne Gordon having his own duties to perform in another college, I did not see more of him than in the ordinary way of intercourse between friends during the four years I passed at Oxford, and from out of that period I retain no recollections but such as are part of my general impression of him formed during all the time I knew him.

"In later life I have been at his Rectory, in Easthampstead, and have served with him on public enquiries.

"On all and every occasion he was the same man, never making professions himself, and no great admirer of many who did, but never failing to do vigorously, punctually, and completely, whatever fell to himself to do.

"It was the same thing in Scholarships as in affairs. No one knew better than he, or could more humourously illustrate with instances, the difference between exactly construing a classic and talking about him, however beautifully, without that precedent condition.

"I do not know that he ever gave any great attention to philology; in real grasp of Greek and Latin, whether to discover the meaning of others, or to express his own, in those languages, in prose or in verse, I know of no one to put before him, and I doubt whether he will have many successors.

"For authorship he seems to have cared but little. It seems strange that I should not possess a line of his in Greek or Latin. But the turn of his mind was decidedly practical, leading him, when he had once mastered a subject, not to dwell upon it, except for use. So, when he got down to his living, twenty or more years ago, he did not betake himself to learned leisure, but to the work of his parish, to the rebuilding of his church, to the farming of his glebe, and to the society of his neighbours, in a favourite neighbourhood, to whom his keen insight into men, and his playful but always kindly wit, could not but make him acceptable; among them were the late Sir William Hayter, and the late Mr. Delane. 'Our parson can preach,' said his admiring Churchwarden, who proposed his health at a local celebration, 'and he can farm.' "

Let me supplement this sketch of his school-life with the following particulars most kindly communicated by his old friend and schoolfellow, the Rev. J. M. Lakin, Rector of Brooksby, Leicestershire.

"Osborne Gordon was a few years my senior, and at school, in consequence, was rather, for his marvellous ability, my admiration at a distance than my companion. All who remember Gordon as a boy will recollect how he seemed always to have time to help a poor youngster, often an idle one like myself, alas! over a difficulty in getting up a lesson, and how, without appearing ever to be at work, he was always ready for class, and always able to do brilliantly what others, whom I could name, worked hard to do, and only in a dull and clumsy way succeeded in doing.

"Being of a singularly spare and weakly frame, Gordon was never distinguished in the play-field, and an accident which resulted in a permanent stiffness of his right elbow incapacitated him for the active exercises of young men, when he had ceased to be a boy. He was fond of riding, but seldom, if ever, wasted time and money, as some of us remember, with little satisfaction, we were wont to do, in the hunting-field. At Oxford I saw but little of Gordon, as he was leaving soon after my college life began, but he was always very specially friendly and genial with old Bridgnorthians."

The Bishop of Manchester, an old and intimate friend, to whom Mr. Gordon was strongly attached, shews his appreciation of the man in the following terms :—

"I often used to regret that with his rare powers, partly from perhaps a natural indolence, and partly because from the fear of seeming ostentatious, he so seldom seemed to care to put out those powers to their best advantage, he was likely to leave so little behind him which would give another generation any idea of what his real mark and capacity were. I have seldom met an abler man : so full of common sense; of a power to grasp things in their reality; of a dry and caustic, but never ill-natured, humour; in his solemn moments of deep and earnest feeling; and of a high appreciation of what was noble, genuine, and true."

It is in the hope of doing away in some degree the ground for regret which the Bishop has expressed that the present publication has been undertaken.

These, it may be said, are the utterances of partial, though discriminating and judicious, friends; but it will be shewn presently what impression he produced upon men who were comparatively strangers to him; and the Press, which has little space or time to spare for men whose names are not familiar to the public ear, found room for him.

The "Times" bestowed two obituary notices upon him, the second of which we print entire, as expressing the judgment which a well-informed critic would be apt to pass upon a man of established reputation, whose merits had already become, in some degree, matter of tradition. But besides his accomplished Scholarship, acknowledged on all hands, there is a trait of character which every notice, whether public or private, equally recognizes. All give him credit for possessing a ready and searching wit: and also for rare forbearance in the exercise of that dangerous gift. He was never at a loss, never disconcerted; always equal to the occasion, whether he was addressing an Academical or a London audience, or an agricultural meeting. But whatever subject called him forth he adorned what he touched upon by the flashes of his wit, without irritation to the most sensitive nerves.

"The Rev. Osborne Gordon, of whom a brief obituary notice appeared in *The Times* of this morning, had passed away from more immediate personal relations with the University for so long a time that in a place so proverbially full of changes those who remember him are in a minority, and even their recollections of him have become general and somewhat listless. And yet in his day Osborne Gordon was a man of much mark in the academical world—a distinguished double-first class man, a brilliant Ireland Scholar, a redoubted Tutor and Censor of Christ Church, a member from the first of the new Hebdomadal Council which replaced the old Board of Heads in the government of the University—the position he occupied and the abilities he possessed placed him in the first rank of Oxford notabilities a quarter of a century ago. He was a sound Greek scholar, and we are reminded of the vigour with which he would extemporize the translation of an ode of Pindar. He was an elegant Latinist, and the tradition survives in Christ Church of the scholarly, facile, clear, intelligible speeches which in his capacity of Censor he had from time to time to deliver in the College Hall. He was a writer of vigorous English, and as a clear and clever draftsman was of great service to the Tutors' Association—a body with which originated many suggestions for the more important educational changes of modern Oxford. He was of most retentive memory, and pungent but not unkindly wit. Stories and epigrams are still afloat in Oxford attributed to him till they shall be assigned to some later humourist. Among his Christ Church pupils were many men distinguished in after life—Lord Salisbury, Lord Harrowby, Sir Michael Hicks-Beach, Mr. Ward Hunt, Mr. Ruskin. To have distinguished pupils is an accident, but to possess their esteem bespeaks merit. He had, however, one failing, if failing it was, to which the very brilliancy and facility of his powers contributed. He was of a temper essentially averse to exertion. He did, and did admirably, whatever he was called upon to do. But he did it without effort, and the exertion involved in what is considered a successful career would have been repugnant to him. In spite of certain eccentricities, which perhaps grew upon him in later life, as was becoming to a college don, he might have commanded success in any career. But he preferred to exercise over his little world an easy and good-natured despotism, tempered with his own epigrams, and to be the soul of common-room life, with its genial humours and local witticisms. Had he been a more ambitious man he might easily have climbed, for he was a sound and moderate Churchman, troubling himself, as we believe, less with dogma than with practice, and a Tory of the deepest hue. He was one of those most valuable men who can write books but do not; who are universally accounted by those who know them capable of the greatest things, but are content with the place in which they find themselves, the work which they perform without trouble, and the career which is its own reward. The College living which Mr. Gordon held for more than 20 years is an illustration of the versatility of his abilities, where he shewed that the career of a college don is compatible with being an esteemed parish priest, a vigorous church restorer, and a welcome neighbour. His connexion with Oxford had been for many years of the slightest, until he was put by Lord Salisbury upon the University Commission in succession to Mr. Justice Grove. At the meetings of this body he was a constant attendant both in Oxford and London, and rendered much valuable assistance in many departments of their work. Mr. Osborne Gordon is to be buried at Easthampstead on Wednesday at 1 o'clock."

The " Daily Telegraph," in a very generous sketch of Mr. Gordon's character, drew public attention once more to an epigram which did much to create his reputation. Apart from its connexion with him, the article in question is of too much interest in itself to be passed over.

" By the death of the Rev. Osborne Gordon, in his 69th year, Oxford has lost one of its most brilliant scholars, and the neighbourhood of Bracknell, in Berks, one of its most popular and respected inhabitants. Born at Broseley, in Shropshire, and educated at its Grammar School, Mr. Gordon did not achieve the feat accomplished by Mr. Brancker of Wadham College, who went up to Oxford from the famous school at Shrewsbury, when Dr. Butler presided over it, and in 1831 won Dean Ireland's Scholarship in a jacket. Nevertheless Mr. Brancker's performance was well-nigh equalled by that of Mr. Gordon, who won the Ireland in 1834, when he had been a little more than a twelvemonth in residence. Since the establishment, in 1825, of the Ireland Scholarship, in which year Mr. Herman Merivale, Scholar of Trinity and Fellow of Balliol, was successful against a strong field of competitors, there has been no lack of exquisite Greek Compositions, original and translated, which have emanated from Ireland Scholars. We risk little, however, in saying that nothing more perfect in expression or touching in sentiment has been written during this century, either at Oxford or Cambridge, than Mr. Gordon's eight lines in Doric Greek 'upon Sir F. Chantrey's monument to two children in Lichfield Cathedral,' which secured for him the Ireland Scholarship in 1834.

"Unlike Mr. Brancker, who got no more than a second class in classics, Mr. Gordon followed up his Ireland victory by taking a brilliant double-first in classics and mathematics. He subsequently became Censor of Christ Church and tutor to many generations of Christ Church men, among whom three members of the present Ministry—Lord Kimberley, Lord Northbrook, and Mr. Dodson—were included. Mr. Gordon was in the habit of saying that no more promising and admirable scholar ever passed through his hands than the late Marquis of Lothian[c]. Upon the death of Dean Gaisford, Mr. Gordon accepted the Christ Church Living of Easthampstead, near Bracknell, where he built a new rectory-house, and long dispensed what Lord Claren-

[c] To the members of the present Cabinet mentioned above as Mr. Gordon's pupils should be added the name of Lord Carlingford, Lord President of the Council.

don would have called a 'flowing hospitality' to his many friends. Remarkable for his witty and incisive conversation, Mr. Gordon leaves a gap in the circle of those who knew him best which is little likely to be filled. Although he had served on many University Commissions, Mr. Gordon was firmly of opinion that, however reformed and tinkered at, the Oxford of the future would produce no such men as the Oxford of the past. His loss will be lamented far and wide, and by none more than by his old and intimate friend, Mr. John Ruskin."

"The eight lines in Doric Greek," which have become classical, have already been made a mark for criticism, and shew the difficulty of determining any literary question even belonging to our own generation. Doric, there is little doubt, was the original dress of this famous Epigram. But Mr. Linwood, in his *Anthol. Oxon.*, has introduced some Ionic forms, whether with or without the author's sanction is uncertain.

Those who are best acquainted with the two scholars think it probable that Mr. Linwood, who had unbounded confidence in his own critical judgment, made the change to suit his own taste, and that Mr. Gordon, in his careless way, let it pass, as a matter of little consequence. Subjoined is the Epigram according to Mr. Linwood :—

"(1.) On Sir F. Chantrey's Monument to Two Children in Lichfield Cathedral.

Ἁ ΜΟΙΡ' ἁ κρυερὰ τὼ καλὼ παῖδ' Ἀφροδίτας
ἥρπασε· τῶν καλῶν τίς κόρος ἐστ' Ἄϊδι;
ἀλλὰ σύγ', Ἀγγελία, τὸν ἀηδέα μῦθον ἔχουσα
βάσκ' ἴθι παγκοίταν εἰς Ἀΐδαο δόμον·

λέξον δ'. ʾΩ δαῖμον, τὰν καλὰν ὤλεσας ἄγραν,
οὐ γὰρ τὰς ψυχὰς οὐδὲ τὰ σώματ' ἔχεις·
αἱ μὲν γὰρ ψυχαὶ μετέβησαν ἐς οὐρανὸν εὐρύν·
σώματα δ' ἐν γαίᾳ νήγρετον ὕπνον ἔχει."

Anthologia Oxoniensis, p. 216, Oxon, 1846.

With this version one furnished by Mr. Fisher from memory agrees.

But Sir R. Lingen, who, if any one, has a right to be heard on this subject, gives the following reading of the Epitaph:—

(2). ʿΑ μοῖρ' ἁ κρυερὰ τὼ καλὼ παῖδ' Ἀφροδίτας
῾Άρπασε· τῶν καλῶν τίς κόρος ἐστ' Ἀίδᾳ [a] ;
Ἀλλὰ σύ γ', Ἀγγελία, τὸν ἀηδέα μῦθον ἔχοισα,
Βάσκε, μελαντειχῆ πρὸς δόμον ἔλθε θεοῦ.

The only variations worthy of notice occur in the first four lines, the rest are the same in all the copies.

(3.) But there is yet another traditional form of the Epigram, for which I am indebted to the Rev. George Gaisford, a scholar and critic, *vi nominis*, who had it from the Rev. Edward Stokes, too early lost to his friends and country, and it was thought to be the original form in which these lines appeared: Sir R. Lingen's variation being introduced to obviate a possible objection on metrical grounds.

---

[a] The form Ἀίδᾳ, in line two, seems preferable to ῞Αϊδι, on the authority of the Epigram of Erinna on Baucis, upon which, as Sir R. Lingen suggests, Mr. Gordon's Epigram was partly moulded.

'Α μοῖρα κρυερὰ τὼ καλὼ παῖδ' 'Αφροδίτας
  ἥρπασε· τῶν καλῶν τίς κόρος ἔστ' 'Αΐδα;
'Αλλὰ σύ γ', 'Αγγελία, τὸν ἀηδέα μῦθον ἔχοισα,
  Βάσκε· μελαντειχῆ πρὸς δόμον ἔλθε θεοῦ.

These lines have perhaps detained us too long.

Soon after his M.A. Degree, in 1839, Mr. Gordon
was called upon to take his share of the college
offices; and till the period of his retirement to Easthampstead, in 1861, he was intimately associated
with all that befell Christ Church.

Dean Gaisford, for whom Mr. Gordon always entertained a genuine admiration, fully appreciated his
brilliant qualities, and constantly availed himself
of his quick apprehension and fertility of resource
on any subject of importance. As a Tutor, Mr.
Gordon at once gauged the intellectual calibre of his
pupils, and adapted his instruction with singular
skill to their several requirements. His particular
taste was for a youth of good natural ability, whose
originality was not overlaid with too much reading:
his own genius seemed to communicate itself to
kindred spirits, and his own vigorous personality
stamped itself upon them. He never squeezed the
orange: and it was to his judicious advice and insight into character, that the influence was due
which he continued to exercise over many distinguished men in after life.

Some great names have been given in the various
notices which appeared soon after his decease in the
public prints: but the list might be almost inde-

finitely enlarged: and there are few departments
of life in which it would not be found that the
leaven of Osborne Gordon's teaching was still at
work.

Mr. Gordon served the University in many con-
spicuous posts—as Moderator, as Public Examiner
in the Schools, and as a Judge in awarding University Scholarships and the Chancellor's Prizes. He
was twice nominated on the Board of Select Preachers,
though on the second occasion he resigned the charge.
He was a Pro-proctor: and on the resignation of the
office of Proctor by the Rev. H. G. Liddell, the present Dean of Christ Church, he was appointed by
Dean Gaisford to fill the vacancy, and delivered the
customary speech of the Senior Proctor on retiring
from office. He was elected on the new Hebdomadal Council, which in 1854 superseded, under recent
legislation, the old Board of Heads of Houses and
Proctors; and, as we shall see by and by, was brought
back to more intimate relations with the University
on the University Commission in 1877.

During his period of residence he frequently assisted his friend, the Rev. Jacob Ley, Vicar of St.
Mary Magdalen (a name even at this distance of
time not to be pronounced without emotion by those
who knew the man), and his Sermons, delivered there,
are still remembered by many of the parishioners
for their vigour and originality.

The dryness of this enumeration may be a little
relieved by the following anecdote, which puts Mr.
Gordon's shrewdness and *bonhomie* in an amusing

light during his earlier tenure of office as Pro-proctor.

It would be inexcusable to reproduce it, except in the exact form in which it was communicated by the same ready and graphic pen to which we have been already indebted.

"The very costly amusement of tandem-driving was indulged in by Undergraduates at the time Gordon was Pro-proctor to such an extent, that the Proctors were determined, if possible, to put a stop to it. In vain for some time they tried to intercept some of the drivers, and to make an example such as might deter others who were inclined to offend in the same way. In a conversation on the subject with one or both of the Proctors of the time Gordon said, 'I will undertake to catch a team to-morrow on any road on which I am told a team has gone out, if you,' addressing a Proctor, 'will go with me, and do what I direct.'

"(The practice, as I well remember, was to send on the leader by a groom, a mile or two out of Oxford, and in returning, at the same point, to take off the leader, and then soberly to drive in to the stables, as though simply from a quiet drive.)

"The Proctor agreeing to go with the Pro, Gordon engaged a fly, drove out with the Proctor, some three miles on, I think, the Bicester road, arrived at the spot he had decided upon, and said to the driver 'pull up.' 'Now,' said he to the Proctor, 'get out.' To the driver, 'Take your horse out of the fly. Push the fly into the ditch.' After such hesitation as one would expect, into the ditch went the fly. 'Now then,' to the Proctor, 'get in.' Into the fly went Proctor and Pro and shut-to the door.

"Scarcely were they settled before up drove two gownsmen in a tandem. 'What,' exclaimed they, 'an upset! Can we help you?' At that moment of kindly proffered help, out in full view of the un-suspecting youths stepped the black-velvet-sleeved Proctor and his coadjutor, with the familiar for-mula, while their caps were raised with more than wonted courtesy, 'Gentlemen, your names and Colleges?'

"Bidding the young drivers to a conference at Christ Church next morning, the fly having been replaced upon the road, the captors turned towards Oxford, followed by the tandem-cart and its occu-pants at a really sober pace. 'There,' said Gordon to his companion, 'you have been trying to catch teams and failed; I told you I would catch one the first time I tried.' You will, I am sure, be prepared to hear that our good and kind-hearted friend Gordon had made it a stipulation beforehand that the drivers of the team, which he by his shrewd stratagem en-trapped, should in no way be punished for their breach of the discipline relating to members of the University still *in statu pupillari.*

"There you have the details of the anecdote which I have been used to think is not a little character-istic of my old friend's amiable cleverness. When his little plan has been told one may say how simple! but how many are there to whom such

c

a scheme would have occurred? And are there not some who would have forgotten to protect the victims of their stratagem against consequences?"

We shall, many of us, like Mr. Lakin, to whom this narrative is due, "think of this little tale with pleasurable interest," and thank him for bringing to light so lively a passage from a Proctor's note-book.

In the summer of 1845 it was the writer's good fortune to be Mr. Gordon's companion on the Continent during a somewhat lengthened tour in Switzerland and Italy. It was his first experience of foreign travel on any considerable scale, and the delight of witnessing some of the grandest scenes of Nature and the masterpieces of Art was greatly enhanced by the keen perception and critical judgment of such a guide. Though Mr. Gordon was not of a robust frame he had an exquisite enjoyment of mountain scenery; and without attempting any dangerous ascents he had, perhaps, a truer appreciation of the peculiar beauties of rocks and glaciers than many who had penetrated further into their secrets. He took great interest in Mr. Ruskin's studies of nature, which he greatly valued, and was constantly bringing his old pupil's theories to the test of experience.

On one occasion, however, his explorations were brought to an awkward termination. He had been spending the day with several Oxford friends on the Mer de Glace, and on returning the party found that they had carelessly come to a fork in the river, one branch of which lay between them and the Inn at Chamounix, only a short distance off in a straight line. The rest were inclined to make a considerable detour, and cross by a bridge further up the stream; Mr. Gordon, however, divesting himself of part of his clothing, tried to wade, but, as the rest of the party feared, was swept away by the torrent, icy cold, and running with great rapidity. His companions, by a common impulse, started off to a point some distance lower down, where the river narrowed considerably, and where they hoped to rescue him; but he did better for himself, and after a time struck out and succeeded in reaching the opposite bank, to the unspeakable relief of those who were watching him. A Savoyard peasant-woman, who had witnessed the adventure, took him under her special protection, and when we reached our quarters, after a long circuit, we had the satisfaction of finding the hero of the day taking his ease in his inn, and, except a few slight cuts, none the worse for his escapade. Those, however, who knew best the danger of his position were much struck by the coolness and address with which he extricated himself from his perilous dilemma [e].

---

[e] It must be confessed that Mr. Gordon was not good company for weak nerves. He was constantly on the verge of a catastrophe *de voyage*, which kept his fellow-travellers in a lively state of uncertainty as to his movements. It seemed utterly hopeless, when he was strolling somewhere about, leaving his effects in utter confusion, that he could be ready for boat or train, or any conveyance dependent on time or tide. But at the last possible moment he sauntered in to the place

In the following year (1846), on the retirement of the Rev. H. G. Liddell, he became his successor both as Censor in Christ Church, and Proctor in the University; and at the close of the official year he delivered the customary speech. It was, as usual with him, a model of terseness and elegance. He had occasion to make several allusions to Cambridge, and congratulated the Sister University, with his wonted force and felicity of diction, upon the recent election of the Prince Consort to the distinguished post of Chancellor. But he passed on to a subject then of absorbing interest—the Irish famine. He dwelt, as might be expected, upon the sufferings and heroic endurance of the peasantry, while he relieved those melancholy details by a brighter picture of the universal sympathy extended to the famine and plague-stricken island; and enlarged with excusable satisfaction upon the excellent spirit displayed by all classes of the University in exerting themselves to mitigate the severity of the visitation.

Perhaps it may not be out of place to add some particulars on a subject to which only general reference could be made in a Proctor's speech. A sumptuary law was passed by common consent amongst Undergraduates limiting desserts at wine-parties—which had been before generally on a much more ex-

of starting with his usual abstracted air and leisurely gait and look of surprise at any symptom of impatience, though how chaos had been reduced to order was a secret known only to himself.

pensive scale—to oranges and biscuits: the retrench-
ment thus effected to be applied to the relief of Irish
distress. This is the only restriction of the kind that
the writer has ever known carried out to the letter:
and this was strictly enforced by public opinion.

At that time (1846-7) third-class trains were
very few, and none running at convenient hours.
The great bulk of the well-to-do members of the
University travelled first class as matter of course;
but in the face of the distress then existing there
was a great change in this respect, and many persons then travelled second class who had probably
never entered a carriage of that kind before. It
must be borne in mind that the accommodation then
provided by the G. W. R. for their second-class
passengers might reasonably be objected to, and was
quite unlike the convenience and comfort of the present arrangements. Remonstrances were in some
cases addressed by strangers to first-class passengers for incurring unnecessary expense, and not
submitting to temporary inconvenience, it being
understood that the difference of the fare was to be
applied in all cases to the cause which was then
uppermost in every heart. Judge of the strength
of the feeling to excuse such a breach of conventional
propriety in punctilious Oxford!

One special circumstance of a more public character may be mentioned in illustration of the prevailing sentiment. There was a considerable balance
at the time belonging to the Oxford Union Society,
which a patriotic Irish Peer, now high in the

public service of the Crown, proposed should be transferred to the Irish Relief Fund. The members of the Society did full justice to the motives of the proposer, with which all sympathized, but the majority did not consider themselves at liberty to deal so with moneys contributed for a different object. The motion was, however, met by a counter resolution, that a subscription should be opened on the spot (in addition to other machinery already set on foot), which it was hoped would more than realise the amount proposed to be alienated from the Society's funds. This was done, and, as far as the writer remembers, the noble mover had no reason to be dissatisfied with the result of his appeal [f].

For some years previous to the Royal Commission of Enquiry into the Universities of Oxford and Cambridge in 1850, there had been a growing feeling amongst those chiefly engaged in Education at Oxford that some alteration of the existing system was required. There were various schemes in agitation, as might be expected in a centre of so great intellectual activity; but the changes formulated might be classed under two separate heads: — (1.) Those which referred to a re-adjustment or re-modelling of the educational system; and, as a means to that end, a revision of the Public Examination Statute then existing. (2.) The extension of the University teaching to classes of students

---

[f] Upon one occasion Mr. Gordon was laid claim to by the sister island, when at a Dublin reception he was announced as The O'Gordon.

not then able to enjoy its advantages. But in discussing the question of University Education generally, a very important subdivision of the subject forced itself upon public attention, and still continues to form one of the problems of the day, viz. the relation of Professorial to Tutorial teaching.

By stress of circumstances the Professors had then (circ. 1850) practically ceased to have any considerable hold upon the undergraduate members of the University. This was owing to no fault of their own. The bulk of the Undergraduates were not sufficiently instructed to profit by such lectures as suited the dignity of the Professor's Chair. The other men who were candidates for distinction in the University had their time thoroughly occupied in preparing for the Schools; and grudged any interference with the course of reading which they thought most serviceable for the end in view. So it was hard to say from what ranks the Professors' audiences were to be recruited.

With the great subdivision of subjects now introduced, and the advance in many branches of knowledge, the difficulty is doubtless by this time much diminished, but no one could be surprised to hear that it still existed in some degree. The College Tutors had, therefore, in great measure, become the recognized teachers in the University, but they were in turn supplemented or superseded by the private Tutors, many of them extremely able men, whose assistance was counted almost indispensable for high honours in the Schools, while the candidates for a Pass degree equally had recourse to help of a more modest character beyond the College Lectures.

One of the chief defects under the old system was the opportunity it held out for idleness during a great part of the Undergraduate's course. There was frequently an interval of a full year and a-half between the Little-go and the Great-go, which a large proportion of the Undergraduates passed in comparative idleness until a few months before the necessary preparation for the Final Schools: and it was justly held that this length of time unaccounted for, during which the Undergraduate was left very much to himself, fostered habits of extravagance and other evils. It was to remedy this state of things that an intermediate examination, called Moderations, was introduced, which has had the effect of remedying many of the abuses complained of under the old system. These remarks are only intended to shew the state of public feeling when Mr. Gordon published a pamphlet on the improvement of the University Statute then in operation, and on the admission of poor Scholars to the University.

The immediate occasion of this publication was a memorial on the subject of University extension signed by a number of noblemen and gentlemen, with Lord Sandon (the late Earl of Harrowby) and Lord Ashley (the present Earl of Shaftesbury) at their head. This object engaged Mr. Gordon's warmest sympathy; he did all in his power to promote it: and though there were doubtless many previous suggestions pointing in the same direction, this pamphlet had the merit of putting the question before the public in a practical form, and paved the way for further progress.

From the extracts given below the reader will be able to see how much University legislation, as it was afterwards carried out, was here anticipated. Mr. Gordon begins with noticing the question of the Professors, which had become more prominent in consequence of a memorial, to which he refers, lately issued by the professorial body.

As the same Academical problems keep constantly recurring in a different shape, Mr. Gordon's remarks may not yet be out of date, though written under the old constitution. There had been an attempt to give the Professors some connexion with the necessary Academic course, by means of a regulation that every Undergraduate should attend one course of Professors' Lectures in " Literæ humaniores," and one in " Disciplinæ Mathematicæ et Physicæ;" the particular subject and professor being left to the taste of the individual. This expedient, however, did not find favour then or at later times.

Mr. Gordon then proceeds: " The subject, however, has not been allowed to sleep. It has occupied the thoughts of many minds in and out of the University, who cannot understand how there should be Professors without Lectures, or Lectures without hearers; and an attempt has lately been made to press it to a decision, by a memorial of the Professors themselves, calling upon the proper Authorities

to give them a chance of doing their duties to their
Founders by providing them with classes. Nothing,
however, can be more liberal than the selection which
these Gentlemen offer, or more modest than their
request. They have enlarged the old columns by
the addition of one or two other subjects, and, as
proposed before, will be satisfied with attendance
on two Courses of Lectures. Still this little is not
granted, and the subject remains to exercise the wits
of University legislators, and to be the theme elsewhere of an annual dirge from a Gentleman, who
having experienced the feelings of a speaker without
an audience, can doubtless enter into those of a Professor without a class."

But as Mr. Gordon considered that the enlargement
of the University, which he contemplated, might also
have a considerable bearing upon the changes proposed in the Examination Statute, he draws attention
to the Memorial from without the University already
mentioned, as his own propositions are founded upon
its suggestions. The passage which he quotes is so
important in itself, and is couched in so moderate
and judicious language, that it will not be without
interest even now :—

"'The Universities,' say the Memorialists, 'take
up Education where our Schools leave it, yet no
one can say that they have been strengthened or
extended, whether for clergy or laity, in proportion to the growing population of the country, its
increasing empire, or deepening responsibilities. We
are anxious to suggest, that the link which we thus

find missing' (between Schools and the Ministry) 'in the chain of improvement, should be supplied, by rendering Academical Education accessible to the sons of parents, whose incomes are too narrow for the scale of expenditure at present prevailing among the junior members of the University of Oxford, and that this should be done through the addition of *new departments to existing Colleges*, or, if necessary, *by the foundation of new Collegiate Bodies.*' After thus stating their general views, they leave the details in other hands, and conclude by 'recording their readiness, whenever the matter may proceed further, to aid by personal exertions, or pecuniary contributions, in the promotion of a design which the exigencies of the country so clearly seem to require.' I know not what may have been the fate of this memorial, but I think that, looking to the high rank and character of the Gentlemen whose names appear at the end of it, and the honourable preference which they shew for our University, every one will allow that they have a right not only to expect a courteous reception, but to be met if possible with free and cordial co-operation. It is in that spirit that I take up the proposition which these Gentlemen have made, hoping that the importance of it, and the necessity of doing something, will be some excuse for the boldness of any one who thinks that he has any thing practicable to offer."

Mr. Gordon takes the subject of improvement in the existing Examination Statute first. He considered it to have been a cardinal error in the last attempt to enforce Professorial teaching, that it had no reference to the Examination Statute. He thought that if Professorial teaching were to be combined with the Tutorial, the Examination Statute must be altered. His observations here depend so little upon the special circumstances of the time for their value, that they will commend themselves to the common sense of the University now, as they did when they first appeared.

"There is," he adds, "a real danger of all systems becoming too systematic, and passing into stereotype; with the perfection of their form they begin to lose their spirit and vitality, and require the re-organization of their old elements, or the infusion of new ones.

"The practical question then which we have to consider, is not what to do with the Professors, but how to improve the Examination Statute. What we want is not to supply *them* with an unwilling audience, but to have the best possible system. At the same time I am persuaded, that the best system is that which will afford them the most useful field for their exertions, and that too by a natural consequence, and not by the force of legal enactment. But if we set our hearts on the formation of classes for the Professors as *an end*, we may succeed perhaps in stimulating the most harmless of that tribe to a ferocity in lecturing quite alien to their natures, but we shall put ourselves out of the way of all practical improvement. If the system is good, and the Professors' Lectures in any branch of knowledge are such as help the student on his way to distinction, they will be attended naturally [g]; if they are not such, why should he be compelled to attend? If on the other hand they lie out of the course of the system, *being good*, it would be a positive evil and impediment to force them into it. I speak here only with reference to those who seek distinction; as to men in general, they would derive no benefit in any case from such Lectures as one who bears the title of Professor ought to give."

The gist of his proposal is that there should be an intermediate School very much on the lines of the present Moderations, and as his object has been in all essential points secured, we will consider the second head of his pamphlet, in which he was equally successful in divining the course of future legislation.

There had long been an uneasy feeling that the University had fallen short of its duty as regarded the admission and maintenance of poor Scholars. A comparison of the then existing Members of the University with the census taken in 1612, shewed that though there had been a general increase, it was not at all in proportion to the increased population and wealth of the country: while the document in question "proved also the diminution, or rather extinction, of a class, which then formed and ought to form, a considerable portion of the University. At that time there appear to have been under various names nearly 500 poor Scholars (out of an aggregate of 2,920, including servants) receiving their education here: at present those who may be considered to

[g] This is now the case as regards Moral Philosophy and Logic.

occupy a similar position are not fifty. It is to the
re-introduction of this class on a large scale that the
Memorialists have referred us, as the only way of
meeting the wants of the country." With this conclusion Mr. Gordon absolutely agrees, and he proceeds to discuss the mode of bringing it about.

"The Memorialists think the good they contemplate may be accomplished in two ways—by the
addition of new departments to existing Colleges, or
the foundation of new ones." To the last suggestion
Mr. Gordon thought there were grave objections;
and these are stated with much force and truth,
and would, under ordinary circumstances, have
proved fatal to such a scheme. For no one had
a right to calculate upon the princely munificence
which once more came to the rescue, and associated
with an honoured name the cause of true religion
and useful learning, in some quarters threatened
with divorce. The splendid exception, perhaps, helps
to establish the rule: and the number of those who
would formerly have been excluded, but are now
admitted to the benefits of the University, far exceeds the modest limit of three hundred, Mr. Gordon's
original calculation as a first instalment; with a capacity, as he truly anticipated, of indefinite enlargement. His concluding remark is as true to-day as it
was nearly forty years ago. "I have supposed the
existence of three hundred poor Scholars in the University. I am almost ashamed at the smallness of
the number, but I have purposely made the lowest
computation. The good, however, that would be

effected by acting even on this moderate scale, can not be represented by figures. It would be the beginning of a system, whereby the Church would strike its roots freely into the subsoil of society, drawing from it those elements of life, and that sustenance of mental and moral power, without which it may last for centuries as an aged trunk, but will never flourish as a tree " by the river's side."

In 1850 came the Royal Commission for Enquiry into the Universities of Oxford and Cambridge. Both the expediency and legality of the Commission were much debated at the time, and the Commission was opposed in a speech of remarkable eloquence by Mr. Gladstone in the House of Commons, on July 18.

This eventful year, which witnessed the death of Sir R. Peel, also gave birth to a movement popularly known as the " Papal Aggression." Upon constitutional grounds it was thought fitting that the University of Oxford should present an address to the Crown against this usurpation. A Delegacy, of which Mr. Gordon was a member, was accordingly appointed for the purpose, and received by the Queen at Windsor, with deputations from the University of Cambridge, and the Corporation of the city of London, on Dec. 10. The excitement on the subject gradually died away after the passing of the Ecclesiastical Titles Bill. At Oxford, moreover, attention was engrossed by the proceedings of the University Commission, which were watched with greater anxiety, as they took a more definite shape.

While this scheme was pending, late in the summer of 1852, the whole of Europe, and it is no exaggeration to say, the civilized world, sustained a shock in the death of the Duke of Wellington. His funeral in St. Paul's Cathedral was a national solemnity without parallel before or since. By the University of Oxford, of which his Grace had been Chancellor from the year 1834, his loss, though for some time anticipated, was not the less sensibly felt. In the Censor's Speech of that year Mr. Gordon referred to the blow which had fallen upon the University, and upon Christ Church especially, of which the Duke was a member, in the death of the Chancellor. Such an event called forth from all quarters tributes of the highest eloquence to the memory of one who had long been the chief Pillar of the State. But it may be doubted whether any speech delivered on the occasion exceeded in force or dignity that of which Mr. Gordon was the author. It is cast in an heroic mould; it is classical in form and sentiment; and hardly bears translation from the Latin, in which Mr. Gordon thought as he wrote. The part of the speech relating to the Duke is subjoined, as evidence that the oration was worthy of the man in whose honour it was composed—the brilliant comparison, or contrast rather, between the two brothers, the Marquis of Wellesley and the Duke of Wellington, both of Christ Church, the former on the foundation,—one of those striking combinations in which history does not repeat itself, found an adequate exponent in the Speaker of the Day.

" Post multa munera, quibus me imparem expertus
sum, nunquam vires mihi atque ingenium magis
defuisse memini, quam cum more solemni ad hanc
orationem elaborandam accessi. Nam si domesticis
rebus, si quid sermone exponendum esset aut illus-
trandum, vix aut ne vix quidem satisfeci, quomodo
in publica causa et communi omnium desiderio, aut
voluntati meæ aut aliorum expectationi respondere
sperarem? Quomodo, quod præstantissimi viri dicen-
dique peritissimi, in senatu plurimisque concionibus,
suas etiam vires superare conquesti sunt, id ego,
omnibus in rebus minor, aut ingenio complecti co-
narer aut oratione attingere auderem? Et tamen in
Cancellarii Universitatis, et illustrissimi civis hujusce
ædis interitu, aut a Censoria consuetudine, scilicet
ut læta et tristia anni exeuntis pro facultate nostra
exponeremus, erat discedendum, aut hoc operis suscipiendum, hic obeundus labor; et periclitando fortasse, potius quam silendo peccandum. In hoc autem
discrimen eo libentius adductus sum, quod res militiæ
a Cancellario nostro splendide gestas, operam domi
in administranda republica egregie navatam, vestra
omnium venia, majori ex parte prætermittere licebit.
Non harum credo rationem a me exigetis. Et tot
profecto tantaque facinora et bellorum miracula, victoriæ ab acerrimis hostibus reportatæ, munitissima-
rum urbium expugnationes, exuviæ ducum, exer-
cituum fugæ et profligationes, debellata unius viri
Asia atque Europa triumphis, hæc non nostri ingenii
sunt, neque facundiæ;

D

Neque enim quivis horrentia pilis
Agmina, vel fracta pereuntes cuspide Gallos

audeat describere. Ceterum inter pacis munera, otiique dulcedines, injussa venit in mentem admirabilis illa triumphorum series, gloriæque illa fere quotidiana incrementa, quæ patribus nostris coram oculis proponebantur, et nobis hæreditario jure, familiaria et domestica devenere. Mallem ad vestram memoriam, quam ad meam ipsius orationem provocatum; sed in ipso Cancellarii nostri nomine, non possumus non recordari, Indiam ab altero fratrum, quem jure nostrum appellare possumus, administratam, ab altero pacatam, et si quid aberat nostris adjudicatum armis, bellum in Hispania longinquum, et assiduo labore confectum, plurimas acies justo prœlio commissas, signum nunquam receptui datum, Lusitaniæ arces tanta constantia occupatas, ubi solus fere atque unicus imperator, molem procellamque belli contra hostiles impetus, contra opinionem patriæ, contra inimicarum partium studia, Fabius alter atque Africanus, diversarum fere virtutum conciliator, cunctando idem atque audendo, sustinebat; tempestatem ab illa arce emissam, liberatam tandem peregrino milite Hispaniam, ultimam denique illam dimicationem, spoliisque opimis nobilitatam, ubi dux summus summo duci, fortunæ filio, si non arma atque exuvias, at belli gloriam et jus victoriæ toties, usurpatum detraxit, Gallicæque aquilæ, relicta præda, nudatæ sordidatæque profugere: ἀντιπάλῳ δυσχείρωμα δράκοντι. Hœc inquam non possumus non recordari, et si terrores minasque ejus temporis respiciamus, formidines omnium, unius robur, Pindaricum illud occurrit animo;

Παῦροι δὲ βουλεῦσαι φόνου
Παρποδίου νεφέλαν τρέψαι ποτὶ δυσμένεων ἀνδρῶν στίχας
Χερσὶ καὶ ψυχᾷ δυνατοί.

"Sed hæc missa facio. Neque enim hæc erant, propter quæ Universitati nostræ cum memoria æterni nominis seipsam consociare placuit; nec quod indolis nostræ erat, castra foro, militiam otio, arma togæ, præponere, aut eam rem in civitate primam esse, propter quam civitas nostra omnium evasit princeps, judicavimus. Esto, quod ait ingeniosus poeta, usurpavit eloquentissimus orator, simul atque novus aliquis motus bellicum canere cœperit, pelli e medio sapientiam, studia de manibus excuti, vi geri rem, sperni oratorem, horridum amari militem; non idcirco militari utcunque gloria florentem, qui nos præsidio tutaretur, quæsivimus. Quamquam haud scio an inter hæc etiam studia quibus dediti sumus, disciplina nostra a militari spiritu et bellicis virtutibus omnino abhorreat. Saltem, si unus et alter tantum a nobis in castrorum stipendia proficiscuntur, illud nunquam Universitati quantacunque flagranti invidia objicietur, aut regi aut patriæ in communi periculo defuisse; nec opinor in formidolosis temporibus, defutura est. Sed non bellorum minæ eo tempore depellendæ erant. Gliscebat civilis furor, pereundi perdendique omnia cupiditas, et legum novandarum insania; plurimorum turbati animi, quidquid aut annis venerabile aut experientia probatum, eo ipso nomine contemptui habitum oppugnatumque ; usu veniebat indies illud,

'Ράδιον μὲν σεῖσαι πόλιν καὶ ἀφαυροτέροις·
'Αλλ' ἐπὶ χώρας αὗτις ἔσσαι δυσπαλὲς δὴ γίγνεται,
Εἰ μὴ θεὸς ἀγεμονέσσι κυβερνάτηρ γένηται.

Postulabat itaque Universitas, qui ante alios hoc sibi desumeret, et vanas hominum libidines ad saniora concilia revocaret. Postulabat Universitas et adhuc fortasse postulat, qui omissa repeteret, desueta instauraret, inutilia recideret, probata atque integra tutaretur. Postulabant omnes, constantiæ, prudentiæ, incorruptæ fidei, nudæ veritatis exemplum ; nec nobis minimæ laudi erit, in eo rerum discrimine ad talis viri auctoritatem confugisse. Memini equidem, nec facile memoria excidet, quanta præclarissimorum virorum frequentia solemnis illa inauguratio celebrabatur ; ornatissimam theatri speciem, favorem vulgi, adolescentium plausus, quorum neminem pœnituit, omnium gratulationes. Ex illo die animi bonorum recreati, spes etiam invitis facta, multis qui de re summa desperarant excitata cura, ne quid amplius detrimenti respublica caperet. Nec, si hæc ultra verum ornare videar, sedecim anni sine fructu perierunt. Crescit inter nos indies, ni fallor, industria, probitas, integritas, constantia officii memor ; et si multa adhuc temerariis hominum expectationibus parum respondere, mirum esset profecto, nisi nonnihil harum virtutum Cancellarii nostri exemplo deberemus. Nemo, credo, nostrum magnificentissimis illis exequiis et funebri pompæ interfuit, quin ita animatus dis-

cesserit, ut patriæ quæ tum pullata principem civem
supremo comitabatur honore, civi qui patriam ita
unice amaverat, Universitati cujus tum personam
sustinebamus, non mediocrem operam et laborem,
sed si quid ingenii præstantius, si quid virium fortius,
si quid industriæ diligentius, impendendum esse fate-
retur. Illustri quidem memoria illa Divi Paulli ædes
insignita et posteris documento futura; nec temere
erit, in densissima urbe, et confertissima orbis terrarum multitudine, inter libera hominum commercia,
et divitiarum contentiones, heroas geminos, alterum
ad alterius latus, alterum terra, alterum mari victo-
rem, pares fide atque officio, qui semel vivi, ut fertur,
consilia de defendenda patria contulerunt, vita jam
defunctos, sed vitæ muneribus absolutis, duo velut
fulmina belli, extinctis ignibus, sopitos conquiescere.
Quorum si monumentum quæritis, circumspicite, non
illud tantum laquearis spatium quod summus archi-
tectus hujus olim Universitatis alumnus gloriæ Dei
Opt. Max. suoque ipsius nomini imprudens con-
secravit—circumspicite potius Britannicum orbem,
immo orbem terrarum egregie factorum testem, et
ingenii cui se haud invitum subdidit, conscium.
ἀνδρῶν γὰρ ἐπιφανῶν πᾶσα γῆ τάφος, καὶ οὐ στηλῶν
μόνον ἐν τῇ οἰκείᾳ σημαίνει ἐπιγραφὴ, ἀλλὰ καὶ ἐν
τῇ μὴ προσηκούσῃ ἄγραφος μνήμη παρ᾽ ἑκάστῳ τῆς
γνώμης μᾶλλον ἢ τοῦ ἔργου ἐνδιαιτᾶται.

"Haud vereor, ne de viro tanto nimius fuisse
videar."

Meanwhile the legislation which resulted from the

University Commission of 1850 was coming on apace. At this critical period the College Tutors who had most considered the subject, formed themselves into an association, of which the Rev. W. E. Jelf, Censor of Christ Church, was the first Chairman, and was on his retirement succeeded by the Rev. E. H. Hansell, Fellow of Magdalen. The association held frequent meetings in different colleges to consider the nature of the changes which appeared most desirable. No regular list of the whole body of members seems to have been preserved: but it may still interest some persons to recall the names of those who served on Committees to prepare recommendations,—

(1.) On the extension of the University.

(2.) On the Constitution of the University.

(3.) On the relation of the Professorial and Tutorial Systems.

The recommendations of these Committees[h] received respectful consideration from persons in authority,

[h] The Committee on (1) consisted of R. W. Church, Fellow of Oriel (Dean of St. Paul's); F. Fanshawe, Fellow and Tutor of Exeter; A. W. Haddan, Fellow and Tutor of Trinity; W. C. Lake, Fellow and Tutor of Balliol (Dean of Durham); H. L. Mansel, Fellow and Tutor of St. John's (late Dean of St. Paul's); C. Marriott, Fellow of Oriel; G. Marshall, Student and Censor of Christ Church; D. Melville, late Fellow of Brasenose; G. Rawlinson, Fellow and Tutor of Exeter (Canon of Canterbury and Camden Professor); S. P. Tweed, Fellow and Tutor of Exeter; and E. C. Woollcombe, Fellow and Tutor of Balliol.

On (2), O. Gordon, Student and Censor of Christ Church; E. Espin, Fellow and Tutor of Lincoln (Chancellor of Chester Diocese); W. C. Lake; F. Meyrick, Fellow and Tutor of Trinity; C. Neate, Fellow of Oriel (M.P. for Oxford City); E. Palmer, Fellow and Tutor of Balliol (Archdeacon of Oxford); G. Rawlinson; J. Shad-

and were not without effect upon the provisions of
the Act, which finally passed, as the result of the
Commission. That Mr. Gordon did not always agree
with the majority of his colleagues appears from
a letter which he wrote to Mr. Gladstone, and pri-
vately circulated, on the part of the Bill relating
to Christ Church. He urged the importance of preserving the continuity of the Studentships, as some
compensation for the smallness of the endowment,
and argued the question with great earnestness and
ingenuity[i]. In this contention, it is needless to say,
he was not successful. In a Postscript to this letter
he mentions his objection to the division of the Hebdomadal Council into Classes. He would rather have
had the election left free, all class distinctions
thoroughly ignored, and every person left simply
to depend on his own abilities and character. "As
it is," he adds, "I cannot help fearing that the Bill
will be more successful in raising and perpetuating
rival classes than in adjusting their claims."

If Mr. Gordon was "a Tory of the deepest hue,"
his toryism was shewn in University questions, by
leading the van in the reform of the Examination
Statute, in opening the privileges and prizes of the
University to poor Scholars, in extending its area, and

forth, Fellow and Tutor of University ; E. Stokes, Student and
Tutor of Christ Church; S. Wayte, Fellow and Tutor and late
President of Trinity.

On (3), O. Gordon; W. Hedley, Fellow and Tutor of University;
W. C. Lake; H. L. Mansel; C. Marriott; F. Meyrick; E. Palmer;
G. Rawlinson.

[i] Vide Note at end of the Life.

in endeavouring to sweep away all restraint upon
the discretion of electors in their choice of representatives to serve upon the Hebdomadal Council.

From the year 1848 to 1852 Mr. Gordon had
been engaged in the service of the University as
Examiner and Moderator, and in 1849 he was nominated on the Board of Select Preachers.

In 1854 he was, as we have seen, one of the
members first elected on the Hebdomadal Council.
In this capacity he was popular by reason of his
genial humour, as he was influential by his shrewdness and power of debate. In a conversation which
the writer had years ago with the late Bishop of
Peterborough, better known in Oxford as the energetic Master of Pembroke, the Bishop spoke unreservedly, as his manner was, of the services which
Mr. Gordon had rendered to the Board.

" Formerly," he said, " he had himself and another
eminent Scholar whom he named, drafted the University Statutes, and put them into Latin (a most
difficult and thankless office), upon the whole with
tolerable success; but when Gordon came we felt,"
he continued, " he was the man, and withdrew in
his favour. He did the work admirably. If any
objection was raised he never argued the point, but
proposed something to meet the objection : he was
never put out of temper by any suggestions, however unreasonable, never at a loss, and ended by
silencing the most captious criticism." Whoever
has succeeded to Mr. Gordon's peculiar functions
on the Board will probably be the first to confess,

that it is not a place in which it is easy to give entire satisfaction.

In 1855 the University of Oxford and the cause of Classical Learning had to lament the death of Dean Gaisford. He was the legitimate successor of the Stephens, the Scaligers, and Casaubons; and with him the great line of European Scholars may be said to have closed. His powerful understanding, his strong common sense, and his unbending principles, had great weight beyond the province which he had made his own: and the kindness of heart, which, as in Johnson, was disguised by a rugged manner, inspired a deep feeling of loyalty and affection to himself personally amongst those who had frequent access to his presence. By Mr. Gordon, who of all officially connected with the Dean probably stood highest in his confidence and regard, the loss was most acutely felt and as powerfully expressed, and the audience assembled at the Censor's Speeches in Christ Church Hall at the close of the year heard a funeral oration worthy of the best days of Roman eloquence pronounced by Osborne Gordon over Thomas Gaisford[j].

Under Dean Gaisford's successor a heavy responsibility devolved upon Mr. Gordon, from the fact that the new Dean laboured under some delicacy of health soon after his appointment, which necessitated a residence at Madeira during two winters, and the management of affairs during his absence was vested in the Sub-dean, Archdeacon Clerke, who admirably

[j] Speech in Appendix.

discharged the duties of the post left vacant, with the co-operation of the Censors. Happily the Dean's health was, after a short time, completely re-established; and he was enabled, amidst his many other avocations, to inaugurate a series of architectural restorations and additions to the existing fabric conceived and executed in the spirit of Wolsey himself.

Mr. Gordon was engaged during the ensuing years in the business of the University, in the Schools and at the Council, as well as in the service of the House.

In Michaelmas Term, 1859, H.R.H. the Prince of Wales was matriculated as a member of the University of Oxford, and was entered on the books of Christ Church. H.R.H. was officially recognized as a pupil of Mr. Gordon, though the direct charge of his education at the University was confided to Mr. Herbert Fisher, now Vice-Warden of the Stannaries. During the remaining period of his residence at the University, and afterwards, Mr. Gordon received repeated marks of gracious consideration from H.R.H., by which he was too loyal a subject not to be deeply gratified.

But he was presently called away to what many will consider the more important labours of his life. In 1860 he was presented to the Rectory of East Hampstead, Berks, in the gift of Christ Church, the only Church preferment he ever held.

It was a position which suited him exactly. He was midway between Oxford and London; he had close at hand parishioners distinguished both in point of rank and refinement; and his humbler neighbours soon learned to appreciate the versatile genius of the new Rector, who was equally at home with all sorts and conditions of men. The country round abounded in the elements of good and varied society, of which he was not slow to take advantage, and to which he lent increased lustre.

When, however, he came into residence in the parish which was to be his home for twenty-two years, he found many and serious drawbacks.

The church was dilapidated; there was only a Dame's School of the humblest type; no habitable parsonage; and the Church feeling of the parish was at a very low ebb, owing partly to the infirmities of the late Rector, a thorough valetudinarian, whose place had not been adequately supplied. Mr. Gordon lived to see a church which for its noble proportions and beauty of decoration has few competitors, with an east window lately presented as the gift of the Downshire family, executed by Mr. Morris from the design of Mr. Burne Jones, which deserves to rank amongst the triumphs of their art.

The Dame's School of thirty children, at most, has been succeeded by school buildings accommodating nearly ten times that number: and a large Rectory-house, well planned and well placed, gives the Incumbent increased facilities in his charge of the parish. It must not be forgotten in this rapid summary that the glebe by judicious building and alteration has been materially improved, and in Mr. Gordon's skilful hands was before long in a state of high cultivation, so that he soon became quoted as an authority on agricultural matters.

But the material has been less than the moral
change: from the state of deadness and apathy,
to the keen interest which Mr. Gordon's searching
and powerful sermons created. His talents, however,
had become too well known to be confined to the management of a country parish. They were soon called
into requisition for the examinations of the Indian
Civil Service, as well as for admission to the Army.

His advice was asked and acted upon by Government
in remodelling the arrangements of the 'Britannia'
Training Ship: as he had also a chief voice in determining the system to be adopted at the Naval School
at Greenwich. Mr. Ward Hunt, at the Admiralty,
reposed implicit confidence in Mr. Gordon, who was
always clear-headed and collected; fully informed
upon the subject in debate, free from prejudice, and
careless of mere clamour.

Upon the election of the Marquis of Salisbury, in
1869, as Chancellor of the University, in succession
to the late Earl of Derby, Mr. Gordon was nominated
on the Delegacy appointed to notify his election to
the new Chancellor. This graceful compliment was
paid to Mr. Gordon, though he had for some years
ceased to be resident of the University, as the Tutor
of the Marquis (then Lord Robert Cecil) during his
residence at Christ Church: whose abilities he early
recognized, and whose future eminence he foresaw.

Mr. Gordon's attitude towards the Education Act
of 1870 never varied. He was distinctly opposed
to a system which allowed only a slight modicum
of religious instruction in the Schools under its
immediate control: and he never saw cause to alter

his opinion. Reference is repeatedly made to the subject in his Sermons, one of which, entitled "The Great Commandment and Education," was published in 1870: and upon the election of Viscount Sandon (the present Earl of Harrowby) on the first London School Board, he addressed a letter to his Lordship with the heading "School Boards and Religious Education:" and the arguments there advanced, if not unanswerable, have never, so far as appears, been answered.

In 1876, under Mr. Disraeli's Administration, Mr. Gordon was nominated to act as Chairman, with two colleagues and a Secretary, upon a Commission to inquire into the constitution of the Councils of the Queen's Colleges in Ireland, and into the position of the Presidents, Professors, and other paid officers of those Institutions.

By the courtesy of the present Chief Secretary for Ireland the writer has had placed at his disposal (1) a letter from Sir M. H. Beach, then Chief Secretary for Ireland, to the Treasury, on the subject of the proposed inquiry. (2.) A letter of instructions from Sir M. H. Beach to the Commissioners on the scope and object of the inquiry. These important documents are printed at length, both on account of their intrinsic value, and by reason of the interest which has been revived in the question: as also because they throw light upon (3) a letter from Mr. Henry Brougham Leech, Professor of Jurisprudence and International Law in the University of Dublin, who acted as Secretary to the Commission, and has borne testimony to Mr. Gordon's mode of dealing with the questions brought before him, in the following striking terms.

(Copy of letter of 29th November, 1875, from Sir Michael Hicks-Beach to the Treasury, relative to the proposed Committee of Inquiry.)

"Dublin Castle, 29th November, 1875.

"Sir,—I am directed by the Lord Lieutenant to acquaint you, for the information of the Lords Commissioners of Her Majesty's Treasury, that the present position of the Professors of the Queen's Colleges in Ireland has recently engaged the anxious consideration of the Irish Government.

"In 1873 a memorial, of which a copy is enclosed, was presented by the Professors of the Queen's Colleges to His Grace's predecessor, Earl Spencer, and other applications of the same kind have been made from time to time. The accompanying extracts from Memoranda by the Secretary of the Queen's University, which I enclose for Their Lordship's information, explain the work and emoluments of the Professors, and state some of the arguments by which their request for increased stipends may be supported.

"His Grace has, however, hitherto refrained from specially urging this subject upon Their Lordships, because he has felt that, following the precedent set in 1863, if an increase in the stipends of the Professors be conceded, it should at the same time be carefully considered whether such increase might not be accompanied by such changes in their position and duties as would materially augment the teaching power of the whole professorial staff, and effect important improvements in the organization of the Colleges.

"His Grace desires me briefly to refer to some important points of this nature which have been suggested to him as deserving consideration.

1. *Class Fees to be abolished, and a Composition Fee to be instituted, to be paid into Prize Fund.*

"1. The income of the Queen's Colleges' Professors is made up by College stipend, allowance from University Chest as University Examiners, and Class Fees. At present a Professor receives £2 from each student attending his instruction.

"It has been suggested that as regards these 'Class Fees,' the present system might be advantageously modified, by allowing the Students to pay a Composition Fee to the College, which should free them to all the instruction of the College (except one or two practical courses in which there are special expenses), and by uniting the Composition Fee into one fund, to be called the 'Prize Fund,' out of which every Professor or licensed Teacher should be paid a fixed sum not exceeding £1 a year for each student attending his class; the remaining surplus being divided among the Professors and other officers of the Colleges according to certain fixed rules.

"In this way the pecuniary interest which a Professor has in the number of students attending his own class would be diminished, but not abolished, while his pecuniary interest in the general success of the College would be increased.

"2. *Professors to be appointed to Faculties instead of Chairs.*

"2. His Grace has been advised that it might conduce to the educational efficiencies of the Colleges if a Professor was not appointed a Professor in a particular subject, but simply a Professor in a Faculty.

"To illustrate his meaning His Grace will give two instances:—There are at present in each College two Professors of Mathematics, a Professor of Pure Mathematics, and a Professor of Natural Philosophy. If they were not so styled in the statutes the College Council could sanction a better division of their duties between these Professors. There are also two Professorships respectively of Greek and Latin, and it is very conceivable that the teaching of these languages and literatures might in some instances be better provided for than by giving the whole of the Greek course to one, and the whole of the Latin course to another Professor.

"It might for many reasons be advisable that the Colleges should be left free in all cases of this kind to make the best practicable arrangement in their power.

"3. *Appointment of Licensed Lecturers other than Professors.*

"3. It has been further suggested to His Grace that it would be also very desirable that the College Councils should have power to license other Lecturers than Professors; and that this power, if granted, would, at an exceedingly small cost, increase very much the teaching power of the Colleges, by enabling the Councils to introduce into the Queen's Colleges much of the advantages which have been found in Germany to result from the addition of 'Extra-ordinary Professors' and 'Privat-Docen- ten' to the smaller staff of 'Ordinary Professors.'

"Should such a system be adopted, it would of course be necessary to consider how far the present occupants of the ordinary Professorial chairs might be entitled to compensation for the loss of that portion of their fees which would go to the new teachers, between whom and themselves the students would be allowed to choose.

"4. *Appointment and Payment of Readers.*

"4. It might also be desirable that a portion of the 'Prize Fund' should be set free for, and allocated to, the payment of Readers who should assist the Professors in getting through the weekly examinations, correction of exercises, and other irksome work.

"5. There are other matters of a less important character, such as the redistribution of offices, the claims of the Presidents and officers for increased remuneration, &c., which are also deserving of serious consideration, but which His Grace does not consider it necessary, more particularly at present, to specify.

"His Grace is of opinion that it is very desirable to the interests of the Queen's Colleges that such points as those above mentioned, together with the

E

claims of the existing Professors for increased remuneration, should be duly inquired into and considered by Her Majesty's Governments.

"His Grace need not point out that, while an improvement in the position of the Professors would afford
a favourable opportunity for carrying into immediate
effect either the particular suggestions that have been
made, or any other changes of the same character
that it might be thought advisable to adopt, it would
be hardly possible, having regard to existing rights,
to make them at once without their being accompanied by some corresponding advantage to the Professors. It is mainly for these reasons that His Grace
wishes the two questions to be jointly considered.

"His Grace feels, however, that without the institution of a careful and searching inquiry upon the
spot, into the circumstances of each College, it would
be very difficult, if not impossible, for Her Majesty's
Government to arrive at a satisfactory conclusion
upon the subject, and that to render such an inquiry
efficient, it would be advisable to obtain the assistance of gentlemen thoroughly acquainted with the
practical working of the professorial and tutorial
system in other Universities within the United
Kingdom. He would therefore suggest to their
Lordships that two gentlemen connected respectively
with an English and Scotch University should be appointed, together with the Treasury Remembrancer in
Ireland, as a Treasury Commission to visit each College
during the work of next term, and inquire into, and
report upon, such points as may be referred to them.

"His Grace trusts that this matter may receive Their Lordships' early consideration, and should Their Lordships approve of the suggestion which he has made, he will be prepared to specify the exact questions which, in his opinion, should be referred to such Commission.

"I am, &c.,
"(Signed) M. E. HICKS-BEACH.

"*The Secretary,*
 "*Treasury,*
  "*London.*"

(Copy of letter of 5th April, 1876, from Sir Michael Hicks-Beach, then Chief Secretary for Ireland, to the Rev. Osborne Gordon and the other gentlemen appointed to conduct the Inquiry into the Constitution of the Councils of the Queen's Colleges in Ireland, and into the position of the Presidents, Professors, and other paid officers of those Institutions.)

"*5th April,* 1876.

"GENTLEMEN,—The inquiry which the Treasury have consented to institute, and which you have kindly undertaken to conduct, has reference to the constitution of the Councils of the Queen's Colleges in Ireland, and to the position of the Presidents, Professors, and other paid officers of those Institutions.

"The principal points suggested to you for inquiry are the following :—

"(*a.*) Whether the constitution of the Councils

E 2

of the Queen's Colleges could be altered with advantage to these Institutions.

"(*b.*) Whether the present mode of appointing to offices in the Queen's Colleges admits of improvement.

"(*c.*) Whether any better distribution of the work of teaching can be effected than at present.

"1. By a better distribution of the work among the Professors themselves.

"2. By permitting the College Councils to license Lecturers in addition to the Professors.

"3. By assigning chairs to future Presidents.

"4. By employing Readers to assist the Professors in their less important duties.

"(*d.*) Whether the remuneration of the Presidents, Professors, and other officers of the College is sufficient, and if not, to what extent, and in what way it should be increased, and whether there are any redundant Professorships, the suppression or consolidation of which might be effected without injury to the Colleges.

"(*e.*) Whether the arrangement in regard to class fees admits of improvement.

"(*f.*) In the event of any changes being recommended, what, if any, arrangements would be necessary to secure the rights of existing officers.

"I need not enter into details upon these points beyond placing in your hands copies of the Act under which the Queen's Colleges were founded, and of the Charter of the Queen's University, and also a copy of a letter addressed by me to the Treasury on the 29th of November last.

" As regards, however, the concluding subject of inquiry under heading (*d*), the Lord Lieutenant is anxious to invite your attention to the reductions and amalgamations that have been already effected in the Professorships.

"Any further information you may desire, and which His Grace has in his possession, shall of course be placed at your disposal; and the Presidents, Professors, and other officers of the Colleges will be directed to afford you every information and assistance in their power, and to furnish you with any returns you may require either before or during your inquiry into each College.

"I have to add that the Lord's Commissioners of Her Majesty's Treasury have been pleased to approve of the appointment of a Secretary to assist you, and that His Grace will communicate to you, with as little delay as possible, the name of the gentleman selected by him for the post.

"I have, &c.

"(Sd.) M. E. HICKS-BEACH.

" *The Rev. Osborne Gordon, B.D.,*
    G. J. Allman, M.D., L.L.D., F.R.S.,
    and H. H. Murray, Esq., &c., &c."

(Copy of letter from Mr. Henry Brougham Leech, Professor of Jurisprudence and International Law in the University of Dublin, to the Under Secretary for Ireland.)

    "49 *Rutland-Square, Dublin,* 24*th July,* 1884.

"DEAR SIR ROBERT HAMILTON,—In compliance with the wish of the Chief Secretary conveyed to me through Mr. F. J. Cullinan, in relation to the Commission upon the Queen's Colleges which was presided over by the Rev. Osborne Gordon, I write a short account of our proceedings therein. The Commission which was issued in April, 1876, was composed of Mr. Gordon as Chairman, Dr. G. F. Allman, now Sir George Allman, F.R.S., who has since held the office of President of the British Association, and Mr. Herbert Murray, then Treasury Remembrancer in Ireland: and I was appointed their Secretary. The Commission dealt with various educational, medical, and financial questions connected with the Colleges, each of these departments being specially represented by the three gentlemen named as Commissioners, while the Chairman was the guiding spirit of the whole, as indeed he was admirably suited to be from his large and varied experience of educational organization in all its branches.

"We started for Belfast in the last week of April, and sitting for nearly a week in each of the three colleges, took the evidence of the Presidents, and Professors, and other College officers, and inspected the libraries and museums. On returning to Dublin about the middle of May, we heard some further witnesses, and then adjourned in order to give time for the printing of the evidence and its consideration, arranging to meet in London for the purpose of drawing up the Report. This meeting took place in the month of July, and we were so occupied for about three weeks.

"The Report was compiled in the following manner: its main portion was drafted by me, in accordance with the instructions of the Commissioners, which were so clear and precise as to make my task a very easy one. Subject to the exceptions presently to be mentioned, these instructions were given by Mr. Gordon. And it was in doing this that he aroused the admiration of his colleagues and myself, by his complete mastery of the subject and the surprising facility and skill with which he handled so considerable a mass of materials. Taking up each topic of inquiry in its turn, he noted down rapidly on a sheet of paper an abstract of his views, stating them as he went along, and arranging them in the most precise and logical order. There was practically no difference of opinion while this was being done, though, of course, some of the points were afterwards discussed at considerable length. It was then my duty to write upon the subject, of which the abstract was thus drawn up, and on the following day what I had written was discussed and amended, and a further abstract of the next topic produced in the same rapid and masterly fashion. This process went on from day to day until the work was completed. I endeavoured, of course, to keep strictly within my instructions, and the heads of the several subjects thus drawn up by Mr. Gordon being so complete and clear, the result was that not much amendment was in general required. In one or two cases, as, for instance, in reference to the question whether the President of the College should hold a chair, the

Commissioners merely stated to me their opinion, and left me to work it out; but the larger portion of the Report was drawn up as I have described, and was thus mainly the work of the Chairman. The part of the Report which deals with the medical branch of the inquiry, and the subjects therewith connected, was wholly the work of Sir George Allman, and the financial tables and statements in reference thereto were drawn up by Mr. Murray.

"I cannot refrain from adding a personal tribute. I shall always gratefully remember Mr. Gordon's kindness to myself, both during the time we were engaged upon this work, and as expressed in the communications which I have received from him since. It is no small privilege to have counted such a man among one's friends.

"I remain, &c.,
"(Sd.) H. Brougham Leech.

"*Sir Robert Hamilton, K.C.B.,*
 Under Secretary for Ireland."

In reference to this and other unpaid services which Mr. Gordon rendered to the State, Sir Michael Hicks-Beach makes the following comment, which will be generally admitted to be alike pertinent and just:—

"What strikes me about his career is, that he did not *seek* prominence, or work: but that he did with remarkable ability, and with great pains, what came to his hand. If he was not called on to do more and higher work was he to blame?"

In the year after the issuing of this Commission,

in 1877, he was invited by Mr. Cross, then Home
Secretary, to supply the place of Mr. Justice Grove
on the Board of Commissioners for the University
of Oxford, engaged in revising the Statutes and
Ordinances of the several Colleges: and upon this
Commission he continued to serve till its work was
finished. He was much gratified by this appointment, and devoted his best energies to a subject upon
which he was so well qualified to advise. Though it
is known that he did not always agree with the conclusions of the Board, he always spoke in the highest
terms of the public spirit and consideration for the University shewn by his Colleagues in their arduous task.

Not long after the lamented death of Professor
Henry Smith, one of the Commissioners, which took
place in February, 1883, Mr. Gordon, in the course
of conversation with the writer, expressed the highest admiration for Mr. Smith's exalted character,
dwelling particularly on his candour, rectitude of
judgment, and liberality of sentiment, with his own
deep feeling of regret at his loss.

He was soon to follow. His constitution had been
more impaired for some years past than his friends
in general had at all suspected. For who could
detect any trace of bodily weakness or decay while
he was under the spell of that vigorous and active
intellect?

A painful circumstance which had occurred in his
own household some time before had weighed heavily
upon his spirits, and may not have been without
its effect in hastening his end. A boy in his service,

in whom he had taken great interest, and whom he
had kept in his employment long after most persons
would have parted with him, had, from some per-
versity of temper or mental defect, been at last
unavoidably discharged. The poor lad left his
master's presence, wished his fellow-servants a
hurried good-bye, rushed to his own room and
shot himself. To Mr. Gordon, the most tender-
hearted and considerate of men to all about him,
this was a frightful blow, from which it is probable
he never quite recovered. He did not sleep for three
nights; he shrunk from observation : and when he
was prevailed upon to keep a long-standing engagement at Milton, was on his arrival utterly prostrate.

It was plain that his whole system had received
a violent shock [k].

Yet in the week preceding his death Mr. Gordon
had been enjoying at his own house the society of
those nearest and dearest to him, and the hospitality, of which we have heard, ran its genial round,

[k] The last time that the writer saw Mr. Gordon in his own home
was in December, 1882, when, in company with the learned and
accomplished Master of Wellington College, he went over to Easthampstead one dismal afternoon to see him. There had been a fall
of snow, several inches deep, overnight, but at some distance from
his house, near the church, they met Mr. Gordon on his way to
the school. He looked, as they thought, worn and aged, but turned
back with his visitors, and welcoming them with his wonted cor-
diality and cheerfulness, entertained them with a packet of correspondence just received from Town, in a tone that quite dispelled
any misgivings on the score of health in the writer's mind.
He is afraid that he sunk several degrees in his companion's esti-
mation by his unrestrained amusement at Mr. Gordon's humourous
comments.

heightened and enlivened by a fund of anecdote and brilliancy of conversation which never failed : when almost with the departure of the last guest the candle burned low in the socket, and the friends who had left their host in the full flow and exuberance of his playful fancy were summoned back in haste to a darkened chamber and a dying bed.

The end came so fast that very many of his large circle of acquaintances were for some time unaware of the loss which they had sustained : and under the circumstances the assemblage by his grave in Easthampstead Churchyard on the Wednesday following his death was not less remarkable for the number and distinction of the mourners, than for the deep feeling by which all present, parishioners and non-parishioners, were moved. Mr. Gordon died on Friday, May 25, 1883. A Funeral Sermon preached in Easthampstead Church on the Sunday following (June 3) by his old and attached friend and former pupil, the Rev. R. Godfrey Faussett, paints Mr. Gordon to the life, and will supply the defects of this sketch.

"With diffidence I speak to you of that dear friend, with whose memory your hearts are full ; who for nigh a quarter of a century past has walked with you here in this house of God. Suddenly his Master has called him to his rest ; and for us, weak mortals as we are, the shock of separation seems all too fresh for words. Something, too, I bear in mind, how repugnant it was to his own characteristic delicacy of nature, as well as to (what I may call) his sober, reverential habit of mind, that aught so sacred, so inscrutable, as the life of a servant of Christ, should be submitted to the rude analysis of an erring human hand. The secrets of the heart are for the most part 'unspeakable words;' they may not, and cannot be uttered. While God alone discerns our spirits, our estimates of each other must needs be at best superficial—well for us if they be not presumptuous also.

"I will try, then, to recount to you some of those outward marks and traits which seem to me best calculated to illustrate the character of our friend.

"I look back to the University, which he served and adorned to the last, and where the best years of his life were spent, and I see a man gifted with so clear and capacious an intellect, that he bore off with ease the chief prizes of his day, and (apparently without effort) assimilated to himself knowledge in all its branches, such as cost others of more than average ability years of laborious study to acquire, yet who was of so generous and unassuming a disposition, that he never despised another's ignorance or stupidity, nor asserted a superiority of which he must—but seemed not to—have been conscious.

"I see a man of so happy and genial a nature, that he was ever the welcomest of the welcome in the society—even of the youngest, towards whom indeed his own fresh sympathies seemed in an especial manner to attract him; but who, while he could laugh unreservedly with the merriest lad among them, never tolerated an excess, or a profanity, in deed or in word.

"I see a man who, apart from his powers of conversation and vast range of knowledge of men and things, possessed so keen a sense of humour, so sparkling and ready a wit, that his presence in his 'common-room,' or at the table of his co-evals, was always the centre and life of the party, but who was never known to utter an ill-natured word, nor do I think he ever harboured an unkind thought.

"Once more—I see the same man sitting with one or another apart, conversing on the most solemn subjects that can engross the heart of man—subjects to which he would pass from some topic of transient interest, almost without change of tone—simply, naturally, readily, as if [not as if, but *because*] his heart was always so attuned to reverence that he was scarcely conscious of the transition. At such times he has done more (I say it advisedly) to confirm the waverer, to reclaim the wanderer, to clear away the doubts (it may be) of (so-called) intellectual scepticism, than any other man could do. He spoke always from the deepest conviction—the conviction of a man devoid of bias or bigotry. The vast resources (not of his learning only, but) of his original independent thought, were at the command of any enquirer; and his 'counsel' was 'sweet.'

"Looking back now along the vista of years, I recognize a character of rare harmony and beauty. I think he was kinder than most men who are kind. I think he was truer and more real than most men who are true and real. Ostentation, affectation, had absolutely no part in him. I have passed over his public work, the many valuable services which he rendered to his University, and to the House to which he was attached. These are matters of fame —no need that I should dilate upon them here. It is not, it never is, upon such monuments that we read the true epitaph of the man. Often his friends (and he had many friends, how could it be otherwise?) have grudged for him that he was not called to higher place and dignity. His versatility adapted him for any place; his ability for the highest. It pleased God to will it otherwise. And yet, humanly speaking, we may acknowledge, I think, that his virtues themselves tended rather to hold him back from promotion. He was too large-hearted to narrow his sympathies to sect or party; too honest to wear the livery of this or that popular enthusiasm of which (though none more ready than he to recognize the merits) his judgment recoiled from the extravagancies.

"Which of us now could wish his life to have been other than it was? Not you, my friends, I dare assert; for though I know but little of what his work was here, knowing the man, I do not doubt he won your hearts. Think of him as he was, the wise, the true, the kind, and thank God with me that his lot was cast with yours. You have often listened to his voice, listen to it still; 'being dead, he speaketh.' He seems to bid us now to sorrow neither for him nor for ourselves; but remembering him as he was, and as he is, to lift our hearts upwards from a world which is fast slipping away beneath our feet."

The following lines, also by an old and dear friend
and pupil of Mr. Gordon, the Rev. R. St. John Tyrwhitt, a name well known in literature and art, breathe
the very spirit of the time and place :—

> "With its familiar clinking sound
>   The rectory-gate behind me fell :
> Some honied drops and scented snows
> From faint rich May and guelder-rose
>   Down-rustling, broke the silent spell
> Of that remembered ground :
> Through masses of dark forest-green
>   All brown and scarlet, brick and tile,
> The house stood rich and warm between—
>   A pleasant place, a little while.
>
> "Sagaciously at ease they fed,
>   With dewlaps deep in summer grass,
> Those well-bred, well-contented kine :
>   They raised no head, but let one pass,
> And never stirred their social line.
> The grey cob shook his head,
> And fretted gently in his stall ;
>   His friend the keen fox-terrier strayed
>   To find the hand he best obeyed,
> And listened for a silent call.
>
> "But all within was hushed and dark,
>   And women wept, and men looked grim,
>   And in a dread and darken'd room
> Mine old best friend lay stiff and stark.
>   'Mid sickening scents and daylight gloom
>   I kissed the lips of him ;
> Had we known *that* in strength and pride,
>   When therefrom truth and learning came,
>   And humour bicker'd forth like flame—
> Should we have laughed or sighed ?

"On the old study-table lay
    An empty album, which had held
Quaint photographs of many a friend
    Far fled and scattered, need-compelled—
Priest, soldier, scholar—all away.
Love here hath but its day,
And comes like life with morn and sun :
    Till the new earth and the new heaven
    Hold all the choir of the Forgiven,—
Till Love make All the mystic One."

In further illustration of Mr. Gordon's character
the following letter is subjoined ; it was written to an
old pupil who had been led astray, in the hope that
he might recover himself; and in its measured and
temperate language is a model of dignified and kindly
remonstrance :—

" Easthampstead Rectory, Bracknell, Sept. 6.

"DEAR MR. —— I have read your sad account of
yourself, of which I will only say I do not quite
understand the points or also the report of the trial.
It gave me great pain to think that one of whom
I once thought so well had fallen so low. I fear
your life for months past has not been reputable,
certainly not consistent with the profession to which
you once devoted yourself. But I do not wish to reproach you ; I would much rather comfort and assist
you. Yours is an advanced age to make a fresh start
in life, but you still may have many years during
which you may redeem some of the time. I cannot
help thinking that there are elements of good in your
character, which may germinate and bring forth fruit.
But you must be prepared for a hard struggle ; I trust

you will meet it, with God's grace to help you, bravely. I assure you nothing would give me greater pleasure than to hear that you were in the way of re-establishing yourself; and if you had any occasion to refer any one to me I should speak truthfully but kindly of you as I now feel. I send you a token of good-will, and I wish it was larger. Perhaps it will be some comfort on your voyage to know that you carry with you even the good-will of one who knew you in happier days.

> "Believe me,
> "Sincerely yours,
> "O. GORDON."

All must hope that an appeal to the better nature urged with so much truth and delicacy has not failed of its effect.

The Rev. E. H. Whinyates, his fellow-worker for eighteen years, says, " During the eighteen years we were together I never saw him once out of temper, and never heard him say a harsh unkind thing of man, woman, or child. The unconscious secret influence he exerted on all with whom he came in contact was most remarkable; he lived but to do good, and had especial influence over the young in his parish, and whenever he could was most zealous in promoting their future welfare. I have been much struck on this my first visit to East Hampstead since his death to find how his influence is still a pervading power, and how generally his loss is deplored both by high and low."

Mr. Gordon's " Short Method " with Parish Councils at a Diocesan Conference in the Theatre at Oxford created much amusement at the time, and put an end very opportunely to a wearisome discussion. His plan, recommended by an invariably successful experience in his own case, was to choose the hour most convenient for all parties, that of luncheon, and at the right moment to propound the burning question of the day, generally of a financial nature, to his host, and always with the happiest results.

None who were present at a dinner given to Mr. Ward Hunt by his personal friends on his appointment to be Chancellor of the Exchequer can ever forget the exquisite ease and address with which Mr. Gordon, on rising to speak, caught the feeling of the hour, and with apt allusion and impromptu strokes of wit, in a vein of subtle and half-unconscious irony held up the glass to many-coloured life. The graceful eloquence of the Chairman (Lord Dufferin), a private friend and political opponent of Mr. Hunt, threw an additional charm over a meeting, the like of which too rarely recurs.

But Mr. Gordon was quite as much in his element with country gentlemen, and tenant-farmers, as with Peers and Privy Councillors, or congressional laymen and divines. At an agricultural dinner at which he was called upon to acknowledge the toast of the Bishop and Clergy of the Diocese, his health was proposed by Mr. Price, himself an eminent agriculturalist, as being "not only a Clergyman, but an agriculturalist: who farmed to a great extent, and very successfully." Mr. Gordon spoke with his usual

point and humour; but his speech dealt too much
with local topics to be admitted here.

He found a congenial occupation in observing
every form of animal life. The habits and peculi-
arities of wild creatures were a constant study with
him: and any exhibition of high courage in man
or beast won his admiration. "He had a favourite black mare, whose vicious tricks," says Mr.
Faussett, "were a source of absolute delight to him,
though he was totally devoid of any conceit as to
being able to ride her." Some bull-terriers, which
afterwards came to a befitting end in Canada, with
their teeth set in a stranger's bullock-cart wheels,
were special favourites with him, from their spirit
and tenacity.

The fragments of his conversation lying about give
but a faint idea of its freshness and originality.
When a pupil on the eve of examination lamented
his ignorance of the details of History, he was con-
soled with the remark, that he would not be hampered
by facts.

He asked a youth whose conceit had led to his
failure in the Schools, "How came you to be plucked
for your Little-go, Mr. A.?"

"They examined me in such trifles, such trifles,
Sir, such trifles (*crescendo*)."

"Trifles to know, but not trifles to be ignorant of,
Mr. A.," was the unanswerable rejoinder.

When his milkman wanted help to replace a cow
that had died of feeding on a Mackintosh cape which
did not agree with her, he pointed out that her diet

had not had the effect of making her milk waterproof. When a lame and unintelligible story came from some members of a certain learned Society in Oxford, he observed that they had such an idea of their intellect that nothing they could understand was good enough for them. He spoke of a certain set of men whose desire for peace was so strong that they were ready to rush into a general war to preserve it. He quoted the dictum of an eminent friend as generally true, that any man who had wit enough to gain any position had usually wit enough to keep it. Or to take as equivalent to many lighter remarks one more serious. "Some of the most conceited persons I have ever known have been those who have suddenly changed their opinions, because *they* have been unable to answer a *novel* argument adduced, as if others could not. In several cases the particular argument was of no real value whatever."

But the result in all such cases is akin to disappointment.

The subtle essence of genuine humour is as evanescent and impalpable as the aroma of a flower, or the spray on the crest of the wave. It dies at its birth. The stars of such rulers of society and masters of debate as the late Earl of Derby, Bishop Wilberforce, and Dean Stanley, already begin to pale, and the next generation will ask wherein lay the secret of their marvellous personal ascendency. So is it with men less prominent, but not perhaps less able. We retain the tradition of their power and brilliancy, but have lost the evidence.

Such illustrations, however, might be multiplied
to any extent; but this Memoir is only intended to
serve as an Introduction to the Sermons which are
the real object of the publication,—that those who
were not personally acquainted with the Author
may know what manner of man he was: that his
profound belief in revealed truth and in every word
of God did not proceed from careless acquiescence or
sluggishness of intellect, but was the fruit of ripe
study and exact knowledge of the Scriptures: the
settled conviction of a mind as acute in weighing
evidence and detecting fallacy, as it was alive to
every phase of philosophy and to every discovery
of science.

His conclusions were those of a man of genius,
not buried in abstractions but conversant with the
practical business of life, with a thorough mastery
of fact on subjects to which he had given special
attention, a wide range of information on all
subjects, and an acquaintance which seemed almost
intuitive with the contents of books that he had
occasion to consult. He had heard and considered
recent speculations upon religious questions, and was
only the more rooted and grounded in the faith once
delivered to the Saints. He could fully enter into
the difficulties of other minds, and regard their errors
and misgivings with allowance and pity, while he held
steadfastly to the doctrines and practice of his own
Church. He had a great dislike to the Romish system,
as opposed, in his view, to the Catholic Faith, nor had
he any sympathy with the extravagances of modern

Sectaries: but ho had a genuine admiration for all that was good and sound in any form of belief, and was in perfect charity with those who differed from him on religious grounds.

It has been very difficult to know what to choose from a great body of compositions, all entitled to a hearing, and no two persons could be expected to agree in the selection. In any case only scant justice can be meted out to Mr. Gordon, who did nothing for display, and only aimed at making his teaching intelligible and useful to his parishioners. Yet it is hoped that the consistency of view maintained throughout these discourses, extending over a long series of years, the clearness of statement, the nice observation of nature, with the admirable exposition of Scripture in which he excelled, will not only interest the reader by the stamp of intellectual power, impressed on every page, but may give back hope and comfort to many a doubting heart, and teach it to anchor upon "the certainty of those things in which it had been instructed."

Mr. Gordon was never married. By a melancholy fatality his younger brother, Mr. Alexander Gordon, to whom he had bequeathed the bulk of his property, was killed by being thrown out of his carriage within a month of attending his brother's funeral.

NOTES.

NOTE to p. 14.

The munificent donation of £5,000 in augmentation of the poorer Livings in the gift of Christ Church by the late Mr. Ruskin was prompted by a sense of obligation to Mr. Gordon on his son's account, which he wished to express in the way most acceptable to him. The presentation was made to Christ Church through Mr. Gordon in these words: "I give it to *you*, Mr. Gordon, as Representative of the College, for the College."

NOTE to p. 22.

Perhaps the interest attaching to the subject may warrant some additional particulars. Since the foregoing account was in type, the writer, who had trusted entirely to his own recollection, has, by the kind offices of the Secretary of the O. U. S., had access to the Minutes of the Meeting, which was held on March 13, 1847. The original proposal came in the form of a resolution to suspend Rule 70, which forbad the application of the Society's funds to any object not connected with the Society. This was moved by Lord Dufferin. To this an amendment was moved by the Rev. W. Thomson (the present Archbishop of York), that the Rule should not be suspended, with the proviso, "that a Subscription List be exposed in the Society's Room for the relief of the sufferers from the Irish Famine."

When the division was taken there were for the Amendment 151, against it 87, so the Motion was lost by 64. Mr. Ward Hunt and other men of note, who have passed away, took part in the debate. Happily the movers both of the Resolution and of the Amendment are spared for the service of their country in Church and State: one as Primate of England, the other as Viceroy of India.

NOTE to p. 39.

Upon this subject a correspondence of some length ensued between Mr. Gladstone and Mr. Gordon : which, though honourable to both parties, would not at this distance of time, even with the requisite authorization, awaken more than an antiquarian interest by its publication.

NOTE to p. 40.

While Mr. Gordon was on the Council he procured the discontinuance of sundry University Sermons out of Term : and by so doing earned the thanks of the overburdened Vice-Chancellor, who assured him that he had made an appreciable addition to his own chance of longevity, and that of his successors.

PREFACE TO SERMONS.

THE selection of the following Sermons has been
determined in many cases by the circumstances
under which they were written. It was thought
right that two of the sermons preached before the
University, as specimens of Mr. Gordon's academical
style, should be included. The last, preached five
days before the Author's death, has been added, as
possessing an interest of its own. The recovery
of the Prince of Wales was naturally an event which
Mr. Gordon would be likely, from his former official
relation to H.R.H., to feel deeply, and a sermon
preached at that time is therefore retained. The
disastrous season of 1879 called forth many conflict-
ing opinions upon the duty and efficacy of prayer,
and a sermon bearing upon Mr. Kingsley's views on
that difficult subject is too characteristic to be omitted;
while other sermons upon prayer generally express
Mr. Gordon's own opinion without qualification. His
judgment with reference to the Romish controversy
and our position as regards Nonconformists is to
be found in other discourses; and passages from
two out of several sermons on the educational scheme
of 1870 are given, as indicative of an opinion which
never wavered on the merits of the system then
introduced.

Besides these occasional sermons others will be

found to treat of the main Articles of the Faith, and various theological topics: some are of more private and personal interest, and extracts have been given in some cases where there was not room for more, in illustration of some opinion or trait of character which ought not to be left unnoticed.

In none of these sermons is there a hint of fine writing, nor the slightest attempt to court popularity; but the mastery of the subject, whatever it may be, the plainness of speech, the distinctness of purpose, the love of truth, with the grasp of Scripture everywhere manifested, will not perhaps wholly fail in other quarters of the effect which they produced upon the parishioners of East Hampstead.

If some injustice is done to Mr. Gordon's memory by a publication, to which he would not have been likely to assent without a thorough revision of the text of the sermons, and probably not at all, the benefit resulting from this expression of original and independent thought may possibly be pleaded as an offset, and redeem the wrong. Many minds would derive more comfort, and be more open to persuasion, by means of discourses intended only for a village congregation, than from more elaborate and studied compositions. The strength of these sermons lies in their directness of aim and the absence of ornament. For its purpose the style is perfect: and it would seldom be possible to suggest a better word for that employed: but it is the style of a writer expressing his meaning in the simplest and most natural terms, rising at times to eloquence without effort, by the mere force or expansion of the idea, but never involved—never confused—never obscure —not shrinking from the most abstruse subjects, when occasion requires, but always knowing where to stop—with accurate and profound learning in reserve, never paraded, but always at command.

With this explanation the following sermons are left to the candid judgment of the reader.

Milton Rectory,
March, 1885.

LIST OF SERMONS.

———◆———

SERMON I.

(p. 81.)

Preached before the University.   (Date uncertain.)

JEWISH AND CHRISTIAN PRIVILEGES AND RESPONSIBILITY.

NUMBERS xxiii. 19.   "God is not a man, that He should lie; neither the son of man, that He should repent: hath He said, and shall He not do it? or hath He spoken, and shall He not make it good?"

SERMON II.

(p. 100.)

Preached before the University during Lent.   (Date uncertain.)

THE TRUTH OF CHRIST THE BASIS OF MORALS.

1 COR. xv. 32.   "If after the manner of men I have fought with beasts at Ephesus, what advantageth it me, if the dead rise not? let us eat and drink; for to-morrow we die."

SERMON III.

(p. 119.)

Trinity Sunday, 1871.

MAN'S PLACE IN CREATION.

GENESIS ii. 7.   "And the Lord God formed man of the dust of the ground, and breathed into his nostrils the breath of life; and man became a living soul."

SERMON IV.

(p. 131.)

Eleventh Sunday after Trinity, 1864.

THE PHARISEE AND THE PUBLICAN.

ST. LUKE xviii. 14.   "I tell you, this man went down to his house justified rather than the other: for every one that exalteth himself shall be abased; and he that humbleth himself shall be exalted."

SERMON V.

(p. 142.)

Twenty-second Sunday after Trinity, 1863.

THE UNMERCIFUL CREDITOR.

ST. MATT. xviii. 32, 33. "O thou wicked servant, I forgave thee all that debt, because thou desiredst me: shouldest not thou also have had compassion on thy fellowservant, even as I had pity on thee?"

SERMON VI.

(p. 153.)

Whit Sunday, 1863.

GIFTS FOR MEN.

EPHES. iv. 7, 8. "Unto every one of us is given grace according to the measure of the gift of Christ. Wherefore He saith, When He ascended up on high, He led captivity captive, and gave gifts unto men."

SERMON VII.

(p. 165.)

July 13, 1879.

REV. C. KINGSLEY'S VIEWS ON THE QUESTION OF SPECIAL PRAYER CONSIDERED.

1 SAM. xii. 17. "I will call unto the Lord, and He shall send thunder and rain."

SERMON VIII.

(p. 178.)

Second Sunday in Lent, 1865.

THE PROFIT OF PRAYER.

JOB xxi. 15. "What is the Almighty, that we should serve Him? and what profit should we have, if we pray unto Him?"

SERMON IX.

(p. 190.)

THE GOD THAT HEARETH PRAYER.

PSALM lxv. 2. "O Thou that hearest Prayer, unto Thee shall all flesh come."

SERMON X.

(p. 200.)

Thanksgiving Sermon, March 3, 1872.

ON THE RECOVERY OF H.R.H. THE PRINCE OF WALES.

JONAH iii. 10. "And God saw their works, that they turned from their evil way."

SERMON XI.

(p. 211.)

ST. MARY MAGDALEN.

ST. LUKE viii. 2. "Mary called Magdalene."

SERMON XII.

(p. 223.)

Whit Sunday, 1882.

JESUITISM.

ST. JOHN vii. 17. "If any man will do His will, he shall know of the doctrine, whether it be of God."

SERMON XIII.

(p. 235.)

CALVINISM.

ST. MATT. vi. 33. "Seek ye first the kingdom of God and His righteousness."

SERMON XIV.

(p. 249.)

First Sunday after Ascension, 1871.

CHRISTIANITY—WHAT?

ROM. viii. 34. "It is Christ that died, yea rather, that is risen again, who is even at the right hand of God, who also maketh intercession for us."

SERMON XV.

(p. 260.)

Eighth Sunday after Trinity, 1869.

WHAT RIZPAH, THE DAUGHTER OF AIAH, DID.

2 SAM. xxi. 14. "And after that God was intreated for the land."

SERMON XVI.

(p. 271.)

Ash-Wednesday, 1862.

OUR CROSS.

GAL. vi. 14. "The cross of our Lord Jesus Christ, by whom the world is crucified unto me, and I unto the world."

SERMON XVII.

(p. 281.)

Twentieth Sunday after Trinity, 1866.

CALLING AND ELECTION.

ST. MATT. xxii. 14. "For many are called, but few are chosen."

SERMON XVIII.

(p. 292.)

August 23, 1868.

CONVERSION.

ROM. vi. 21. "What fruit had ye then in those things whereof ye are now ashamed?"

SERMON XIX.

(p. 304.)

1871.

POWER MAKYTH MAN. AMERICAN PRESIDENTS.

1 SAM. x. 6. "And the Spirit of the Lord will come upon thee, and thou shalt prophesy with them, and shalt be turned into another man."

SERMON XX.

(p. 316.)

July 27, 1877.

AN OLD MAN'S REASON.

1 ST. PETER iii. 15. "Be ready always to give an answer to every man that asketh you a reason of the hope that is in you with meekness and fear."

SERMON XXI.

(p. 327.)

Dec. 1878 and 1879.

SIR W. HAYTER AND MR. DELANE.

ISAIAH xl. 1. "Comfort ye My people."

SERMON XXII.

(p. 338.)

(Last Sermon preached, Trinity Sunday, May 20, 1883, died May 25.)

TRINITY IN UNITY.

REV. iv. 8.   "Holy, Holy, Holy, Lord God Almighty."

EXTRACTS FROM UNPUBLISHED SERMONS.

(p. 350.)

APPENDIX I.

(p. 365.)

LATIN SPEECH AS SENIOR PROCTOR, EASTER TERM, 1847.

APPENDIX II.

(p. 373.)

CENSOR'S SPEECH ON DEATH OF DEAN GAISFORD,
MICHAELMAS TERM, 1855.

SERMON I.

Jewish and Christian Privileges and Responsibility.

NUMBERS xxiii. 19.

" God is not a man, that He should lie ; neither the son of man, that He should repent : hath He said, and shall He not do it ? or hath He spoken, and shall He not make it good ?"

THE truths of divine revelation are in their nature essentially different from any developments of human reason or inferences from human experience. They are not in any way anticipations of, or supplementary to, the progressive results of our own exertion, but relate rather to an order of things into which our natural powers, however improved by cultivation, are unable to penetrate. Unless this point is substantially conceded the believer in revelation will find it difficult to determine what its peculiar subject-matter is. No one at least in the present day will contend that we are to refer to it as a standard of political or physical truth. It might be urged with greater show of reason that its office is fulfilled by the establishment authoritatively of a purer code of morals; and it may be allowed at once that Christian morality so far exceeds anything imagined or practised by the heathen that it may be called not unfairly, by contrast, a new and distinct system. Yet the idea that this is, in its isolation, the sum and end of revealed truth has led many to the conclusion that a great part of its volume is irrelevant and vain. This consequence is indeed openly embraced by those bolder spirits, who reject in their very profession the idea of definite doctrine, and still more impressively because unintentionally illustrated, by the history of those bodies, which, thinking to avail themselves of the moral precepts of Christianity without recognizing their source and strength, find themselves carried down imperceptibly by the bent of an unsanctified nature to the positive denial of those first truths of religion which in their pride they refused, or in their indolence neglected, to maintain.

The Christian, however, will assume that the great end of revelation is to give us that knowledge which by nature we cannot have, the knowledge of "Him that dwelleth in light unapproachable," whom we in vain "seek to find out by searching," whom no man hath seen at any time,—the knowledge of what He is in Himself, so far as we can "see now through a glass darkly," of the mode of His being, and the nature of His attributes, as far as we are capable of understanding them—the knowledge specifically of His relation to us, and all those His wondrous acts to us which call forth all the feelings of love, fear, dependence, adoration, due from the creature to the Creator. To know this is the true sum of Christian knowledge; to give it its due effect upon the heart, the true realization of Christian life.

But this it is in which men have failed from the

beginning of the world. Heathen, Jew, and Christian, each in his degree must plead guilty to the charge "that knowing God, they glorified Him not as God, neither were thankful." Knowing Him, or having the means of knowing Him, they gave Him not the glory of acknowledgment, and gave the word of His knowledge no access to their hearts. "Thus their hearts were hardened, and their knowledge departed from them." And so it is still: how few of us are there in whose mouths the language of St. Paul, speaking of the love of Christ, would not be descriptive rather of what we ought and would strive to feel than of what we actually do feel. Yet who will suppose that St. Paul spoke of anything more than what should be the habitual warmth of a Christian's heart, while we are happy if we can put it for an instant under the most sensible sunshine of God's love. Nay, it might appear that St. Paul himself was not perfect in that feeling compared with that disciple who enjoyed the peculiar privilege of being the one whom Jesus loved. At all events, how small the number of those who realize in fact and feeling the full blessing of their Christian citizenship! And so with the Church of old. At what period of their history was it adequately impressed upon the Jewish mind that they were what they were, "a chosen generation, a royal priesthood, a holy nation, a peculiar people, to shew forth the praises of Him who called them out of darkness into His marvellous light?" *We* indeed read their records with the tokens of God's presence imprinted upon

every page.   The cloudy pillar of fire; the thunders
of Sinai; sins repeated and avenged; miracles recurring till they became familiar; laws of nature suspended till it was not a thing unheard of that the
stars in their courses should fight for the captains
of the Lord; nations dispossessed and exterminated;
those mighty kings, whose entire history is a memorial
of the power of God's love and the weight of his
displeasure; the national decline and fall; the clouds
of divine vengeance, rising at first no bigger than
a man's hand on the verge of the horizon, yet sweep-
ing gradually onwards towards the Holy City, till
at last they gather in a dark mass, and overwhelm
the nation in destruction: all these remind and impress upon us the conviction, that it is God's own
people that we are reading of, "and that He hath not
so dealt with any other nation."   Yet the Jews who
lived in the midst of these marvels were to a great
extent insensible of them, or misinterpreted their
meaning.   In their early history they felt their distinctions as burthens and impediments to their inveterate desire of living after the manner of the heathen
round them; at a later period, when they were on
the point of losing them, they regarded them as testimonies to their own superiority, and a justification
of spiritual pride.

Yet however little we can learn of the true character of the chosen people, from any expression of
their own consciousness upon the subject, we may
endeavour to place ourselves for a moment by the
side of the great prophet, himself not one of the

Lord's people, who looked down upon the tents of
Israel from the high places of Baal, and had revealed
to him in a trance the future destinies of the nation
whom he was called upon to curse. Balak, King of
Moab, saw only in the invaders of his land "a people
come out of Egypt." He knew little more of them
than that they covered the face of the earth, and
threatened in his own emphatic language, "to lick up
all round about them as the ox licketh up the grass
of the field." So he sent for the son of Beor to curse
his enemy; "for I wot that he whom thou bless-
est is blessed, and he whom thou cursest is cursed."
Nor had the prophet any personal objection to reaping
the wages of iniquity. Warned as he was, he still went
his way. But when his sacrifices were completed,
his tongue refused to do its work: "How shall I
curse, whom God hath not cursed? or how shall I
defy, whom the Lord hath not defied? For from the
top of the rocks I see Him, and from the hills I behold
Him: lo, the people shall dwell alone, and shall
not be reckoned among the nations. Who can count
the dust of Jacob, or count the fourth part of Israel?
Let me die the death of the righteous, and let my
last end be like his!" Again, from the field of
Zophim, on the top of Pisgah, and a third time from
the top of Peor, the word was changed from cursing
unto blessing. "Balaam the son of Beor hath said,
and the man whose eyes are open hath said: How
goodly are thy tents, O Jacob, and thy tabernacles,
O Israel! As the valleys are they spread forth, as
gardens by the river's side, as the trees of lign aloes

which the Lord hath planted, and as cedar trees beside
the waters. God brought him forth out of Egypt;
he hath as it were the strength of an unicorn. Blessed is he that blesseth thee, and cursed is he that
curseth thee." Lastly, in still more solemn tones, ere
he went unto his people, he warned the idolatrous
king of what should be hereafter. "I shall see Him,
but not now: I shall behold Him, but not nigh:
there shall come a Star out of Jacob, and a Sceptre
shall rise out of Israel, and shall smite the corners of
Moab, and destroy all the children of Sheth."

Such was the vision of the future unrolled before
the prophet's eyes. To us it may be a profitable
task to enquire briefly into the substance of what
he saw, and the principles on which his language
is to be interpreted. One point we may assume at
starting, that he saw and spoke of a reality. Otherwise the wildness of the place itself, the remoteness
of the time, the distant view of the mountain-land of
Moab, the orderly beauty of the tents of Israel seen
far below in the valley, might be looked upon as elements of a great poetic scene, such as might easily
be connected with a man whose mysterious character
and troubled communings with his own heart, and
solitary sacrifices thrice repeated, well accord with
those ideas which in older times regarded poetry as
a special gift of Heaven, and invested bard and prophet with common attributes and name. This view,
however, may be dismissed at once. It was no
creation of fancy that arrested the prophet's gaze.
It is impossible to resist the conviction of reality

which his words force upon us, "He hath said which heard the words of God, and knew the knowledge of the most High, falling into a trance but having his eyes open." The question seems what it substantially was: one part of it indeed is sufficiently explained by the history of Edom, Seir, and Amalek. Still it is obvious that this is but a part, and not the most important one; his language must appear cold and exaggerated, if its meaning is restricted to the overthrow and annihilation of the accursed race. Far beyond any temporal victories must be the blessing of those words, "He hath not beheld iniquity in Jacob, neither hath he seen perverseness in Israel: the Lord his God is with him, and the shout of a king is among them." Was it then, we ask, that Israel which lay visibly before his eyes, or was it some ideal Israel, of which they were but the faint shadow and resemblance, in which the Lord saw no iniquity or perverseness? Was the soul of the prophet filled with the sense and power of holiness, embodied and triumphant in the host of Israel? Was it not to them as a people, but to the cause which they typified imperfectly, that the promises pertained? It may be so. Doubtless theirs *was* the cause of God; *their* enemies the enemies of God. Doubtless they were imperfect representatives, and so far failed to attain the fulness of their blessings. Yet allowing this, we must be careful not to deprive this and prophecy generally of its positive character and specific references; bringing it down more or less to an abstract statement of the laws by which God

will judge the world, pointed, perhaps, at some special
occasion, but in its fulfilment independent of it.   It
is true indeed that the general laws of God's Providence must be involved in prophecy; but this may
well be because prophecy refers to events, and the
events are determined by those laws: and the question is whether its primary end is to declare those
events, or the laws which they illustrate.   That it
should declare them so far as to become a kind of
anticipated history is not to be expected; for it is
no part of the idea of prophecy that its predictions
should be intelligible before events have supplied
a key to its interpretation.   It is enough for us that
we see its meaning when it is fulfilled.

But apart from general considerations on the nature of prophecy, into which I will not enter, there
seem to be special reasons for bearing in mind the
positive aim of the prophecy of Balaam, arising both
from the character of the man himself, and the un-
deniable fact of his having received direct instruction
from the Spirit of God.   A good man from the convictions of his own heart might have foretold the
final triumph of a good cause, and by consequence
of the people associated with it, in that language
of faith which has more than the dignity of prophecy.
An ignorant man again might have been moment-
arily impressed with the sense of goodness, and
become, as it were, the unwilling instrument of
blessing a cause with which he had no sympathy.
But Balaam was neither of these: he neither loved
what is right and holy, nor was he ignorant of it.

It is unnecessary to make any remark upon a character so much studied in this place, or upon that mystery of iniquity inexplicable in terms, but illustrated by his conduct, and I fear too often by the experience of the hearts of every one of us. Who, however, can fail to recognize in that idea of righteousness which the prophet Micah has preserved, "to do justly, and to love mercy, and to walk humbly with thy God," the very points which our Lord Himself insists upon as the weightier matters of the law, "judgment, mercy, and faith?" There was then no want of knowledge in the mind of Balaam; nor do these ideas appear to have been imparted to him at the time, but rather to have been in his habitual possession. That sad and solemn aspiration, "Let me die the death of the righteous," could only have been suggested by the working of his own mind upon the facts before him. He spoke out of the fulness of his heart; it was no forced confession or involuntary acknowledgment of truth, but the sincere though inoperative wish that "his last end might be like theirs." And it is in this light, I presume, that Bp. Butler regards it, as there would be nothing extraordinary in his uttering sentiments inconsistent with his conduct, if they were simply due to the power of inspiration, and not to be identified with the convictions of his own heart. It was not then knowledge of the truths which was communicated unto Balaam in the vision of the Most High; nor yet was it the triumph of Israel as the *ideal* representative of a righteous cause. We cannot

suppose so wide a separation of the prophetical from
the historical Israel. For when was it that Israel
realized in any degree that beauty of holiness which
it might be supposed to represent? True, their foes
were destroyed before them; Amalek punished for
ever; Seir fulfilled its destiny, and Edom became
a possession—but where was the righteous nation,
the zeal in the cause of God, the love of His Holy
Name, the willing mind, the faith, and the obedience? On the contrary, is not the complaint from
first to last of the hard heart, and stubborn neck,
of abominations repeated without end, of rebellion
and ingratitude, till at last the whole body became
a mass of festering corruption, full of wounds and
scars and putrifying sores? Nor indeed can the
distinction between the prophetical and the historical
be maintained without danger of destroying the very
force and point of prophecy. It may be conceded
that they generally, but not universally, employ a
different language, and see things from a different
point of view, that prophecy speaks of the blessings
and glory, history of the sins and humiliation, of
Israel.   And this difference naturally makes us
anxious to discover the corresponding objects that
will enable us to recognize the truth of both. But
surely this is to be sought for, not in the distinction between the Israel of prophecy and history,
but in that double character which belongs to every
man and nation more or less distinctly, as he has
received more or less of the free gifts of God. What
description can be too glorious for that nation in

the midst of which it has pleased the Lord to dwell? What description, on the other hand, can be too dark for that polluted people, which, invested with such glorious powers, so signally abused them to its own destruction, and the dishonour of God's Holy Name? This was the vision which unrolled itself before the eyes of the Prophet from the Eastern Mountains. He saw the wings of God's love spreading over the people of his choice, "even as the eagle fluttereth over her young, spreadeth abroad her wings, taketh them, beareth them upon her wings." He saw them as the Lord's portion, and blessed them as he saw them—holy, just, righteous, and invincible. He saw them such by virtue of the power that was sustaining them; for how could they be otherwise whom the Lord had chosen? The arm of the Lord was with them, to go forth conquering and to conquer. "Surely there was no enchantment against Jacob, or divination against Israel." But he saw not "that Jeshurun should wax fat and kick, that he should forsake God which made him, and lightly esteem the rock of his salvation;" he saw not "that the time would come when God should hide His face from them— a froward generation, children in whom is no faith." He saw not, "that a fire should be kindled in His anger, and burn unto the lowermost hell, the sword without and terror within, to scatter them into corners, and make the very remembrance of them to cease upon the earth." He saw, in short, their blessings, but he did not see their sins. And this view will

surely be more effective in its application to our
hearts than any generalization of revealed truth,
not to mention how consonant it is with the teaching of Scripture elsewhere, that the same place and
the same person may be the subject of the highest
gifts and the most fearful condemnation. For the
Christian cannot read the history of the Jew without being reminded of that still more favoured people,
which has taken their place in the economy of God,
and of which we are members—the Church of Christ.
Nor will it occur to him to doubt but that greater
gifts, and a larger measure of His grace, are poured
into his bosom than enriched the people that He
loved of old. What then if some Balaam were
placed upon an eminence to survey again the tents
of Israel? Would not his spiritual eyes discern
much greater things than all the glories of the
heights of Pisgah? "Prophets and wise men desired to see those things which were once seen,
and which the eye of faith may still see, and did
not see them." What was all the inheritance of
Israel, the ark of the covenant, the mercy-seat,
the visible majesty of the Most High, compared
with that presence which made the glory of the
latter house greater than the glory of the former
house, and which is inseparable from the very life
and being of the Church? What is a people chosen
out of all the nations of the earth, to a people created,
as it were, out of nothing, "which in times past,"
as St. Peter says, "were no people, but are now
the people of God?" What was that Church of the

Wilderness or of Mount Zion to that Church in which all nations shall be gathered into one—to worship the Lord in Spirit and in Truth — sanctified with the precious blood of Christ, "that He might present it to Himself a glorious Church, not having spot or wrinkle or any such thing, but that it may be holy and without blemish?" Surely, if this is our spiritual inheritance, any considerations would be valuable which would compel us to recognize it more faithfully than is common with us. Surely if the Church is an actual body, bound together in its parts by closer ties than those of friendship, family, or country, even by that life which, having its spring in Christ the Head, is the source of life to each communicating member, great must be not only our loss but also our guilt in thinking or speaking of it as a mere name, or aggregate of individuals, or representative of an idea.

And this warning is more necessary in an enquiring age which refuses to accept anything as fact, except that which can be supported by sensible evidence. And so to our sorrow it must be confessed that the attributes of the Christian Church can hardly be inferred from the aspect of the Christian world, and we can well conceive the infidel enquirer looking back upon the last 1800 years, and sneering on the presumption of those who claim to themselves the name of saints, and have done so much to vitiate their claim. Nevertheless, the Christian will remember that the Word of God standeth sure; that "He is not a man that He should lie, nor the Son of man

that He should repent;" that His promises are without repentance, and that the Church which He has
purchased is to be characterized by His gifts, and
not by our miserable shortcomings.   But I would
speak more practically, not of the Church itself as
a whole, but of ourselves as individual members,
though it may be hard to separate the two.   The
aspect, indeed, and character of the world around us
is such as to suggest a question.   Is there such a
thing as the company of the redeemed?   Is the seal
of God's love a pure imagination?   Is the cross of
Christ a shadow on the clouds, or is it the very
sign by which we are to fight and conquer, "and
the kingdoms of this world shall become the kingdoms of the Lord, and of His Christ?"   Are the
graces of divine ordinances, which are presumed of
every one that has been admitted into the fold of
Christ, fictions or facts?   Is Christianity itself anything more than an improvement of what has gone
before, destined to serve the purpose of human
progress for a time, and to be absorbed itself into
some new system of more comprehensive truth,
compared to which its feeble light is but as the
first streak of the morning to the brightness of the
perfect day?   Or is it rather that light which
lighteth every man that cometh into the world,
and will light even unto the end of time?   Is this
the true fold in which we may abide for ever, feeding
on green pastures, and drinking freely of the waters
of comfort, or is it but a resting-place for the day,
offering only a brief refreshment on a pilgrimage

we know not whither? These questions touch the interests, and should touch the heart, of every man; and it is impossible to conceal from ourselves that they are being asked and considered extensively throughout the world, receiving such solutions as might be expected, when men depart from the standard of God's revealed word, and recorded promises, and become a law and standard to themselves. By the avowed sceptic, by the philosophic enquirer, by the statesman, by each man who frames his system for himself, the power of Christianity is measured by its visible effects or by the individual consciousness, rather than by the guaranteed gifts and promises of God. Yet if men would consider they could not help seeing that they are neither doing justice to themselves, nor "rendering to the Lord the homage due unto His Name," in thus making their own weakness the limit of His spiritual blessings. The language of St. Paul is exactly parallel to that of the text: "What if some did not believe? shall their unbelief make the faith of God of none effect? God forbid: yea, let God be true, but every man a liar." The advantage of the Jew would still have been the same, though no Jew ever reaped it. Circumcision would not have profited the less, though it had become a brand of condemnation to every one that bore it. Far as men have departed from the service of God, "there has been always a remnant, according to the election of grace." In all times "God has raised up witnesses to His truth in the persons of His faithful servants." Yet those 7,000 men that bowed not the knee to Baal *added* nothing to the truth of which they were the witnesses.   Nor would a single one of the blessings of Israel have lost any of its virtue, though every child of Jacob had departed from the God of his fathers.   And so with us: those covenanted helps, which are the mainstays of every Christian soul, are not to be determined by any reference to general experience.   It is enough for every one who is working out his own salvation in fear and trembling to know that they are sufficient for him.   No growth in grace can make them more, no despite done unto the spirit of grace can prove them to be less.   He that hid his pound in a napkin, and had it taken away, still *had* received it.   The fact remained, and the grace of God would still be a fact in the midst of an apostate world.   How careful, then, ought we to be, lest any observation of our brethren around us, lest any experience of human weakness or human depravity, lest any false and plausible philosophy, lest any consciousness of sin working in our own hearts, should lead us to disturb the verities of Christian faith.   The creed of Israel was historical; it embodied the great facts of their deliverance, and was to be handed down from generation to generation by a perpetual ordinance.   "He made a covenant with Jacob, and gave Israel a law, which He commanded their forefathers to teach their children; that their posterity might know it, and their children which are yet unborn; to the intent that when they came up they might shew their children the same."

The creed of the Christian is the history of his spiritual deliverance. The facts which it records, even in their most formal enunciation, cannot be separated from their spiritual significancy and effect upon our condition. Article by article we trace a positive change in the prospect and condition of human nature, corresponding to that great "mystery of Godliness" whereby God was "manifested in the flesh, justified in the spirit, seen of angels, preached unto the Gentiles, believed on in the world, received up into glory." Did Christ take upon Himself the form of a servant, and bear our nature upon earth? It is united with Him now in one person at the right hand of God. Did He become obedient unto death, even unto death upon the cross? Then reckon we ourselves also to be dead to sin with Him. "Nay," says the Apostle, "ye are dead, and your life is hid with Christ in God." "For we are buried with Him by baptism unto death; that, like as Christ was raised up from the dead by the glory of the Father, even so we also should walk in newness of life." Did He cast off the garments of the grave and rise again to incorruption? "Then, if we have been planted together in the likeness of His death, we shall be also in the likeness of His resurrection." Yea, already "Christ has risen from the dead, and become the first-fruits of them that slept." Has He ascended unto heaven? He has "gone before to prepare a place for us, that where He is we may be also." Has He taken captivity captive? Then are the captives free. Has He

H

received gifts for men? Then has He poured them out upon His Church, "yea, even on the rebellious also, that the Lord may dwell among them." Has He promised "to be with it always, even unto the end of the world?" Then assuredly "where two or three are gathered together in His Name, there is He in the midst of them." One great duty, therefore, which we in particular owe to ourselves, to this generation, and to the children that are yet unborn, a duty which the signs of the times mark out as a special one in an age of growing unbelief, is to preserve whole and uncorrupt the faith "once delivered to the Saints." It is true indeed that no neglect of ours, no spirit of compromise with error, no wickedness of the world, no apostasy, though it should be universal, can touch one jot or one tittle of that truth which shall endure for ever when heaven and earth have passed away. The truth is not dependent upon us, but we upon the truth. But we are constituted stewards, and may be unfaithful to our charge. Stewards we certainly are, and shall have to give account as such, when "the Lord shall come and reckon with His servants." And the enquiry in that day will not be simply, *what* we have to give our Lord, but whether we can restore with usury those very talents which we have received. This is a responsibility we cannot evade; the number is recorded against us; no denial of ours, no forgetfulness, will alter a single unit of its sum. It is well, therefore, to reckon with ourselves now; otherwise our judgment will not be that of Tyre and

Sidon, but of Chorazin and Bethsaida, which saw the mighty works which would have moved the very cities of the plain to repent in sackcloth and ashes, but repented not. Let the Christian, therefore, whom, like Capernaum, the grace of God has exalted unto heaven, so measure and preserve his exaltation, that when the time comes to fix his place for ever he be not cast down into hell. This he will do by God's help, if he bears it constantly in mind. God has not only made us a peculiar people, but has plainly told us so. It is only by remembering what we are that under His grace we can hope to become what we should be—partakers in fact and fruition, as we are by right and title, of the inheritance of the saints in light.

SERMON II.

The Truth of Christ the Basis of Morals.

———✦———

1 COR. xv. 32.

*"If after the manner of men I have fought with beasts at
Ephesus, what advantageth it me, if the dead rise not? let us
eat and drink; for to-morrow we die."*

AT a time of the year when the name of self-denial
is often on our lips, and the idea of it familiar to
our minds, and the practice possibly has some place
in our daily lives, it will not, I think, be an unprofitable employment of some portion of an hour if I
enquire, or at least suggest an enquiry, into the
grounds and principles on which the duty so pro-
minently put forward at this penitential season is
to be maintained. I speak not of the wisdom of
devoting special times and seasons to a stricter
discipline and sterner practice, but of the denial
of the lusts of the flesh in itself, not as a matter
of purer taste, not as on the whole adding more to
the sum of human happiness than it detracts from
it, not as more consistent with the dignity of human
nature, but as a Christian duty; and that again not
peculiar to this time, not giving a party-coloured
appearance to the Christian life, but running through
its whole texture, still existing though unseen, pene-

trating the substance when it is not detected on the surface, and only brought out into relief by the incidence of those lights and shadows which are cast upon it by the varying associations of the Christian year. It is indeed a condescension to our imperfect natures, that we are allowed and encouraged, on fitting occasions, to give play to particular affections, and to cultivate particular tempers, the exclusive or excessive development of which would destroy the harmony of the Christian character. For the right affection of the heart towards its Maker and all heavenly things is neither joy nor sorrow purely, not hope nor fear: yet is there a time for all things; there is the night of sorrow and the morning of joy, the depression of fear and the confidence of hope, each in its turn and its degree; by partial and oblique movements we must be content to make a slow but sure advance in holiness and the love of God. Perfect love is a simple, direct, and impulsive feeling, casting out as alien whatever it does not absorb as akin unto itself, but in its growth and imperfection it admits of analysis; it is the result of many forces, the combination of many elements, reverence, ambition of God's love and approbation, delight in the hope or consciousness of it, fear of His displeasure, each of which has an influence and expansion of its own[a]. As then, though a real growth in grace can be nothing less than "the edification of the whole creature, till in the unity of the faith and of the knowledge of the Son of God he come

[a] Butler, vol. ii. 195, (168).

unto a perfect man, unto the measure of the stature
of the fulness of Christ[b]," yet this is effected not by
the simultaneous growth of the whole building, but
by adding, as it were, stone to stone—as in teaching, line is laid upon line, and precept upon precept;
and, as in the ways of Providence, affliction and prosperity each have their message from the Most High;
as in the government of ourselves we sometimes
suffer ourselves to rejoice freely, sometimes wet our
couches with our tears, so may we, as it seems fitting,
take some particular duty and affection, isolate, en-
large upon, enforce it, without being supposed either
to exaggerate its importance, or ignore the existence
of others and its relation to them. We may not
only impress and apply, but we may analyse and
examine, we may trace back a duty to its command
and authority, and a feeling to fundamental proposition, be it one of fancy or of truth[c]. I say its *proposition* rather than its *object*, because though it is most
truly said that "we are so constituted as to feel
certain affections upon the sight and contemplation
of certain objects," and again, "it is by reason that
we get the ideas of the several objects of our affections," yet it is clear that the ideas we thus get
are *truths*, and admit of being expressed in propositions. Thus allowing practically that it is *the
God of love* contemplated as an object that lights
up and keeps burning the fire of love within the
hearts of His saints, yet the true account to be given
of their affection is that they have thoroughly appre-

[b] Eph. iv. 13.   [c] Butler, vol. ii. 195, (169).

hended and embraced the proposition that "God is love." In the same way Bishop Butler, to whom I have alluded above, shews that "the duties and feelings which we owe to the Divine Persons in the Gospel revelation arise from the relations in which those persons stand to us[d]," and to us, therefore, individually from our recognition of those relations. "By reason is revealed the relation in which God the Father stands to us; hence the obligation of duty which we are under to Him. In Scripture are revealed the relations which the Son and Holy Spirit stand in to us; hence the obligations of duty which we owe to them. How these relations are made known, whether by reason or revelation, makes no alteration in the case, because the duties arise out of the relations themselves, not out of the manner in which we are informed of them. The Son and the Spirit have each His proper office in that great dispensation of Providence, the redemption of the world,—the one our Mediator, the other our Sanctifier. Does not then the duty of religious regards to both these divine Persons as immediately arise to the view of reason, out of the very nature of their offices and relations, as the inward goodwill and kind intention, which we owe to our fellow-creatures, arises out of the common relation between us and them?" Thus, then, those spontaneous offerings of the Christian's heart—reverence, honour, love, trust, gratitude, fear, hope to Godward, and derivatively to men as children

[d] Butler, vol. i. 182.

of *the One Father of us all, and of our Lord Jesus Christ*, really rest upon the Articles of the Christian Faith; and it is possible, and may be necessary, to trace them back unto their source. For the sake of both it may be necessary to show that all duty and right feeling presuppose the apprehension of truth, that they are distinct and correlative. It will even become so, if the disposition to translate the language of divine truth into principles and rules of human duty, to confound the one with the other, or to depreciate truth—if men can be induced to take the same view of their duties—should spread extensively among us.

Will it then be deemed unprofitable to enquire as I have proposed into the real grounds of Christian self-denial, of the duty in obedience to which, and the feeling according to which, we are bound, not as rational beings simply, but as followers of *the Lord Jesus Christ*, to use this world as not abusing it, to live in it and yet not be of it? Will it be said that it is worse than waste of time to disturb the foundations of a building that is standing fast, that we may assume a duty that is in some sort generally recognized as our starting-point; that the office of the preacher is to impress, enforce, persuade, to draw the heart by the cords of love rather than fetter it with the chains of critical discussion; that we must thankfully avail ourselves of the existence of right feelings and true ideas, and rest content if we can make them deeper and more effectual? Will it be urged, that where all allow in general terms the duty of denying *all ungodliness and fleshly lusts,* it is even dangerous to raise any question of principles, and to lead men to ask themselves why they should be temperate when by habit and disposition they already are so? And indeed it would be a sign of a cold and unloving heart not to prefer the warmth and glow of the Christian's life, unconsciously exhibiting itself in the pulsations of love to God and man, to the naked, and in itself unattractive, structure that supports his frame. I should not envy the man who is ignorant, or thinks nothing of the direct influence which heart has upon heart, that holy feeling is to be called into operation in those whom we address by the manifestation of holy feeling in ourselves, that men are to be guided up to high and noble resolutions by our acting on the assumption of their susceptibility to such impressions, or who seeks to create them by the bare force of unexceptionable logic. Heathens were never converted by such means. Nevertheless, it becomes us in this place, where we are called upon not only to advance in personal holiness, but to arm ourselves as practised warriors in the cause of Christ, to walk round the walls of Sion, and mark well her bulwarks from every possible point of view, and to be prepared to act in positions in which we would not voluntarily place ourselves. Cherishing all Christian sympathies, and living in them, we must learn even to retire from their influence, and place ourselves without their pale, to view the Christian simply as a phenomenon, to enquire into his motives and his hopes,

and establish the reasonableness of his conduct without prejudice or predilection. Why does he walk
along the path of life, alone amid a crowd, his step
unlike that of other men, his eyes bent upon the
ground, his hands folded on his breast, and the cross
upon his brow? What unknown purpose, what
strange resolve, what silent call wraps up the secret
of his pilgrimage? It is for the Christian minister
to solve this problem: himself the mystery, he must
also be its explanation. It is obvious that the missionary in a heathen land must be a pure phenomenon; as such, if he does anything at all, he must
excite attention and cause enquiry. Will he then
answer the questions which his coming will suggest?
He must put himself in the place of those he has
to teach, and become a phenomenon unto himself:
how else shall he convert those into whose feelings
he cannot enter? Nor will it be enough to wait
for the effect of time and rational reflection on the
minds of his hearers; from the very first he must
shroud himself by an effort of imagination in the
darkness which he comes to dispel; he must know
experimentally the desolation of a soul *without God
in the world* while he is the beam of His knowledge
and the herald of His will; he must feel of himself,
" How beautiful are the feet of them that preach
the gospel of peace, and bring glad tidings of good
things [e];" he must retire into the valley of the shadow
of death and welcome his own coming as an angel of
life; and even so, though in a less degree, must

[e] Rom. x. 15.

he be prepared to exercise his ministry even in the Christian world. For that which we so call is not wholly Christian. So far as there are principles at work within it hostile to Christianity it is yet Pagan, and must be treated as such. Wherever evil is at work we must place ourselves in the centre of its operation, and survey the doctrine that we preach and all its bearings, as they present themselves to those whom we have to gather or reclaim into the fold. We must not expect sympathy, but be prepared to justify the faith to stubborn hearts and unrelenting wills. We may be called upon to debate and maintain what are to us first principles and axiomatic truths, as though they were new and undetermined questions. Where nothing is conceded we must be careful to assume nothing. The economy of teaching and the emergency of warfare may place us in a strange position; we may even be compelled in an extreme case to wrest from men's minds truths which they do hold, if they hold them not according to the analogy of faith. It may be our office to place a fearful alternative before the world. "See, I have set before thee life and good, death and evil [f]." An alternative of such a nature seems to be offered in the words of the text, "If the dead rise not, let us eat and drink, for to-morrow we die." Strange words from an Apostle's lips! Is there no compromise for human nature? Must it needs be *exalted unto heaven, or cast down into hell?* May it not remain of the earth earthy, and not sink

[f] Deut. xxx. 15.

into the sensual, devilish ? Is the hour of our trial
come, and the choice between the doctrine of Christ
and the very formula of Epicurus ? Surely it is His
voice that bids us *eat and drink, for to-morrow we die ;*
for though the words themselves may be found in the
Prophet Isaiah, yet it seems more probable that the
sentiment in St. Paul's mind, writing to the luxurious
Corinthians, was associated with that Gentile Philosophy
which was nowhere more practically carried out than
in that ancient city.   And this view seems borne out
by the quotation which immediately follows from
a heathen poet; but, however this may be, the scope
of the words is obvious, and independent of the source
from which they are derived.   What strikes the
mind with astonishment is that they should have
been adopted by St. Paul.   What! we are tempted
to ask, did the great Apostle of the Gentiles really
mean us to infer that besides the *obedience of the faith*
there is no rational course, no course at all for man to
follow, *save the life of the beasts that perish ?* We will
not suppose that he spoke of anything like grossness
of self-indulgence ; the words do not necessarily imply
that ; they may mean nothing more than a pure,
innocent, and virtuous, though Epicurean, existence.
Still we ask, is that the life St. Paul, as a heathen,
would have chosen for himself? Were the tendencies
of a sensual nature so thinly covered by an education
after *the strictest sect of the Pharisees ?* Were there
no higher pleasures than those of sense to attract
and engage his mind ? We cannot, I think, conceive
St. Paul, so noble, so unselfish, so intellectual, so

ardent in the cause of truth, so ambitious after the natural man, even to have drunk of these last dregs of Grecian Philosophy. But if we consider him as a Christian teacher his words sound yet stranger to our ears. True, he writes with the hope of immortality before him, as one who, knowing that the pleasures and fashion of this world endure but for a season, "keeps under his body" accordingly, "and brings it into subjection, lest when he has preached to others he himself should be a cast away." Yet his words seem to be wanting in an earnest and disinterested love of that law which he observes and fears. They fail to put us in mind of the glorious liberty of the sons of God. They savour almost of the feeling of those who regretted the time when "they sat by the flesh-pots of Egypt, and did eat bread to the full[g]." They fall far short of the oft-repeated song of the Patriarch of Israel: "O how I love Thy law, it is my meditation all the day[h]." "How sweet are Thy words unto my taste; yea, sweeter than honey to my mouth[i]." "Thy testimonies have I taken as an heritage for ever; they are the rejoicing of my heart[k]." "I have longed for Thy salvation, and Thy law is my delight[l]."

But these ideas vanish when we consider St. Paul as speaking, not of himself individually, or of his own tastes and disposition, but with a true appreciation of the general tendencies of human nature. There is no necessity for supposing that he himself

[g] Exod. xvi. 3.   [h] Ps. cxix. 97.   [i] Ibid. 103.
[k] Ibid. 111.   [l] Ibid. 174.

would have passed a life of sensuality in any form, even if he had not known that for *all those things God would call Him unto judgment.* Rather we may believe that as a heathen he would have been found among those nobler spirits who argued and proved that even in this lower world the destiny of man is somewhat higher than that of the beasts of the field, that he is invested with larger powers than those which can be pressed into the service of sense, the exercise of which in itself would be a source, not only of the purest, but of the most enduring, happiness. But while his own heart would have told him of the dignity of the higher elements of human nature, his knowledge of mankind would not have suffered him to fall into the delusion that the sense of that dignity in the general mass is sufficient to prevent them from sinking into the lowest depths of degradation. Acknowledging and illustrating the natural pre-eminence of mind over matter, and of knowledge over sense, he would have felt that the question in which all are interested is not *that*, but whether the two are so proportioned in our actual constitution that this natural pre-eminence can be maintained. He would have seen that the discovery of the law of our nature is one thing and obedience to it another. He would not have used that inflated and unpractical language in which heathen philosophers indulged, and some Christians strangely imitate, about the supremacy of mind and the superiority of intellectual pleasures. If an idea of his own dignity had arisen in his mind it would have found expression in the language of surprise and abasement. "What is man that Thou art mindful of him, or the Son of Man that Thou so regardest him? Thou hast made him a little lower than the angels, Thou hast crowned him with glory and honour. Thou madest him to have dominion over the works of Thy hands, Thou has put all things under his feet. All sheep and oxen, yea and the beasts of the field. The fowls of the air, and the fish of the sea, and whatsoever passeth through the paths of the seas. O Lord our Governour, how excellent is Thy name in all the world [m]." But sadder thoughts would soon have intervened when he turned from the gifts and powers with which he was adorned to the evil working in his own heart; and the true voice of his struggling humanity would have broken out in the cry of despair and agony, "Wretched man that I am, who shall deliver me from the body of this death!"

St. Paul, therefore, did not mean that it was but to eat and drink and be merry while the day lasts, because when night comes our souls may be required of us; but that where the truth of Christ risen from the dead was not received, the tendency of human conduct would be in that direction. The alternative in his mind, taking an extensive survey of the world, lay between Christ crucified and the lusts of the flesh. Many perhaps doubt whether such alternative is one of reality or argument. They may urge that men have been known to live in temper-

[m] Ps. viii. 4.

ance, soberness, and chastity, without the reception
of saving truth; that they have not found it necessary;
that individuals, societies, and even nations alien
to the Name of Christ have given examples of those
virtues, putting the conduct of Christian men to
shame. Moreover the general laws of morality have
been demonstrated in times of ignorance on grounds
independent of the Christian faith. Now as to persons
living in a Christian land, but not receiving the *truth
as it is in Jesus,* so far as they are affected by the
atmosphere around them, deriving life from it which
they will not acknowledge; so far as their conduct
is influenced even by particular doctrines which they
hold imperfectly and unconsciously, to that extent
it is an illustration of the truth of what I say.
Beyond that influence, their virtues, of whatever
kind, are those of heathens; among whom, if the
lives of men holy in their degree are quoted, if it
is urged that dark as they were, and feeling blindly
after truth, no philosopher ever commended a life
of self-indulgence, whatever the issue of his teaching
—allowing this as may be, it is not asserted that the
alternative existed to those to whom it never was
proposed. Yet even as regards them, it seems an
arbitrary act of ours to cut them off entirely from
that source of light, in the full beams of which *we
live, and move, and have our being.* Surely, when we
assume that those men purified their hearts and invented systems of partial truth by the unassisted
exertion of their natural powers, we must be influenced by some false idea of what we could do

ourselves under like circumstances, forgetting *that we have nothing which we have not received.* St. Paul, it is true, speaks of "the Gentiles doing *by nature* the things contained in the law, and becoming a law unto themselves," but we must remember that St. Paul uses the current language, and that the word *nature* in its Christian application expresses only *facts* and not principles, and is of itself no adequate account of anything. Indeed St. Paul himself teaches us that it was not because the heathen neglected to use their natural powers to discover and originate to themselves "that which may be known of God," and which God Himself shewed to them, but, "because knowing God, they glorified Him not as God, and changed His truth into a lie, and did not like to retain Him in their knowledge, that He gave them over to uncleanness through the lusts of their own hearts, and to vile affections, and a reprobate mind." This much, at all events, we know, that God did give a law to Adam, which he transmitted to his children, but we do not know that it was ever lost and re-discovered, nor is it probable that it could be; history at least supplies no instance of a nation falling so low as the loss of the knowledge of God supposes, and rising again without external aid. The system of the philosopher most studied in this place is based upon the antecedent fact of moral knowledge already existing in the world. The appetite of the child is trained into the habit of temperance by the wisdom of the parent; but the parent must have received that wisdom by trans-

I

mission, nor does it appear how consistently with
the theory it could have been originally obtained.
Two contrary habits cannot be in formation at the
same time, and all will allow that the tendency of un-
regulated appetite is to grow into a habit from the
hour of one's birth. The wisdom, therefore, that is to
rule our conduct must be traced to an external source;
and the idea of man having reclaimed himself from
lawless barbarism by his own powers, or been
charmed out of it by the force of an eloquence that
could not have existed in such a state, is not only
contrary to the history of human nature as disclosed
in revelation, but involves within itself impossible
contradictions. The real basis, therefore, of heathen
morality, whether it was recognized or not, was
the tradition of the law of God. Tradition supplied
the ideas, ideas became matters of speculation to
reflecting minds, speculation developed into philosophy, philosophy withered into effete systems and
lifeless forms when it claimed an independent existence, and ceased to derive nourishment from the
parent vine of which it was an offshoot. Yet how
little philosophy really added to the knowledge of
mankind is clear from this, that the best and wisest
of the heathen, when the hour of his trial came,
virtually confessed that knowledge failed him, and
that faith alone, the antecedent of all true philosophy,
carried him, like a ship-wrecked mariner, over the
waves of this troublesome world to the haven of
his rest. If, then, the secret of such truth and virtue
as the heathen had is to be sought for in the re-

vealed law of God, can we, with our knowledge, doubt that this revelation is due solely unto Him who in the fulness of time came to supersede all former messages from God to man by the republication of that law, and to be Himself *the way, the truth, and the life?* Those gleams of light that flash upon the eye in the darkness of the ancient world, were they not in some way reflections from many a clouded mirror and through absorbing media of the true Light that lighteth every man that cometh into the world? Possibly some heaven-directed eye may have caught upon the clouds that limited the view of other men, some early glimmering of that dawn which the rising of the Sun of Righteousness has brightened into perfect day. But, however this may be, is it not probable that He who in the beginning created all things that are, who formed the eye and framed the ear, was also the same that taught men knowledge? that He, the Lamb of God, slain from the foundation of the world, was also from that epoch the messenger of the Most High and the Prophet of His law—the παιδαγωγός of mankind—who, according to Clemens, gave unto the world the law of Nature, and to His peculiar people the law of Moses. "Deriving from the same fountain both the first and second precepts which He gave, He neither suffered those who were before the Law to be without Law, nor those who minded not the Philosophy of the Barbarians to do according to their will. He gave to the one Precepts, to the other Philosophy, and concluded them in unbelief unto His coming, when whosoever believeth not is without excuse."

With these words I will finish my discourse, when I have briefly noticed the practical conclusion to which all that I have been saying tends. If in times of past ignorance all imperfect knowledge was in some way connected, however remotely, with the perfect, how can we to whom " has been revealed the mystery hidden from the foundation of the world," set aside that association now? Are we, in dealing with mankind, to make ways of our own, or to follow the example of St. Paul, who, furnished as he was with heathen and Judaic lore, determined to *know nothing but Christ Jesus and Him crucified?* He did not cast aside his learning, for he still felt that it was a gift of God; but all that he knew before, all detached and fragmentary truths fell into their places round the new idea, and Christ became unto him *all in all.* Armed, therefore, with the sword of this faith he went forth, not to spread abroad a new philosophy, not to reform the morals or humanize the manners of mankind, but with "grace and apostleship for the obedience of the faith among all nations in His name." And it is this warfare which we are called upon to wage against the carnal lusts of the flesh. Shall we, then, trust to heathen armoury, to probable arguments of philosophy, or plausible economies of truth, the spear and the shield that have been wrought by

human hands, or shall we go forth in the spirit of
David against the uncircumcised Philistine with that
small but deadly weapon which He who sends us
to the battle has supplied? The history of the world
holds out no promise of permanency to schemes of
ingenuity and combination. The shore that borders
on the stream of time is strewed not only with the
wrecks of thrones and principalities and powers,
but of philosophic systems which have resisted the
force of human passion for a time, and yielded to
the storm and flood. One barrier yet remains which
we have the assurance of God never shall be shaken.
It is for us to take our stand upon it for offence and
defence. Mark the spirit of the Apostle's teaching,
"If the dead rise not, let us eat and drink, for to-
morrow we die." He trusts to the doctrine of the
resurrection of the dead to counteract the tendencies of human lusts. But this is not merely the
notion of a future state of retribution certified and
established; but the doctrine of our union with
Christ, in that He took our nature upon Him, and
"by rising from the dead became the first-fruits
of them that slept." It may be that the alternative between this doctrine in all its fulness, and
a life of sensuality is before the world. Certainly
in the consummation of all things, when men and
angels shall look back upon this warfare as a thing
that has passed away, and view it as a whole, the
truth of it will be known, and the company of the
redeemed will give glory to God, and confess "that

this is the victory that overcometh the world, even our faith." May God incline our hearts to do our duty in the contest, so that, sharing its labours we may win its crown, and be more than conquerors through the might of Jesus Christ our Lord.

SERMON III.

Man's Place in Creation.

———◆———

GENESIS ii. 7.

"And the Lord God formed man of the dust of the ground, and breathed into his nostrils the breath of life ; and man became a living soul."

THIS is the divine account of the origin of man. And I have taken this account of his origin for my text, rather than that verse which you have just heard in the first chapter, because it seems to me more particular and circumstantial. It seems indeed to answer a question that might reasonably be asked as arising out of the first notice of man's creation. "So God created man in His own image, in the image of God created He him." How was this creation effected? My text, I say, supplies the answer. There was a double process. First the dust of the earth was taken and formed as by a mould; and then into the nostrils of the figure thus framed God breathed the breath of life. By this double action the work was complete, and "man," as the Scripture says, "became a living soul." Now observe it is not stated here that man was created directly out of nothing. The materials of man existed before man existed himself, just as the clay exists before the potter is able to shape his vessels from it. There was the dust or substance of the earth ready for the Creator's hand, there was the breath of life existing eternally in the Being of the Creator, ready for His will. There is such a thing as absolute creation, though man was not the subject of it, and the very idea of it transcends and perplexes our imagination. "In the beginning," before the first date of time, "God created the heaven and the earth." This is the first, the most awful utterance of revelation. The whole material and immaterial universe—all that we see and all that eludes or lies beyond our sight—was called into existence out of nothingness by the Divine command. Let us confess at once, on entering the temple of God through this portal, that we cannot understand it, or rather, that if by faith we do understand that the worlds were framed by the word of God, then this the very first demand upon our faith is also the very greatest. Have you considered, or will you now consider for one moment, what creation really is? You are familiar with many changes of form and character and condition of material things. You see, for instance, water changing into vapour, and vapour into water, coal into smoke, and heat, and flame. You must know also that the grass with which the fields are clothed is changed into the flesh of animals which becomes the food of men, and that flesh again into the substance of our bodies, and so on by the recurrence of a perpetual series as long as the world shall last. And from your sensible

experience of these things you would not be surprised if one were to tell you of other more subtle
changes, of which you have as yet no knowledge.
You would, I doubt not, be prepared to believe
that all the objects and all the 'phenomena of nature
that we see around are the results of new combinations and change; and that there is no reason
for supposing that there has been any actual addition
to the sum of things, or diminution from it, since
God, in the beginning, spoke the word, and the
heavens and the earth were created. Indeed, if you
will consider a little in your own minds you must
feel how inconceivable an act of absolute creation is.

If at least you can conceive any small portion of
space, absolutely empty and devoid of matter, you
will feel, I am sure, that no thought of man, no
inventive ingenuity, no mechanical or other power,
is capable of producing within that space one single
particle of matter that had no existence before. How
then with the vast space of heaven, above, below,
around, and all the infinity of worlds that have their
place and order and motion assigned to them therein?
One thing only is more inconceivable than the creation of the universe, and that is, that it should be
in existence without having been created at all.
Common sense will always choose the least of two
difficulties—and the word of God, as usual, takes
the side of common sense—when it assures us that
"In the beginning God created the heaven and the
earth." In the sequel, therefore, of the chapter you
have just heard, you are reading, not so much a re-

cord of absolute creation, as of the order and process
by which things were brought into such a condition
as to make the earth fit for the occupation of man.
All persons seem to allow that there is a general
correspondence between what we read here and the
evidence of the changes through which the structure
of the earth has passed, and that the author of the
Pentateuch must have been, for his day, an advanced
student of natural philosophy. On the other hand,
people seem to have a pleasure in pointing out where
the great lawgiver has failed, and committed himself
to statements that cannot be reconciled with the discoveries of modern science. And while some rejoice
over this as destroying the whole book of revealed
truth, or at least reducing it to the level of an obso-
lete speculation, others tell us, in a patronizing sort
of way, that Scripture was never intended to be the
vehicle of scientific knowledge. Now to me all knowledge is scientific, that is to say, when imparted to
my mind, it makes me to know something, be it
much or little, which I did not know before, and
that is the meaning of the word *scientific*. But passing this over, and having a firm conviction that every
word of Scripture is absolutely true, when it is understood as the Holy Ghost, who is its author, designed
it, I must protest against the intention of Scripture
being thus limited or defined in this arbitrary way.
If you want to know the intention of Scripture you
must go to the volume itself and find out there what
it actually is and says; and not to the surmises of
your own mind as to what it may be expected to be

and says. Whatever Scripture says that it intends
to say, and if it makes statements about the natural
world, it intended to make those statements; and we
would rather doubt our own convictions, and distrust
our own understandings, than accept, as an apology
for its supposed errors, that it has gone into matters
which are outside its own proper province. All that
we are concerned with now is the account that God,
having in the beginning created the heaven and
the earth, left the earth for a time—we know not
how many countless ages would count for less
than a second in His eternity—" without form and
void. And darkness was all the while upon the face
of the deep; and the Spirit of God, either during
that whole period, or as a prelude of the work that
was to follow, moved on the face of the waters." And
then we are told how, by a series of formative actions,
light and darkness were separated, the waters divided,
some taking their place in air, some gathering themselves into seas, the earth stood firm and solid out
of the surrounding water, and became the seed-bed
for plant and herb and tree; how the sun and moon
took their appointed offices in heaven; and how the
successive generations of animal life, in all their
exuberance, were called into existence to increase
and multiply, and people the new organic world,
which we will, now that it is furnished, venture to
call creation; and how, lastly, when everything else
was finished, man himself appeared upon the scene.
The painter, the sculptor, all in fact who practise
even in the lowest degree any effort of creative art,

have in their own minds some idea that they have shaped out, and are able to contemplate, before they attempt to apply their hands to canvas, or clay, or marble. And here is the idea which the great Author of all conceived and designed before He proceeded to embody it in the formation of man. "And God said, let us make man in our image, after our likeness." And not only was the idea of this Being thus determined, but his rank and position fixed in the scale of created things. "And let them have dominion over the fish of the sea and over the fowl of the air, and over the cattle, and over all the earth, and over every creeping thing that creepeth upon the earth." It is due to our own infirmity, and part of it, that though God's thoughts are not as our thoughts, nor His ways our ways, we can only speak of Him, or be spoken to concerning Him, in the same language that would be used if we were speaking concerning men; and it is but natural to ask, to what agent working with Him, or subordinate to Him, did God communicate the plan of His great design, " Let *us* make man in our image?" And on this day we recognize by the light of the Gospel in the very opening chapter of Revelation the inscrutable mystery of the ever-blessed Trinity, three Persons and one God, as concerned in the work of creation. We read directly here, "The Spirit of God moved upon the face of the waters," as an agent of life and power. And in the first chapter of the Gospel of St. John, which seems to have a determinate relation with the first chapter of Genesis, commencing with the same words, "In the *begin-ning*" the "*word*" which was then with God, and which was God," will not suffer us to doubt as to the person to whom the purpose of the Father's will was announced. "The same"—the Word, i.e., who became Flesh and dwelt amongst us—"was in the beginning with God. All things were made by Him, and without Him was not anything made that was made."

Now I will allow that the account we have— the design of this Lord of Creation as man has been called—is one that is dangerous to argue upon, lest you should both fall short of and exceed what is intended. "Let us make man in our image, after our likeness." We cannot imagine that it refers to man's natural form, excellent as it is and wonderfully made, for we dare not confine the Creator to the mould of the creature. And if we look for the resemblance rather in the rational soul, we must not forget that even in that respect it may not be quite safe to compare ourselves very closely with Him. Our idea of God, defective as it is, must come to us through the medium of our consciousness of ourselves; we cannot invest Him with attributes entirely different in kind from those which we feel ourselves to be in possession of. And the Divine command, in some degree, assists and justifies human incapacity. "Be ye perfect, even as your Father which is in heaven is perfect," enjoins upon us the imitation of God, and therefore implies a likeness to Him. Man can only think of God as a Being

in some way like unto himself, and even in the present state of our nature the soul of man bears some
faint resemblance to his Maker.   Understanding,
memory, and imagination exhibit a faint shadow of
divine wisdom and knowledge.   The will acting upon
and controlling matter in an inexplicable manner,
bears some resemblance to the almighty effects of
His absolute Will.   Conscience seated as a judge
within the breast exercises a function which connects
it directly with the great Judge of all; while a derived
and imparted immortality reminds us of Him who
is self-existent and eternal.   Again, our sense of
justice, our feelings of love, charity, kindness, establish a kind of likeness between us and Him who
is all just, all merciful, all good, as well as almighty;
and generally, as we approach the character of Jesus
Christ, which by His aid it is possible to do, in that
respect we grow nearer to the Divine image of Him
in whom dwelt all the fulness of the Godhead bodily,
while at the same time we are reminded, by the enormous difference between us, that we can never come
up to that image till the "new man is thoroughly
renewed in righteousness and true holiness."   But
whatever perfection of nature is implied in "the
image of God," in which we were created, this,
at least, is implied, that man is not to be considered
as one of a series of animals, though the very highest
member of that series; but that as regards his place
in creation, he stands absolutely pre-eminent and alone.
He is not the best of animals, for he is no animal
at all, but a being of different order.   He has an

affinity with animals as regards bodily structure, just as he has affinity with angels as regards spiritual power; but as you do not on that account call him an angel, so it is a false description of him to speak of him as an animal. The series of organic life which embraces the creatures of the flood, and of the air and field, is summed up and brought to a close. There is a pause in the work, and the great Creator, ere He calls into being him to whom He intends to give dominion over all that He has made, seems to take into counsel the other co-eternal Persons of the Trinity, one of whom shall be the Redeemer and the other the Comforter of that creature in his fallen state, whom they concurrently sent into the world in "their own image," and thus "man became a living soul." The heathen did not know all this, and the Jew knew it imperfectly; for it could not be expected of him that he should decipher the book of Revelation as clearly as ourselves. But as the fact of a higher origin separates us from mere animals, so the sense of this origin, both among Jew and heathen, has been the source of all that is great and noble among men; and where this sense is lost the fact itself seems to be obscured and effaced. We tell you that you are sons of God, even in your natural state, in a sense in which no animals are, though they too are His creatures. You are sons of Him by nature, and if you belong to Christ you are doubly sons of Him by Grace. This is what we tell you, and what the Scripture tells you and me; but we belong to a simple and unlearned time,

and when your children come to be better educated
than you or I they may be told a very different
tale.   And what this may be I may as well tell
you now.   You will be told that all this is an idle,
unreal dream of superstition and self-complacency;
that man has no such origin, no special prerogative
of heavenly birth; that his descent may be traced
back, and back, and back, through countless ages, to
a shapeless, helpless creature, half animal, half vegetable, that attached itself for protection to some firmer
object in the great ocean; that this creature—by
a process of self-aid known only to itself—improved itself into a fish, was, I suppose, ennobled
in an ape, and at last fought its way to the Headship
of Creation in the form of man.   This genealogy
is drawn out for us, by a very able hand, and if it
is true it is very important that you should all know
it.   But he has not told us at what stage in the process of this creature to its present condition an immortal soul was infused into the animal frame, or
whether, in fact, he has any soul beyond the animal
life, which is shared by other creatures.   One thing,
however, is clear: mere animal life could not grow
into an immortal soul by degrees; either it was, in
fact, in the frame at some particular time, about
which we should wish to be informed, or it does not
exist therein at all.

But meanwhile what will be the effect of this
teaching, if it takes hold upon our minds?   It
is idle to say that it is a mere scientific speculation, which ought not to have any practical effect

upon our conduct; that we are what we are now, and that it does not matter how we became so. If what is said is true, it is a most practical truth; and it is quite right that a vain delusion should be dissipated. If this is our origin and our nature, it would be wise to live according to it, as St. Paul argues. "If the dead rise not again, let us eat and drink, for to-morrow we die," and that is the end of us. Many animals live happier lives than many men, and are better cared for. Higher gifts in some cases only bring greater capacity for greater suffering, and if we are only animals it would be better for us to be even as they. I do not understand philosophers, but it is impossible that the mass of men can receive this account of themselves without being degraded in every part of their nature. I think I can even trace a tendency to this in the weak and disjointed argument of the very able man who has lately brought this account of his own and our existence before the public view. Pride, it is said, goes before a fall. The pride of human will, and human achievement, and human power, was never raised to a higher pitch than at the present day; and it is strange to see it accompanied as it is, by an infatuated passion for human degradation. You and I may not be able to argue, and may be perplexed by the arguments of other men, but you can guard and maintain in your own person the rights and the dignity of human nature. And you will do this effectually if you will bear in mind that it was this very nature which our blessed Lord as-

K

sumed to His own person. He took not on Him
angels, nor the brutal nature of fishes or of apes,
but He took upon Him the seed of Abraham. "The
Word which was with God, and which was God,
was made flesh and dwelt among us." The very
thought of this will preserve you from the low and
degraded estimate of yourselves which it is attempted
to force upon you. You will not say, in the language
of Job's abasement, "I have said to Corruption, Thou
art my father: to the worm, Thou art my mother
and my sister," but will rather be exalted by the
true humility of David.

"What is man that Thou art mindful of him, and
the son of man that Thou visitest him?

"Thou hast made him a little lower than the angels: and hast crowned him with glory and honour.
Thou madest him to have dominion over the works
of Thy hands: Thou hast put all things under his
feet.

"O Lord our Governor, how excellent is Thy Name
in all the world."

SERMON IV.

The Pharisee and the Publican.

———◆———

ST. LUKE xviii. 14.

"I tell you, this man went down to his house justified rather than the other : for every one that exalteth himself shall be abased ; and he that humbleth himself shall be exalted."

THE parable that is brought before us in the Gospel of this day [a] differs from every other in an important respect, viz. that it is based, not upon an imaginary, though possible event, but on one that must have been of daily occurrence. Two men went up into the temple to pray. Thousands must have done the same every day, for prayer was part of Jewish life, and the temple was the place where prayer was appointed to be made. Its courts were thronged, and this is our Lord's own description of His Father's House, "My House shall be called the House of prayer." But the force of the parable consists in this : that these two men are typical or representative characters—representing, that is, two different classes of men, two different tempers or spirits, in which it is possible to approach God in prayer, and in which men actually do approach Him. There is such a thing as indolent and thoughtless prayer, prayer in which the words come mechanically from the lips, while the heart is far away on other

[a] XI. Sunday after Trinity.

things; but of this mockery of prayer nothing is said
in the parable. Both of them were thoroughly in
earnest, and sincere—deceived, the one of them perhaps, by the consciousness of his own sincerity. But
the one of them was a Pharisee, the other a Publican.
No words could suggest a stronger contrast of character than these to the Jewish mind. The one,
of the strictest and most exclusive caste, separated
from the body of his nation by conceit of himself, by
the respect of others, and by his very name which
implies separation; a man of professed and external
holiness—exact in every observance of the law, and
receiving from others the confirmation of the opinion
which he held of himself; a man who expected all
the deference that he found, and who found all that
he expected; one for whom men made room in the
market-place, and resigned the chief place in the
synagogue; one who, if he thought himself holier than
others, found his countrymen quite as ready to con-
cede, as he himself was to advance, the claim. The
other belonged to the most despised and degraded
class, hated by their brethren as the mercenary
ministers of a foreign power, the gall of whose yoke
had eaten deep into their necks; collectors of taxes
that went to the benefit of a foreign capital, and
whose collection in town and country, at market and
landing-place, brought home daily to their feelings
that they were no longer a free people, and that they
had fallen from their high place among the nations
of the world. We have rich and poor here, high and
low, and the extremes of society are far enough apart;

but I fancy that nothing we can see or even imagine now will give us any adequate measure of the distance that separated the genuine Pharisee and the Publican.

Still there was one link remaining to testify that they were children of the same father, and joint citizens of the same peculiar people. In the hallowed courts of the Lord's House, into which no stranger could be admitted, they both felt themselves at home; rich and poor, high and low, there met together, and confessed by the act of their meeting that the Lord was the Father of them all. But they carried with them in their hearts and characters the difference that was stamped upon their external professions and their lives. The one in some fixed and ostentatious attitude, composing himself so as to be seen of men— for that seems to be implied by the expression—wrapt up in himself and his own holiness, spoke really to himself, while his language seemed to be addressed unto God. And we may conceive him running over in his mind his list of friends and acquaintances, and the vulgar throng whom he despised, and deriving fresh matter for pride from each comparison, till at last his eye fell upon the poor publican, who was absorbed in the confession of his own sins, unconscious that he was attracting, even for a moment, the attention of so great a man. And then his idea and measure of himself was completed, and in the satisfaction that he felt at the standard he had attained he was disposed not to pray, but to give thanks unto God, with a strange kind of sincerity. " God, I thank

Thee that I am not as other men are, extortioners,
unjust, adulterers, or even as this publican. I fast
twice in the week, and give tithes of all I possess." Meanwhile, what was this publican doing?
We do not know the secrets of his heart, or the memories of sin that dwelt there. Perhaps he had
avoided the ordinary vices of his class, that were
touched upon by John the Baptist when the Publicans came to be baptized, and asked what they in
particular should do towards the reformation of their
lives—"Exact no more than that which is appointed
to you." Perhaps he had escaped this special temptation. Perhaps, on the other hand, he was carrying
the burthen of some more strictly personal sin. Or
in his low estate he might have been humbly walking
the way of righteousness, and striving to serve God
with a perfect heart. But whatever his virtues or
his failings, his sins or his graces, one thought only
filled his heart as he stood unconscious of aught else,
in the customary attitude of prayer; the fire was hot
within him, "he dared not so much as to lift up his
eyes unto heaven, but he smote himself upon his
breast," and at last he spake with his tongue—few
words, but all the feelings of his heart were discharged with them—"God be merciful to me a sinner." And "I tell you"—is the lesson of this parable,
"This man went down to his house justified rather
than the other. For every one that exalteth himself
shall be abased, and he that humbleth himself shall
be exalted."

Now this parable suggests several very interesting and practical questions, which it would be impossible to consider fully in a single sermon. Let us confine ourselves to one very obvious one. What was it in the prayer of this Pharisee, what defect or element of sin was it in his heart, that made his prayer unacceptable to God, and sent him home with his own good opinion, but without that comparative justification which his poor brother found, whose cry for mercy proved that he had no thought of self beyond the confession of his sins?

For do not let us hastily take up the notion that this Pharisee was a bad or profligate man, and gave himself a false account of his life and conduct, a man who assumed the garb of religion to cover the deeds of iniquity; one of those whited sepulchres, so fair outside, and so full of ravening and uncleanness, on whom our Saviour pronounced the sentence of eternal woe. Had he been so, his prayer would have been simply an abomination to the Lord, and, according to the fearful imprecation, would have been "turned into sin." But there is no reason to believe that he was deficient in that legal righteousness which was all that a Pharisee aimed at, and which was sufficient to satisfy and feed his pride. There is no reason why he may not have been all that St. Paul described himself to have been in the days of his ignorance, not only a "Hebrew of the Hebrews," and, as touching the law, a Pharisee; but like him burning with "zeal" for all that he thought right, and "as touching the righteousness which is in the law blameless." Nor need we interpret it to his disadvantage, that whereas he is said to have "gone up to the temple to *pray*," there are no words of prayer recorded from him, but only "thanksgiving." For prayer and thanksgiving are necessarily connected together, and in fact both are included under the idea of prayer, either being incomplete without the other, as St. Paul in more than one place declares, e.g. "Be careful for nothing, but in everything by prayer and supplication with thanksgiving let your requests be made known unto God." Nor yet was he wrong in giving thanks to God that he had not fallen into the vices of men whom he saw around him, that he was not an extortioner, or unjust, or an adulterer. Those who take the darkest view of his character will hardly believe that he was in reality what he thanked God that he was not. And if he fasted twice a week, which would be a voluntary self-denial, not required by the law, and gave tithes of all that he possessed, or rather acquired, while the law probably only exacted a tithe of the fruit of the field, and the produce of cattle, all this would tend to shew a hearty and a generous obedience to the law, as far as it commended itself to his conscience. So far, then, from condemning this part of his conduct, we would maintain that he had cause for thanksgiving, and the cause existing, he could not be wrong simply for offering it. Indeed, I think a reflecting person cannot read or hear of the commission of any sin or crime without an instinctive feeling of thanksgiving, whether expressed or not, that hitherto he has been preserved at least from

that; and when we meet the most degraded of our
kind, we should be impressed, I think, not only
with pity and with fear, but we may not let them
pass without a thanksgiving, that we have not yet
been degraded, and a prayer, that we may never
yet be degraded, to their miserable level. For who
can look into his own heart honestly without feeling
that deep buried there lie the seeds of every sin,
ever ready to germinate into life, and wanting perhaps only the stimulus of temptation, or the sunshine
of opportunity to make them bring fruit unto death?
Some persons must be conscious that they have halted
on the very verge of a great crime, and they know
not why; others who did not seem more bent upon
it went on and perished, but an invisible hand
stayed their course at the very edge of the pre-
cipice—they recoiled from the black depth and were
saved. "Two people were working in one field,
one was taken and the other left." Shall the saved
find no voice to give God the glory? And if we
know not that we have been so near to deeds which
our souls abhor, may we not have been just as near
without our knowledge? And if we have never
been near such deeds at all, surely it is the greater
mercy the further we have been kept from them.
If, for instance, when we have been angry without
a cause, we may thank God that our anger did not
run on into any deed of violence, may we not thank
Him much more that we have never been angry
without a cause? And if we have never been near the
commission of what I will call *crime* as distinguished

from sin, may we not remember how influences that
once surrounded us, and acted on us, suddenly or
gradually passed away, or ceased to act; how, perhaps, some evil companion was removed from our
side, by what seemed accidental then, or how reflexion was forced upon us by some trifling thing
or even chance word; and so we collected our
thoughts and considered our ways, and became,
as the world says, very different persons from what
we were or might have been? And shall we take
all this to ourselves, and give God no thanks for
His goodness? He that is no "adulterer, or unjust,
or extortionate," may without sin be conscious that
he is not, and thank God—for all this he might
have been; and if to the absence of these gross
vices he has added virtue, knowledge, temperance,
patience, godliness, charity, he cannot be entirely
ignorant of the gifts of God within him, but he
will be most ungrateful, and can hardly be said to
have some of them, if he does not acknowledge them.
There is such a thing as innocence of the grosser
defilements of the flesh, and he that is so far innocent must know that he is so; and there is such
a thing as growth in grace. It is possible to feel
the working of the Spirit of Christ within us,
"mortifying the works of the flesh, and our earthly
members, and drawing up our minds to heavenly
things." Great and unspeakable comfort do such
thoughts bring to godly persons, kindling their
love to God, and confirming their faith of eternal
salvation to be enjoyed through Christ. Shall they

then be looked for as a matter of course, and received without a word or thought of thankfulness?

Far from it; for the first rise out of sin, for every step we make, as we are working out our salvation in fear and trembling; for every escape from danger, if near, and for the absence of it, if distant; for every temptation that we have not felt, if kept far from us, that we have overcome if it has assailed us, for all that we have or are, if it be anything that is good, not unto us be the praise, but unto Him, who is at once the Author and Finisher of our Salvation.

But this Pharisee did not recognize this truth, and while with his lips he was thanking God "that he was not as other men are," in his heart he was taking all the glory to himself. He had built, or fancied he had built, a ladder by which he could ascend to heaven, and he was admiring the work of his own hands, and counting its steps. By the rigid discipline of his whole life, and by voluntary sacrifices not required by the law, he was accumulating merit day by day, till he should gather up a mass of it, which would ensure him, as of right, an everlasting reward. It is by a happy combination that we have presented to us in the Epistle the language and the idea of another Pharisee of a very different kind. The one thanking God that he is not what other men are, and the other confessing, "By the grace of God I am what I am," but implying equally that he is different from other men, seem not at first sight to be very unlike each other; but they are as far asunder as the poles of heaven. For St. Paul had learnt this lesson, the very alphabet of which the Pharisee had yet to learn, nay, could not learn at all, till he had unlearnt all that he thought he already knew: "If any man could have confidence in the flesh," St. Paul could above all others. But now he says, " What things were gain to me, those I counted loss for Christ. Yea, I count all things but loss for the excellency of the knowledge of Christ Jesus my Lord, and do count them but dung, so that I may win Christ, and be found in Him, *not* having my own righteousness which is of the law, but that which is through the faith of Christ, the righteousness which cometh of God by faith."

This was the lesson that the Pharisee had to learn, and herein is the failure of his prayer, that all that is good, be it of high or low degree, cometh from God, cannot be put down to ourselves, though God accept it through Christ, and that nothing that we can do can merit heaven. Those who are heavy-burthened with sin can at least cry, " God be merciful to me a sinner," and He will hear them ; but the best will only say—and the better they are the more deeply will they feel it—" By the Grace of God I am what I am."

And those who have fought the good fight, and feel now that their course is finished, will know through whose power they have conquered. And while they "look forward to the crown of righteousness which the Lord the Righteous Judge shall give to them that love His appearing," they well

know what worship the Redeemed will offer, and
"how they will cast their crowns before the throne,
saying, Thou art worthy, O Lord, to receive glory
and honour and power, for Thou hast created all
things, and for Thy pleasure they *are*, and were
created.

SERMON V.

The Unmerciful Creditor.

———◆———

ST. MATT. xviii. 32, 33.

" O thou wicked servant, I forgave thee all that debt, because thou desiredst me : Shouldest not thou also have had compassion on thy fellowservant, even as I had pity on thee ?"

THE ideas of sin and debt, of payment and punishment, or retribution, have always been closely connected together in the mind of man. This fact is borne witness to by language ancient and modern, by a kind of innate sense of justice, by law and practice all over the world. Where we sin against a neighbour, that is to say, do any wilful injury to his person, property, or character, the law will in many cases award him a compensation, treating us in every respect as though we were in debt to him, and enforcing the payment. And where the crime is transferred from the sufferer to the law itself, where the broken law in its majesty is contemplated as the party that is injured by the wrong, we become indebted to the law, and the law takes from us satisfaction in proportion to the wrong done ; it may be in money, it may be by the infliction of some equivalent pain or penalty, it may be, in an extreme case, by the shedding of blood. Then we say that a life has been forfeited by the law, and the miserable man whose crime has brought him to this extremity, will, if he be truly penitent, accept his fate in heart and soul, and offer his life as a willing atonement—and the only one he can offer—for the evil that he has done, giving God the glory that He has brought a sinner to justice in this present world, and trusting to the atonement which he cannot offer for forgiveness of that vaster debt which he owes to Him whose justice is far stricter than that of human law.

Now Holy Scripture not only sanctions but takes up and employs for our instruction this close connection of the idea of sin and debt, payment and punishment. In fact our Lord Himself expresses Himself in these terms, in that version of His own prayer which St. Matthew has recorded in the Sermon on the Mount, "And forgive us our debts, as we forgive our debtors." And I need hardly point out how practical and easy to understand this representation of sin is. It places man at once towards God in the relation of a debtor towards a creditor. It is in itself a terrible relation to stand in towards Him; and the idea of it, before the voice of peace and reconciliation was heard, and still now in lands where it is not heard, drives the miserable victims of superstition to seek atonement of their sins by self-inflicted misery and torture, as though they might thus hope to pay their own debt, and appear clean before the eyes of Almighty God. And if we are relieved from the tyranny and agony of such an idea, it is not that the idea itself is false or baseless, far from it; we are still debtors in ourselves, hopeless debtors to One who is of purer eyes than to behold iniquity, whose justice is infinite, and whose knowledge reaches to the faintest imaginations of our hearts; but God Himself has paid the debt, and made the atonement, blotting out the record of our sins, and redeeming us, not by corruptible things, as silver or gold, "but with the precious blood of Christ as of a lamb without blemish and without spot."

Let us see how this idea of debt is worked out in the parable before us, and then dwell for a few moments on the practical lesson which the great Teacher Himself has drawn from it. The parable does not stand by itself as an abstract lesson, but it comes direct from the Saviour's lips in answer to questionings that were disturbing the disciples. He had just been teaching them how an offending brother was to be dealt with: "If thy brother shall trespass against thee, go and tell him his fault between him and thee alone; if he shall hear thee thou hast gained thy brother, but if he shall not hear thee, take with thee one or two more, that in the mouth of two or three witnesses every word may be established. And if he shall neglect to hear them, tell it to the Church; and if he neglect to hear the Church, let him be to thee as a heathen man and a publican." Not one word to justify or satisfy any angry or unkind feeling; the offender must be dealt with somehow, but, in the extreme case, he must be excluded from the Church, from which

virtually he is already excluded by his own un-
christian temper. And with what feeling is the
heathen and publican to be regarded? not with
enmity and scorn by the disciple of the Friend of
publicans and sinners, but with pity still and love,
so that if he whose words are listened to when he
speaks in kindness the first time to his brother will
have the blessed satisfaction of "gaining his brother,"
there will still remain at the last the hope of "restoring the publican," and converting the heathen:
that work which is its own reward of converting
a sinner from the error of his ways. In this treatment all abandonment of personal feeling is supposed from the first; and that being presumed, our
Saviour's directions apply simply to the method of
dealing with him; but St. Peter, speaking no doubt
for his brethren as well as himself, wishes to know
if this is all, how many times this may be repeated,
and when some concession may be made to the feelings of a man smarting with the remembrance of
repeated wrong. Now some of the Jewish teachers
had a strong tendency to bring life and conduct in
all their details under the control of positive rules,
and it appears that they had resolved, as they thought
on the authority of Scripture, that a personal enemy
had a claim on our forgiveness for three successive
offences and no more; but a very good man who
would not be disposed to cut down his obedience
to the very least that the law would accept, might
extend his forgiveness to a fourth; so that when
St. Peter asked, "How often shall my brother sin

against me and I forgive him? Until seven times?"
he thought, no doubt, that he had "named a perfect
number, beyond which no forgiveness could be required
or even conceived." And now comes the answer to
this question in the parable; that heavenly lesson of
forgiveness which these men were soon to practise
in a world that hated and persecuted them, so that
they might be made like unto Him in all things, alike
in enduring and in forgiveness of wrong; "forgiving others," so He spake again through His Apostle,
"even as God for Christ's sake had forgiven them."
The lesson, which is on the surface of the parable,
comes upon us with greater force when we look more
closely into it. For it would be a reasonable argument to a person of ordinary good feeling that he
should shew to another the same amount of kindness which he himself has received; and even the
hard world would condemn a person who should be
severe in exacting a debt from another, from the
like of which he himself had just been excused.
And most men would rejoice in an opportunity of
repaying in this way the kindness or indulgence
by which they have been benefited. But here there
is no equality or even proportion between the sums
owed by the two debtors. The one is enormous—
ten thousand talents—which sounds to our ears a
large sum, and is to be reckoned by millions; the
other is but a paltry sum of three or four pounds.
And what does this contrast tell us? and is it for
nothing that sums so specific and so widely different
in magnitude are given? Surely it teaches us that

sin in the sight of God is an infinitely greater out-
rage to His holiness, and more abhorrent to His
nature, than any wrong that man may receive at
the hands of his fellow can possibly be to him; that
though the world may be full of violence and wrong,
of deceit and fraud; though man may be in arms
against his brother and thirsting for his blood; though
nation may be divided against nation and house
against itself, yet all the mutual injury which this
implies is to be counted as nothing, compared with
the exceeding sinfulness of sin, compared with the
intrusion of sin into the world which God created
good, that sin of which we are the heirs and partakers. And yet all this load of debt God forgives
freely, so much greater is the mercy that God shews
than that which man refuses to shew. He forgives
and has compassion because His servant falls at His
feet and worships Him. And He forgave freely, though
His servant in the extremity of distress is ready to
make promises of payment, and engagements that
it is impossible for him to fulfil. "Have patience
with me, and I will pay Thee all." He asks for time
and patience while his debt is accumulating on him;
but he gains more than he asks or hopes for, an absolute discharge. But here let me remind you that
the parable deals only with the fact of this *absolute*
forgiveness. It is *absolute* as regards the man himself, i.e. it does not depend upon any arrangement
made with the man himself, but it is not absolute
to the entire exclusion of any condition or means.
God does not pardon sin absolutely in that sense,

because we repent of it, or because we move His
compassion by our tears and prayers. If it were
so, Christ would have lived and died, if not in vain,
yet without any need of such a life and death. It
is a dream of our own that God, out of the stores of
His infinite mercy and love, might pardon sin at once
without atonement, without mark of His displeasure;
nay, that it is more consistent with His nature that
He should do so, than that He should exact or accept
the penalty from another. This is nothing less than
to put our ideas of what ought to be in the place
of the knowledge that is offered to us of what really
is; but what man, conscious of the weakness of our
common nature, will presume to say how it would
be most consistent for a God of infinite purity,
justice, and love, whose attributes in their infinity
seem almost to contradict each other, "who will
by no means clear the guilty, and yet keepeth mercy
for thousands, forgiving iniquity and transgressions
and sin," to deal with the enormity of human guilt?
Either Scripture is written for nothing, and Christ
Himself suffered for nothing, and the Apostles
preached and suffered too for nothing, or there
was a difficulty in the forgiveness of sins which the
human mind perhaps cannot understand, and which
Divine wisdom only could overcome. Sin could not
be wiped out at once as though it had never been,
or the sinner pardoned or restored by the pure benevolence of God. Either, I say, Scripture is de-
ceiving us, or there was a tremendous problem to
be solved—though we may not be able to enter

into its difficulties—how is man to be pardoned? how can the work of sin be undone, and yet sin condemned and punished? how can God be at the same time just, and yet the justifier of the unjust? And Scripture deceives us more if this was not done for us by a Divine person, who out of pure love took our nature upon Him, subjected Himself of His own free will to all its sufferings and afflictions, rendered a perfect obedience, and died for us on the cross, being made sin for us, though He knew no sin Himself, and then ascended into heaven, where He can plead the sweet-smelling sacrifices which He Himself offered unto God, leaving us the assurance that "if while we were enemies, we were reconciled to God by the death of His Son, much more being reconciled we shall be saved by His life." Either this is the Gospel we have to preach, the Gospel it is called of "reconciliation," or else we know not what we say, and "Christ crucified" is a mere name. But it will be no *mere* name, but a name, or rather a power, of "hope and faith and joy and salvation" to those who in humility and truth look into their own hearts, and conscious of the evil that is dwelling there, ask that question which has been an anxious one for man ever since the foundation of the world, and is only trifled with by fools now,—"Wherewith shall I come before the Lord and bow myself before the most High God?" Those that know themselves best will know best that they can come to God only through Christ, that all they have to plead is His merits, not their own

efforts or repentance, that they have access to the
Father only through Him, and can only offer up
praises and thanksgivings in His Name; that they
can have nothing without Him, but with Him have
everything they need, "Wisdom and righteousness
and sanctification and redemption."

With us who have the sense of this reconciliation
how can any evil feeling or unforgiving temper find
a dwelling-place in our minds? Yet this man of
whom we have been reading goes from the presence
of his Lord, and finding some fellow-servant who owes
him some trifling debt, and appeals to him in the
self-same words, words which must have recalled to
him the mercy he had received, will have no compassion on him, but casts him into prison till he should
pay his debt. The common feelings of humanity
rise to protest against his conduct, and his fellow-
servants, in their indignation, report it to his Lord.
And so his own debt, his forgiven debt, revives and
returns upon him; and he is delivered over to the
tormentors till he should pay all that is due. It
is no simple punishment for his inhumanity and
ingratitude that he has to bear, but the entire work
that has been done for him is undone—grace, pardon,
love, are forfeited, and he falls back into the condition of an unredeemed man. "So likewise shall My
heavenly Father do also unto you if ye from your
hearts forgive not every one his brother their trespasses." It is a lesson to us all, for envy and malice
and cruelty gain too ready an entrance into our hearts,
and what room is there for the Spirit of Christ when,

they have possession? To do unto others as we would
that they should do unto us is a high and perfect
rule of conduct; it tells us to put ourselves in the
place of another, and to treat him as we would then
wish to be treated: but to do unto others as God,
for Christ's sake, has done unto us is a higher and
more perfect rule still. And if men would really
walk as the redeemed of the Lord, as God's adopted
children, sealed with His Spirit and bearing with
them the recollection of all that has been given them
and all that has been forgiven, we might hope for
something like peace upon earth and good will among
men.

There is a change in our Lord's expression when
He speaks of the unmerciful servant which should not
escape our notice. " So likewise shall *My* heavenly
Father,"—*Mine*, observe, and not *yours*, for in forgetting the mercies you have received you put yourselves
out of the family of God, and virtually deny your
relationship, just as you confirm and establish it by
deeds of mercy. " Love your enemies, and do good
and lend, hoping for nothing again, and your reward
shall be great, and ye shall be the children of the
Most High, for *He* is kind unto the unthankful and
the Evil." For ourselves we have mercies past to
think of, and sometimes we are appealed to by them,
" forgiving others as Christ forgave you," and as we
look to mercy hereafter; and sometimes the appeal
is this, " Forgive and ye shall be forgiven." But
the son of Sirach points out how we may make the

past mercy fruitless, and put ourselves beyond the pale of the future.

"One man beareth hatred against another, and doth *he* seek pardon from the Lord? He sheweth no mercy to a man who is like himself, and doth *he* ask forgiveness of his own sin?

SERMON VI.

Gifts for Men.—Whit Sunday.

EPHES. iv. 7, 8.

" Unto every one of us is given grace according to the measure of the gift of Christ. Wherefore He saith, When He ascended up on high, He led captivity captive, and gave gifts unto men."

THE Psalm in which you have just joined according to the services of the day will have told you whose those words are to which the Apostle is referring. The Psalm itself, it is believed, was composed on the occasion of conveying the ark from its dwelling-place on the threshing-floor of Araunah, to its final habitation on the Holy Hill of Sion. But as that ark, though the work of human hands, was the token of God's presence with His people, as its conveyance to the place which God desired above all other places to dwell in for ever was typical of the ascent of a more triumphant conqueror than David into a more enduring seat than the earthly Jerusalem, so is the entire Psalm in the highest degree prophetical of greater events than any that were destined to be accomplished in the city of David. It spans, indeed, in a marvellous manner the whole range of time, from the very beginning of God's dealing with

His people, to the final consummation of all things. It commences with the very words of Moses—used day by day as the ark shifted its place in the wilderness—"Let God arise, and let His enemies be scattered;" it carries us onward to the triumphant entrance of the Saviour not into the holy places made " with hands, which are the figures of the true, but into heaven itself, now to appear in the presence of God for us."

But I would call your attention to the singular distinctness of the prophecy as quoted by the Apostle, with some noticeable variation of terms. " Thou hast ascended up on high, Thou hast led captivity captive, Thou hast received gifts for men, yea, for the rebellious also, that the Lord God might dwell among them." " Thou hast *received* gifts for men " is the expression of the Patriarch. " He led captivity captive, and *gave* gifts for men," is the version of the Apostles—*giving* thus taking the place of *receiving*. I shall recur to this hereafter, at present it is enough to notice it.

The Psalmist you see connects together in the closest possible manner the act of ascending up on high and giving or receiving gifts for men. And if we turn to the pages of the New Testament we find this connexion so uniformly maintained, both in thought and language, that the two acts seem to be almost confounded into one. We cannot account for this harmony, except by the fact that the same Spirit which spake by the prophets of old was given in full measure to the Apostles on the day of Pente-

cost. Nothing else can explain this marvellous unity.
It was not only the strangers that were in Jerusalem
on that particular day, devout men as they were from
every nation under heaven, Parthians and Medes and
Elamites, strangers of Rome, Jews and proselytes,
that heard in their own tongues the wonderful works
of God, many languages proclaiming the same truth.
It was the harmony not of a single day, but of many
hundreds of years, many voices but the same Spirit,
and the Lord God long since filled His holy Prophets
with the same Spirit, with the first-fruits of which
His Church was endowed as upon this very day. So
that if we find St. John expressly stating "that the
Holy Ghost was not yet given because that Jesus
was not yet glorified," or St. Peter after shewing that "God had raised up Jesus, according to
the Prophets," and pointing out as a necessary consequence that "*therefore* being by the right hand
of God exalted, and having received of the Father
the promise of the Holy Ghost, he hath shed forth this,
which ye now see and hear;" (for David, he says,
whose sepulchre is with us unto this day, is not
ascended into heaven, but he saith himself, "The
Lord said unto my Lord, Sit thou on My right hand
until I make thine enemies thy footstool." He could
not, therefore, be speaking of himself, but of some
greater One;) if, I say, we find this in the New Testament, we shall not be surprised if we find the
Psalmist connecting together the ascension of that
greater One, and the gifts of the Spirit in the Old Testament, or the prophet Joel, determining, so to speak,

the pouring out of the Spirit upon all flesh to the last days—the days when the great work of salvation had been finished, and the Author of our salvation had been received up again into the glory which He had with the Father before the world was. It was on the very day of the delivery of the law from Mount Sinai in the wilderness, that the Church of God received the far higher endowment of the Spirit. Ten days only elapsed before the promise of the Father was fulfilled. The same arrangement of time that regulated the dealings of God's Providence with His ancient people was observed and carried out in His dealings with His new. They counted fifty days from the Passover to Pentecost, we count fifty from the great Atonement to Whit-Sunday. Our blessed Lord had promised His disciples that when He went away He would give them another Comforter, that should abide with them for ever, even the Spirit of Truth. But till He was taken away the gift which we now commemorate as a fact seems to have been withheld by a kind of necessity of God's spiritual kingdom. The Holy Ghost it appears could not be given unto men while the Son of Man Himself was walking among the children of men. Therefore, when sorrow filled their hearts at the very thought of His departure, He assures them "that it was expedient for them," a positive advantage to them, that He should go away, as though a very hindrance to their good would be removed by His departure, "For if I go not away the Comforter will not come unto you, but if I go away, I—i.e. I myself—will

send Him unto you." And this will enable us to
understand how the *receiving* of the Psalmist corresponds to the *giving* of the Apostle. The Son will
pray the Father, and He will give us another Comforter. But the gift cometh through the Son, and
the Son sendeth Him. The gift is from the Father,
but because all good things come to us only through
the Son, therefore the Son sendeth *Him.* He proceedeth from the Father and the Son: "When the
Comforter is come whom I will send unto you from
the Father, even the Spirit of Truth which proceedeth
from the Father, He shall testify of Me." And
again, "He shall glorify Me, for He shall receive of
Mine and shew it unto you. All things that the
Father hath are Mine. Therefore I said that He
shall take of Mine, and shall shew it unto you."

But there is a part of the Psalmist's prophecy
which I have not yet noticed, and which is not
quoted by the Apostle, not because it is unimportant,
or has no bearing upon ourselves, but because it was
not the custom to quote prophecy in full, only to
indicate how holy men of old spoke as they were
moved by the Holy Ghost. "Thou hast received
gifts for men, yea, for the rebellious also, that the
Lord God might dwell among them." God, that
is, who maketh the sun to shine on the evil and on
the good, did not confine the special favour that
He shewed to His own peculiar people, to those who
truly served Him with a perfect heart. Now the
whole career of His people is nothing less than
a history of God's Spirit striving ever with the

rebellious spirit of man. It was the same before
their time: "God saw that the wickedness of man
was great upon the earth, and that every imagination of his thoughts was only evil continually."
And He said then, "My Spirit shall not always strive
with man." And when the flood had swept away
that generation from its surface, and one just man
only with his family was preserved to replenish the
earth, the strife began anew with the new spring
of the human race; of the three branches of that one
stem that was permitted to multiply, one was soon
cut off, and thrown aside, and the descendants of
Ham bear to the present day the burthen of their
parent's curse, "Cursed be Canaan, a servant of
servants shall he be unto his brethren." And when
God left the rest of the world to walk in their own
ways, though even then He left not Himself without
a witness, and chose out one particular family for His
inheritance, the strife continued there only in a more
aggravated form. The prophet whom Balak con-
sulted, when he looked upon the goodly tents of
Jacob, and his tabernacles spread forth as gardens
by the river-side, filled with the sense of the blessed-
ness of those whom God has blessed, could not
restrain his imagining of what that people so highly
favoured was or ought to be. "He hath not beheld
iniquity in Jacob, neither hath he seen perverseness
in Israel." But those who were commissioned to
speak of them and to them, when they had been
proved by prosperity and affliction, held a very different language. "Son of man, I send thee to the

children of Israel, to a rebellious nation that hath
rebelled against Me: they and their fathers have
transgressed against Me, unto this very day. And
thou shalt speak unto them, whether they will hear or
whether they will forbear, for they are most rebellious." Rebellious children, impudent and stiff-hearted
—these are but a few of the reproaches that are cast
upon God's chosen people by the prophets who were
sent to recall them into the way of righteousness.
In the most glorious Psalms the mighty works of
God stand side by side with the rebellions of His
people, as if to shew us that where His mercies are
greatest there man finds the greatest opportunities
of sin. "Then believed they His words, they sang
His praise." But in the next verse, "They forgat
His works, and waited not for His counsel. They
despised the pleasant land, they believed not His
word." "They joined themselves to Baal-Peor. They
angered Him at the waters of strife. They were
mingled among the heathen and learned their works;"
so that when the page of their history is full, and we
have read through the record of their crimes, when
the cup of their iniquity is full, and the hour of
their desolation at hand, our own judgment finds
expression in the dying words of the first martyr,
"Ye stiffnecked and uncircumcised in heart and
ears, ye do always resist the Holy Ghost: as your
fathers did, so do ye."

And yet God dwelt among this rebellious people,
and fixed His seat upon the Holy Hill of Sion,
even amidst the iniquities of Jerusalem. No re-

bellion of His people, however aggravated, could destroy the reality of the gifts that He bestowed upon
them. They were there not by their own option, but
by His act, whether they would or no, with their
blessings if they received and used them rightly,
with their curses if they neglected or abused them.
So much was left in the power of man, and so much
only, to make him a savour of life, or a savour
of death unto himself, but he could not affect the
reality of the gifts by ignoring them.

Therefore, when Jerusalem had become utterly
abominable, when her kings were apostates, and the
whole nation, as Isaiah describes it, one mass of
corruption, full of wounds and bruises and putrifying
sores, it was still the Holy City, for God was in the
midst of her. All that God had given her was hers
still, continued hers, because none but the Lord
who gave had power to take away. The day of
forfeiture, it is true, came, but it came when God
pronounced the sentence, and from His sentence,
not from any act or sin of man. God dwelt there,
not so long as it might seem to be a fitting dwelling-
place for the Most High, but according to the times
that He hath put in His own power. It is said that
before her place was left unto her desolate, strange
voices from the most holy place were heard in the
courts of the Lord's House. "Let us go forth from
hence." And then God departed from her for ever,
and Jerusalem was trodden down by the Gentiles
till the times of the Gentiles be fulfilled. But till
then the gifts of God were without repentance, and

their inheritance was entire. They were still Israel, though all were not Israel who were of Israel; to them appertained the adoption, though they shut themselves from the household of God—the glory of God's presence that is, though they dishonoured Him—the covenants, though they broke them—the giving of the Law, though they made it of none effect—the promises, though they would not have them—the fathers, though they did not the work of their fathers—to sum up all, "of them as concerning the flesh Christ came;" though "He came unto His own, and His own received Him not."

Now there is an exact parallel to this in our own case. When St. Paul quoted the words of the Psalmist, and thereby fixed their meaning, it was enough to say, "He gave gifts for men." All the rest was implied, or rather was expressed, beforehand, "Unto every one of us is given grace according to the measure of the gifts of Christ." The grace of God, that is, is not special to any particular number of persons, but universal, to all of whom and to whom the Apostle is writing; to those who walk as children of the light, and to those whom he still finds it necessary to warn, that they walk not as other Gentiles walk, in the vanity of their minds, "having their understanding darkened, and alienated from the life of God through the ignorance that is in them, because of the blindness of their hearts." These gifts are gifts unto the Church, and they are shared by many who are unworthy members of the Church: nay, they have a wider range even than this. On

M

this day of Pentecost they that received St. Peter's word gladly were baptized, and the same day there were added to the Church three thousand souls. And afterwards we are told that there were added to the Church daily such as should be saved. But there must have been many times three thousand Jews, from every nation under heaven, who heard the solemn appeal of St. Peter: "Repent, and be baptized every one of you in the name of Jesus Christ for the remission of sins, and ye shall receive the gift of the Holy Ghost. For the promise is unto you and to your children, and to all that are afar off, even as many as the Lord our God shall call." They who received the gift were condemned or justified by the use they made of it hereafter, but they who rejected it were not thereby exempted from the duty and danger involved in its offer. Were I speaking to Jews or heathen it would be the same now. Those who preferred darkness rather than the light, because their deeds were evil, would bear the consequences of their evil deeds, done in despite of light. But I am not speaking to heathens here, or those who will be tried as heathen, not to those to whom little has been given, and from whom little will be required, but to those on whom God has poured out all the riches of His grace freely. You are members of the family of Christ by adoption, though you may be wasting your substance, and living the lives of prodigals. You are incorporated members of His Church, and all that He has given unto His Church is yours, though you profit nothing by it. The name of Christ is yours, though you may dishonour it. Eternal life is yours, though you judge yourself unworthy of it. The blood of the covenant is yours, though you count it an unholy thing. You have been once enlightened, you have tasted of the heavenly gift, and been made partakers of the Holy Ghost, though you have fallen away, and cannot again be renewed unto repentance. The past cannot be undone, and God's gifts, slighted and despised, it may be even profaned, cannot leave you as though they had never been received. No doubt the idle and unprofitable servant, who hid his Master's talent in the earth, would have been very thankful if he could have declined receiving it. But it was thrust upon him, and he was condemned, though he returned it whole, because he had done nothing to increase it. What, then, will be the judgment of him who wastes his talent? He at least thought it a valuable thing, and one to be preserved. But what of those who have nothing at all to shew, not even what they have received, in the great day of account? What of those who shrink from the table of the Lord, and from the communion of His Body and Blood, and dare not touch them because their lives are evil? Can their evil lives invalidate the offer of these gifts, or destroy the guilt of rejecting them? It cannot be; do not deceive yourselves in so grave a matter. Be assured that by all God's gifts, by all that you have received—by all you might have received and would not—you will be tried, condemned, or justified. Will it be any answer to plead that we have not profaned God's Holy Communion, when the charge is that we have never lived in it? Just as he that receiveth not the witness of God which He gave of His Son maketh him a liar, so he that refuseth that gift of God profaneth that gift by not receiving it. But Christ Himself pleads with us to come to Him, and His very invitation is the highest gift, even to the disobedient and rebellious, a free unbought and undeserved grace to as many as the Lord our God shall call.

Let us throw our souls open to all those holy influences which the Spirit brought down upon the Church of Christ this day, to convictions of sin, to motives of holiness, to truth, to purity and love. And let us who stand fast in the grace of God take heed that we receive not the grace of God in vain.

SERMON VII.

Rev. C. Kingsley's Views on the Question of Special Prayer considered[a].

---

1 SAM. xii. 17.

" I will call unto the Lord, and He shall send thunder and rain."

THE Archbishop of Canterbury has, I am informed, issued letters to the Bishops, recommending prayer to be offered for the blessing of finer weather, to mature and enable us to gather in the fruits of the earth; and I am sure there are those among you who will join in that prayer with as great earnestness as in any prayer you have ever offered in the course of your lives. Nevertheless, the question of prayer for rain or sunshine, or for anything else that appears to depend upon the physical laws that govern the universe, is a very serious one, and, as it seems to me, goes a good deal deeper than is generally supposed — affecting, in fact, the whole principle of prayer for anything. If we turn to Scripture we have certainly not many instances of prayers such as I am speaking of. Samuel stood in a peculiar relation to God, as the Prophet and the Judge of His people. He appealed to God, as we read last Sunday, and He answered by rain and thunder in harvest. It was a miracle, and had its

[a] July 13, 1879.

effect as such upon the minds of the people, so that they greatly feared the Lord and Samuel. The answer to the prayer of Elias is referred to by St. James as an instance of the general power of the "effectual fervent prayer of a righteous man." "He prayed," says the Apostle, "that it might not rain, and it rained not upon the earth by the space of three years and six months. He prayed again, and the heaven gave rain, and the earth brought forth her fruits." And lest it should be thought that the greatness of Elijah as a prophet, and his holiness as a man, gave him an exceptional privilege in the matter of this prayer, St. James adds, as it appears to me, that "he was subject to like passions as we are," so that whatever he prayed for we have on proper occasions the same right to pray for. Nevertheless, the question of prayer for such things seems to me to be a very difficult one, and the practice of it one that is not commended to us on ordinary occasions, so that in fact it may become a sign not of faith, but of want of faith in those that offer it. And some years since a very distinguished clergyman, and almost a neighbour of us, the Rev. C. Kingsley, got himself into a good deal of obloquy by refusing to offer it, and as nobody can doubt that he was a good, holy, and faithful servant of Christ, it will be worth while to consider what his reasons were, though I do not entirely agree with them. First he declined to read the prayer for fine weather unless ordered to do so, because it seemed to him to imply an opinion that we are wiser than God. That prayer speaks of a plague of rain and waters as a punishment. "But how do we know that it is a punishment? and if so, for what? It is well that we should have the judgment of God before us on all occasions, and no consideration that can induce us to amend our lives can be out of place. And if we think of the special sins of the day, and the vices of society, and of the luxury, and dishonesty, and corruption that prevail among those who ought to be examples to others, there seems to be enough to make a thoughtful mind tremble for the days that are coming. But how do we know that the excessive rains that make us so anxious are a judgment? Are we quite sure that they are not a boon and a blessing? A certain quantity of water is as necessary to the earth as blood to our living bodies. It rises from the sea in clouds, and falls to the earth as rain, not to the same extent in all years, but so as to give a regular average, and this is kept up not year by year, but taking one year with another. Perhaps we may think it would be a good thing if we had exactly the same quantity every year, and falling at the same time; but this would be, in fact, to suppose ourselves wiser than God. Man does not live by bread alone, but by all the laws of nature, which are in truth the words of God. Can man live on food without drink, or on the two without air, or on the three without heat? No! nor on all four without a hundred other wholesome influences, of many of which the wisest man can only guess, but which altogether go to make up the health of man. How do we know but what the rains are not restoring to us many a wholesome influence of this kind which we should want without them? How do we know that they are not washing away day by day the seeds of pestilence in man, and beast, and vegetable, sowing instead the seeds of health and fertility for ourselves and our children after us? How do we know that when we are asking for bread we are not really asking for a stone?"

The cholera was threatening at the time these words were written, and Mr. Kingsley asks with pertinency, "How do we know that in asking God to take away these rains we are not asking Him to send the cholera in the year to come? I have long been of that opinion. I have long thought that one or more dry summers, keeping the springs at their low level, would inevitably bring cholera or some other pestilence; and if that particular guess be wrong, this I believe, and this I will preach, that every drop of rain which is now falling is likely to prove, not a plague or a punishment, but a blessing and a boon to England and to Englishmen."

These considerations are the reflexions, not of an irreligious, but of a most religious and God-fearing mind, and that of a high and noble order, and as such are deserving of our careful regard. They come from a spirit of humility and patience, that can wait in faith till it sees the goodness of the Lord. They are, if you like so to take them, a confession of ignorance. But where I am ignorant,

I prefer the confession of it to the presumptuous pretence to knowledge. He speaks of himself, and I speak of myself: "Who am I that I should judge another?" I blame no one else for praying for rain or for fine weather, particularising, if he likes, exactly where he wants each to prevail. I am content with the general form of the Litany, "That it may please Thee to give and preserve to our use the kindly fruits of the earth, so that in due time we may enjoy them." But I have no objection to the special prayer when it is ordered by authority, and I hope I use it in faith, that the Maker, Creator, and Sustainer of all things will order them for the best. Still I cannot go entirely along with Mr. Kingsley in all that follows. What he means he has expressed in the fewest possible words. "Every shower," he says, "and every sunbeam is fore-ordained from the beginning of the world." If this is the case, we need not trouble ourselves about the objection that in praying for such things we make ourselves wiser than God. We are simply asking, not for that which is unwise or presumptuous, we are asking for that which is impossible. And such I know is the opinion of many men in the present age. Everything past or future is absolutely determined by fixed law. The chains of causes and effects cannot be broken; everything continues and must continue according to the ordinance by which it was framed, serving Him, if we believe in Him, and fulfilling His Word. Now I will observe of this idea that though it *may* be irreligious, and probably is so in many minds, yet it is not necessarily so. It removes God from the place which we give Him, as a dispenser of special providence to man; but it credits Him with a wisdom and a power which enabled Him so to construct the system of things, that it should neither require nor admit of any further interference even from Himself. The manufacturer here constructs a chronometer; it goes round the world and comes back in perfect time. It is self-correcting and self-adjusting, and requires no touch from the hand of the maker. He has done with it, and it is independent of him when he has once sent it out of his shop. There is nothing irreligious in supposing that God has finished the whole system of the world, with the same perfection of workmanship, that it may go on for ever, adapting itself, without correction, to every need of every creature that forms a part of it. It might even be said that we are enhancing His power and wisdom by entertaining such an idea of Him. True it removes Him from us, as a Father who careth for His children, as one to whom we can pray and speak; there is no room for fervent love and adoration in the amazement which so vast and complicated a machine must create.

Yet I do not say that this is irreligious; it is only not consistent with what God has revealed to us about Himself. And the recognition of a general law as ordering the world is, to my mind, perfectly consistent with the action of a special providence overruling and possibly reversing that law. Did the storm on the lake of Gennesareth arise necessarily from causes that had been in operation from the foundation of the world, and of which it was the outcome? and shall we attribute its sudden cessation to the same causes, forgetting Him of whom the simple people of Galilee remarked, "What manner of Man is this that even the winds and the waves obey Him?" And it is hard to say how far this theory is to be carried if you once recognize it. Depend upon it, you will have to make distinctions in its application which it will be very difficult to maintain, and people must have clearer heads than they generally possess, if they are to be saved under this idea from the tyranny of universal fatalism. The language of Scripture, and the lessons of experience, and the prayer of faith, seem to me to be perfectly consistent with each other. We are certainly living under the rule of law; if we were not so we should not know what to do from day to day; we should have no certainty of to-morrow's sunrise; our calculations of seed-time and harvest would be all disarranged, and idle speculation would take the place of ordinary prudence. But because we are living under law, is that any reason why when we feel its excessive pressure we should not seek relief from Him who is able to give it? Is the prayer that God's great army of locusts, as it is called in the book of Joel, may be carried away, an idle one, and the promised restoration of the years that this locust hath eaten, and the consequent abundance, to be considered a mere sequence of natural causes? or were the people right in believing, as God Himself declared, "that He had dealt wondrously with them?" or, when what was called the thundering legion under Marcus Aurelius was perishing from thirst, and the Christian soldiers in it knelt down and prayed, and the rain fell at once in abundance, which was right, those who took it as a matter of course, if there were any such, or the heathen Emperor who attributed the deliverance to the prayers of soldiers who happened to be Christians, and stopped the persecution of Christians in consequence? It does not appear to have occurred to the Emperor, though he was a philosopher, that that rain had been ordained to fall at that time and place from the foundation of the world. At the same time it may be allowed that these physical blessings are not what we ought to pray for most earnestly and constantly, though I think it is lawful to pray for them. "Seek ye first the kingdom of God and His righteousness, and all these things shall be added to you." But the reason of this distinction is not to be looked for in the supposition that the things which the Gentiles seek are not equally at the disposal of God, but in the relative value of the things themselves. Seek for those things which are most valuable and necessary first, and trust to God for the rest, taking the ordinary methods to provide them without anxiety. Trust in Him, and they will come either in the ordinary way, or by His special providence. Whichever way they come it will make no difference to you, nor in fact will there be any difference of authorship, for anyhow they will come from Him; and it was not on the score of special mercies which they did not recognize that the heathen world was condemned, but for ordinary blessings which they received, though they were without excuse for not seeing in them their Author; "who knowing God, glorified Him not as God, neither were thankful." But when Mr. Kingsley speaks of the things for which we ought mainly to pray, we can go with him entirely, and I use his beautiful language. "Let us have faith in God, and not break out before we know the facts and the truth into hasty and ungrateful complaints that He is plaguing and punishing us, when all the while He is most probably preserving and blessing us, as He is wont to do. Let us not cry to Him greedily and blindly for fancied blessings which may be real curses, and for the seeming bread, which may prove to be nothing but a stone. We should not give such gifts to our children, neither will God to us. But for this let us cry, for the good gifts which can do us nothing but good, which He has promised freely to all that ask Him; for His Holy Spirit, for the Spirit of wisdom and understanding, the Spirit of counsel and might, the Spirit of knowledge and of the fear of the Lord, the Spirit which is good for all men and for all ages, and in all places for ever; the Spirit which will help us to be sober in good times, cheerful in bad times, brave, prudent, and industrious in all times, as men who know that they have a Father in heaven, who has made the earth right well, and has given to man, if he will use

it with reason, dominion over it." But in maintaining
that material phenomena are inflexibly determined
by causes that were set in motion at the foundation
of the world, I am afraid that Mr. Kingsley has admitted a principle that other persons will carry
a good deal further than he intended. It involves
at least this distinction, that God governs the material world in one way, and the spiritual world in
another. The material world is governed by general
law, the spiritual world by personal and individual
influence. The material world is one great machine;
each individual man is a free moral agent, and is dealt
with as such. But though there may be this distinction of things, this distinction of government is, as it
appears to me, very difficult to prove. The fact that
we are able to investigate and discover the laws of
the material world, and are daily advancing in the
knowledge, whereas we cannot discover the laws
which prevail in the spiritual world, does not prove
that there are no such laws, and we may be arguing
simply on our ignorance. "The wind, indeed, or
rather the Spirit, bloweth where it listeth, and ye
hear the sound thereof, but ye cannot tell whence it
cometh or whither it goeth, so likewise is every one
that is born of the Spirit:" which words seem to
place the action of the Spirit beyond the rule of law;
and perhaps they are as regards our knowledge, but
it does not follow that it is without law absolutely.
The words may simply mean that it has laws of its
own which we cannot discover, as the wind and the
weather certainly have, though practically they are

undiscovered still. But natural science has made
great advances since Mr. Kingsley wrote the words
I have been commenting upon, and there is a tendency in philosophy clearly apparent to bring even
moral emotions and dispositions under the same laws
as mechanics. The language we are compelled to use
in speaking of human conduct rather favours this idea.
We speak of the motives of a man's actions, thereby
recognizing a kind of resemblance between a force
acting on dead matter and the inducements which
act upon a living soul. But dead matter has no
personal will, and a living soul has. Therein lies
all the difference, and we must be careful of our
language and our thoughts. But the most advanced
teachers of natural science seem to ignore this distinction, and to push the rigour and severity of law
into the very inmost recesses of the human soul.
Thus one of them suggests "how the religious
feelings may be brought within the range of physio-
logical enquiry." Perhaps you do not understand
this kind of language, but you will understand me
when I tell you that it implies this, that the presence
or absence of faith, hope, and charity, in a human
soul is to be accounted for in the same way as the
presence or absence of measles or small-pox in the
human body. Everything, according to them, de-
pends upon the relation and arrangement of mole-
cules, i.e. of the ultimate particles of matter of which
our bodies and everything else is composed, and,
they tell us, every mental and moral fact is in relation to some molecular fact, so that if we can explain

these molecular facts, we have explained the mental
and moral facts. This again is, I daresay, strange
language to your ears, but you will understand me
when I say that it reduces those Christian graces
I have mentioned to an affection of matter. They
are no longer graces at all, but certain subtle conditions of the human system, and may be rather compared to electrical phenomena. They belong to
matter and not to soul, or rather there is no soul
to which they can belong. Therefore, I say, Mr.
Kingsley's idea of the absolute sovereignty of law
is likely to be carried, and has been carried, much
further than he intended, and we want some reason
for the line he draws between the government of the
domain of matter, and the government of the domain of spirit, and of mind and soul.

I do not exercise myself upon great things, and
know that there is a knowledge that is much too
deep for me, I cannot attain to it; but I cannot
help observing the thoughts that are afloat in the air,
and am thankful that they are not my thoughts.
That the general government of the world is according to law is a matter of experience. That the
method in which God deals with the spirits of men
is not to the same extent according to law, is more
than I would venture to say.

But I know that the special character and prerogative of God is that "He heareth prayer," and
I am not disposed to narrow the range of that prayer.
And whether our prayers are general or particular,
as that which I have offered up to-day, I am sure

that He maketh all things work together for good to them that love Him; and whether you deem it right to pray for this or that special thing or not, I will only say, "Be not faithless, but believing;" and commit yourself with faith and without philosophy to the Lord of all material creation, to the Lord of all flesh, and of the Spirits of all flesh.

SERMON VIII.

The Profit of Prayer[a].

JOB xxi. 15.

*" What is the Almighty, that we should serve Him ? and what
profit should we have, if we pray unto Him ?"*

SUCH were the words and sentiments put into
the mouths of profane and wicked men. They
shocked the moral sense of the patriarch Job, but he
was unable to answer them. It was a problem to him
that he could not solve, and he asked in vain why
things were suffered to be as they were. "Wherefore do the wicked live, become old, yea, are mighty
in power?" It seemed more consistent in his eyes,
more suitable to his idea of the goodness and majesty of God, that evil should cease at once from
the earth, and the workers of it be destroyed, than
that it should triumph even for a time over good,
and that bad men should seem to enjoy more of
the favour of God than those who were washing
their hands in innocency, and striving to walk blameless in His sight. And he was still more shocked
when he found men prospering in this world, and
making that very prosperity the ground of their
denial of Him to whose hand they were indebted
for every blessing they enjoyed, for the absence
of every evil from which they were free. "What
is the Almighty," they said, "that we should serve

ᵃ Second Sunday in Lent.

Him? and what profit should we have if we pray unto Him?" They had all they wanted, and they were conscious that they were not serving Him. Why should they change their course of conduct? Prosperity came to them in the way of nature, just as effects follow from their proper causes; and what further advantage would they gain if they prayed unto Him?

This book of Job is a wonderful book, full of a deep and meditative philosophy; so much so that there seems to be hardly a question that has ever stirred the heart of man concerning the deep things of God and His relation to us, His providence and our liberty, His power and our defiance of it, His holiness and our corruption, that is not opened, and in some cases closed also, by it. Closed, perhaps, I can hardly say—though answered for the time—for questions of this sort will ever revive and continue to exercise the mind of man. Why is God all powerful, and yet suffers that which He most hates to exist? all good, and yet looks on while evil is triumphant? all wise, all merciful, infinite in His perfections, knowing no variableness or shadow of turning, and yet suffers Himself to be entreated by prayer? We, when we are entreated, may well change; anger is softened and wrath appeased, and we come to a better mind; fierce resolutions are melted down, and our feelings are turned from cruelty and indifference to tenderness and love. It is a redeeming feature in our nature that we can yield to prayer, a glorious victory over ourselves when we

do it; but it is so mainly, because our minds are
evil, our tempers violent, our resentments strong,
our wishes selfish, our love cold. When we yield
to prayer we are in a better frame; but that implies
that we were once in a worse, the change is in us
from worse to better. But we can imagine no such
change in God; the purposes of perfect wisdom must
be eternal, the rule of perfect justice cannot swerve
from its own line, the measures of perfect love cannot
be enlarged. There are, it must be confessed, difficulties in the way of prayer, if we make it simply
a matter of reasoning; but they are as nothing if
we will trust the impulses of our hearts. When we
are told, for instance, that God is an unchangeable
Being, the same yesterday, to-day, and for ever—
the same, not only in His nature and attributes,
but in His counsels and purposes—that every good
gift is from above, and cometh down from the Father
of lights; but that God doeth as He will, and is
degraded by the supposition that He can be moved
to send His gifts by clamourous petitions; that He
is not a man that He should alter His purposes, nor
the Son of Man that He should repent: hath He
resolved that He will not do it, and will He do it
at the request of a vain man? Hath He determined
to do it, and shall His purpose be made void, because
frail and impotent man desires the contrary? When
we are told that among men change of purpose
denotes weakness and infirmity, for that he that
changes his mind changes it either for the better
or for the worse; to change for the worse shews

want of wisdom, to change for the better shews
that he who makes the change was in the wrong
before: shall we charge God with that which is
a weakness in man? How can God alter His counsels for the worse when there is no weakness or
iniquity in Him? how can He change them for
the better when they are always perfectly good and
wise?

It is not always wise to start questions which it
is not easy to answer, and which, perhaps, might
not suggest themselves if they were not so started;
but as I believe that many persons are hindered
from prayer by the idea that it does not profit, and
that some such objections as those stated are at the
bottom of this idea, it is worth while to consider
not so much whether there is anything or nothing
in them, as whether a great deal more may not be
said on the other side. We cannot take any single
attribute or perfection of God, and follow it blindly
to whatever conclusion it may seem to lead us.
The Divine nature is a mystery to us, and can
only be known so far as God pleases to reveal Himself. But He can only make Himself known to us
by investing Himself with human attributes and
feelings, though at the same time "His thoughts
are not as our thoughts, nor His ways as our ways."
We cannot conceive of God at all without running
some risk of bringing Him too near to ourselves,
or removing ourselves too far from Him. When
we talk of the arm of God being stretched out or
revealed, or of His face being turned away from

us, no one is so ignorant as to suppose that this
language, which expresses with perfect accuracy the
actions of men, can be applied with the same strictness to the actions of God. We all understand
that by the "arm of the Lord" is meant His power,
and by His countenance turned towards us or away
from us, His favour or His displeasure; but there
may still linger in our minds the more subtle error
that His favour, His displeasure, His love, His pity,
His wrath, are to be tried by the same measure,
and their workings traced in the same manner as
our own. On the other hand, we must not fall into
the more dangerous error of denying unto God the
attributes which He takes unto Himself, and in the
exercise of which He declares that He finds delight.
Where it is revealed to us that "God is Love" it
is better to conceive of Him according to the most
exalted idea of human love, than to repel His image
from us by the thought that the love of the Creator
to His creatures cannot be such as the love of His
creatures to each other. When we are told that
"like as a father pitieth his children, even so hath
the Lord pity upon them that fear Him," it is intended that we should throw ourselves upon the
love and mercy of our Father which is in Heaven,
with the same feeling, or rather with more confidence, more hope and love, than we should throw
ourselves upon our fathers, who are on earth. But
if God's love is infinite we must not infer from it
what we should think might follow from infinite
love. We must not, for instance, extend it to the

pardoning of confirmed and unrepentant sinners. It is enough for us that "He gave His only Son, that whosoever believeth on Him should not perish but have everlasting life." Nor if God's justice is infinite may we extend it to the punishment of sinners who believe and repent, though they can offer no satisfaction for their sins.

In the same way, because God is unchangeable we are not to suppose that He will not hear our prayers and be moved by them. What if His purpose was from the first to be moved by them, is it weakness or imperfection to be so moved? The unchangeableness of God cannot be better proved by reason or by Scripture than His readiness to supply the wants of those who truly call upon Him. If we think it an imperfection in God to depart from a declared purpose, would it be a smaller one to be deaf to the prayers of His servants, or unable or unwilling to help them? Certainly constancy is a virtue, but when a man is highly exalted above his fellows, it adds nothing to his character to be inexorable, but quite the contrary. It may not be easy to reconcile the fact of God's purposes being unchangeable with the fact of His being prevailed upon by prayer, but both are proved by the same principles of reason and revelation, and we must not deny the one, lest by implication we should overthrow the other. The two, it may be, are contrary in our minds, but we must bear the contradiction, till we see Him as He is face to face, and then we shall be able to understand how they are reconciled and united in the Divine Nature.

Prayer is to be understood, not by talking about it but by praying. They who know by their own experience that God does hear and answer prayer will not be much moved by any general argument to shew that He does not; and those that do not pray themselves cannot expect very convincing evidence of the experience of others. We cannot shew the invisible hand which reaches out blessings to us; God does not manifest Himself to our senses, dealing favours to those who make supplications to Him; though we receive what we ask, we cannot prove to others that we receive *because* we ask. This is matter of faith, which can hardly be expected from those who have not tried it, but matter of faith and certainty to those that have.

Shall we say that there may be entire trust in God without prayer? Certainly there may. We may be always trusting in God, but we may not be always literally *praying*. But that would be a strange trust that was maintained without prayer, and a strange mark of confidence in God that we abstained from troubling Him with our requests, assuming that if we were worthy of His favour He would grant it, though not asked; if we were not, it would only be presumption to ask Him. But what is *trust in God?* Is it a carelessness about Him? Is it the same thing to trust in God, and in any material support on which we may happen to be resting? We shew our trust, for instance, in a bridge over which we may be crossing by never thinking of it. We walk over it unconcerned, as though it were solid land, and when we trust a person without reserve in our dealings

with him, we are apt generally to forget him, but
we think much about those whom we distrust; they
become to us a cause of anxiety, and if our interests
are involved in theirs we cannot get them out of our
minds. But a trust in God brings Him ever before
us; we are conscious of our dependence upon Him,
that our life is in His hands, that we are living under
His protection, that we are His people, and the sheep
of His pasture.

If we believed that this world and this system
of things in which we live were carried on by a fixed
law or necessity without the Providence of God, we
might well put that kind of trust in it which we
should give to a great machine that was carrying us
from place to place; but that is not the kind of trust
that we repose in God, when we think of Him as
a Creator ever mindful of the wants of His creatures,
and as a Father ever anxious to protect His children.
This trust shews itself not in forgetting God, but in
having Him ever present to our thoughts. And this
feeling is of the very essencé and life of prayer. He
that says that if we have this feeling we need not the
utterance of prayer, may say the truth, for prayer
consists not in the bending of our knees, or the
service of our lips, or the lifting up of our hands
or eyes to heaven, but in the lifting up of the soul to
God. But few of us are equal to that constant devotion of life which makes our whole life one continuous prayer; the very needs of this world interfere,
and we are glad to retire into our chambers and be
still. Our Saviour has given us a fixed form of

prayer, the soul is steadied in prayer by the very attitude of the body. The very place we are in has a tendency to compose us to prayer; and the greater our general confidence in God, the more particular and definite will become the petitions of our prayer. The habit of prayer may be vague and general in its utterance at first, but it will become specific and definite in the end. God has no need that we should tell Him our wants, but by encouraging us to make them known unto Him He teaches us how to make them known unto ourselves. It is something to feel what our real wants are, and this feeling which is quickened by prayer sends us back again in prayer to Him. It is not humility but presumption that declines or neglects to ask, and those who ask in obedience to His command have really that humility which those falsely pretend to who expect God's blessings without asking. If God grants His favour only to the worthy, it may be that in His esteem part of this worthiness consists in " a spirit of prayer and supplication," which again is His gift; and if it is argued that the unworthy will ask in vain, it might be true that if we depended upon our own worthiness we might have reason to despair of receiving; but God, through Christ, will save us who are unworthy if we plead the merits of our Saviour against our own demerits and undeservings.

It may be that we do not always receive, or at least feel that we receive, an answer to our prayers; but what an encouragement we have in the Gospel of the day. This poor woman of Canaan, child of an accursed race, might well have thought herself beyond the covenant of mercy, beyond the range of grace, yet she had boldness to approach the Saviour, and declared her faith in the mission of the "Son of David." No voice of comfort answered to her prayer: the Son of David was deaf to her entreaty, till His disciples, either in compassion for the sadness of her case, or desirous to be rid of her importunities, became her advocates. The answer seemed to be fatal to her hopes, and would have struck down at once one less determined to persevere. Still she pursues her request, but instead of finding any sign of relenting she is answered with a proverb, that seemed at the same time to upbraid her with her unworthiness and to chide her presumption. "It is not meet to take the children's bread and to cast it unto dogs." Nay, but the dogs' portion will be enough for her; she will not rob the children of their own. "Even the dogs eat of the crumbs which fall from their master's table."

The very trial of our faith by the withholding our petitions or the delay in granting them is oftentimes a blessing, and importunity is made the condition of our being heard, not because it pleases God to continue us in our misery, but because He wills to draw us closer unto Him. Prayer brings us into such a frame of mind as religion is intended to create within us. We cannot be frequent and serious in prayer without becoming better, and it is not any change which our prayers make in God, but the change they make in ourselves, which is the cause of their success. God's will is ever for our good, but He hears our prayers, or delays to hear, so as to do us the greatest good, not as we wish, nor just when we ask, but as is best for us. And that is best which most calls out and strengthens our faith, not that which brings the quickest satisfaction to our wants. It is God's purpose not that we should fly to Him at once at the first sense of want, lightly asking, and lightly receiving, but that we should make prayer a serious and an earnest thing, using every effort we can make in the direction of our prayers, and thereby ascertaining our real needs. We must not even ask for our "daily bread," as idle men doing nothing to procure it for ourselves, but we must join to our prayers all industry in the use of such lawful means as Providence has placed within our reach. And if we pray that we may not be led into temptation, without watching and shunning occasions of sin, our prayers will go up not as a remembrance but as a mockery to God. We acknowledge in the collect of the day that we are "not able to help or keep ourselves," but we cannot expect to abide safe "under the shadow of the Almighty," unless we are careful to do all that we can do for our own preservation, though we may not be able to do all that is necessary. God will not save us without our own concurrence, and if we have prayed to Him to-day "to keep us outwardly in our bodies, and inwardly in our souls, that we may be defended from all adversities that may happen to the body, and from all evil thoughts which may assault and hurt the soul," let us remember the exhortation that follows on this prayer:

" We beseech you, brethren, and exhort you by the Lord Jesus, that as ye have received of us how ye ought to walk and to please God, so ye would abound more and more."

SERMON IX.

The God that heareth Prayer.

PSALM lxv. 2.

" O Thou that hearest prayer, unto Thee shall all flesh come."

I SPOKE to you lately of the power and efficacy of prayer in the hour of distress and temptation. The remarks I made were suggested naturally by the consideration of the temptation of our Lord. No stronger instance, no more constraining example, could have been adduced. If He, the Son of God Himself, in whom dwelt all the fulness of the Godhead bodily, felt both the need and the strength of prayer; if He passed whole nights upon the mountain in the earnestness of prayer; if in His agony He prayed more earnestly, till His sweat was as it were great drops of blood falling to the ground; if in the days of His flesh He offered up prayers and supplications with strong cries and tears unto Him that was able to save Him from death, and was heard in that He feared, what can we, weak and sinful creatures who have no strength of our own, whose impulses to good are feeble, and to evil strong, we who have the tempter not without us only, but within us, in the lusts and imaginations of our own hearts, what can we do without prayer? what may we not hope to do with it? How solemn is that repeated warning of the Saviour, "Watch and pray, that ye enter not into temptation." The Three

were literally asleep when He roused them by these
words, and the words cannot be taken too literally.
In the silent hour of night, when thought and action
are suspended, when for the time the world is dead,
and we unto the world, as though it had ceased to
exist, the soundless tread of the tempter is approaching, coming like a thief of the night, and we must
shake off slumber and be upon our guard. But here,
too, prayer is the great protection against the enemy,
builds up an unseen barrier that he cannot pass, surrounds us, as it were, with an atmosphere in which
he cannot breathe or act, lightens the darkness of
the night around our souls, and so confounds the
powers of darkness; and they who fall asleep in
prayer may assuredly say with David, "I will lay
me down in sleep and take my rest, for it is Thou
Lord only that makest me dwell in safety." And
so, taking these few words of David for my text, I
propose to say something on the nature of prayer
generally, inasmuch as it can never be severed from
any of our needs and occasions, and least of all from
the hour and the very thought of temptation.

It is a remarkable title, that by which David here
addresses his Maker: "O Thou that hearest prayer,
unto Thee shall all flesh come," and we may be sure
the inspired Psalmist did not use it without a distinct consciousness of its meaning. When God
is addressed by any special attribute there is always
a close connection between that attribute and the
favour that we ask at His hands. We do not
appeal to God as to one of whom we know nothing,

and from whom we have only a vague hope of receiving aid; but we appeal to past mercies and deliverances, making them, as it were, the basis of our expectation of new mercies. There is implied ever in prayer a full faith in the constancy and faithfulness of God. There is implied in it necessarily an act of faith, and the more definite the faith, the more earnest and effectual the prayer. When the Jew appealed to the God of his fathers, the God of Abraham, Isaac, and Jacob, he professed a full belief in all that He had done for his fathers, and a full assurance that He would never forsake their children. When we feel the burthen of our sins too heavy for us to bear, we appeal to Him as a God of mercy, full of compassion and forgiveness, because we believe that His nature cannot change, and that all the mercy and loving-kindness which He has shewn to others will be also extended to ourselves. When suffering from calumny and wrong our hearts fly for refuge to His justice, and we "commit ourselves to Him that judgeth righteously." In every act of prayer so much at least must be implied, that "He is One who heareth prayer." It is a distinctive attribute of the Divine Nature, and in the full apprehension of this the Psalmist combines the title with a deep and pregnant prophecy: "O Thou that hearest prayer, to Thee shall all flesh come;" or, as Isaiah expresses himself more fully, "All flesh shall come to worship Me, saith the Lord." Men shall be taught the true nature of God, that He does not hide Himself from their wants and necessities, that His ears are ever open to their prayers, ever waiting to be gracious; that He is ever near them and round their paths, and then in the sense of His presence men shall worship Him in spirit and in truth, and "My House shall be called a house of prayer for all nations, saith the Lord." It is possible that in addressing God by this title the Psalmist had before him the deaf and dumb and senseless idols whom the heathen around adored as gods, and you may remember, perhaps, the scorn and contempt with which these false deities and their worshippers are spoken of both in the Psalms and other books of Holy Writ. "They have mouths but they speak not, eyes have they but they see not. They have ears but they hear not, noses have they but they smell not. They have hands but they handle not, feet have they but they walk not, neither speak they with their throat. They that make them are like unto them, and so is every one that putteth his trust in them." And there is a strong and cutting irony in the language of Isaiah, where he describes the idol-maker cutting down a tree in the forest, using part of it for fire, and part of it for other purposes. "He burneth part in the fire, with part thereof he eateth flesh, he roasteth roast and is satisfied. And with the residue he maketh a god. He falleth down to it and worshippeth. He prayeth unto it and saith, Deliver me, for thou art my god. None considereth in his heart, neither is there knowledge or understanding to say, I have

o

burnt part of it in the fire, yea, I have baked bread
upon the coals thereof: I have roasted flesh and
eaten it, and shall I make the residue thereof
an abomination? Shall I fall down to the stock
of a tree?" And there may perhaps occur to some
of you that wonderful scene where Elijah defied
the assembled prophets of Baal. From morn till
noon they cried unto their god, they cut themselves with knives and lancets in their fury, but
there was no voice or answer. "Cry aloud," said
the true prophet in the calmness of his faith, "for
he is a god; either he is talking, or he is pursuing,
or he is in a journey, or peradventure he sleepeth
and must be awakened." And then his own prayer
in contrast, "Lord God of Abraham, of Isaac, and
of Israel, let it be known this day that Thou art God
in Israel, and that I am Thy servant, and that I have
done all these things at Thy word. Hear me, that
this people may know that Thou art the Lord God,
and that Thou hast turned their heart back again."

Most truly, then, did He vindicate His name as "He
that heareth Prayer." But if David had before his
mind the contrast between the God whose servant he
was and whom he feared, and the deaf and senseless
idols whom the heathen worshipped, we are not to
suppose that this is all he meant, when he appealed
to God as One that heareth prayer. No doubt he had
larger views before him, and truer and higher notions
of the Divine Nature than could be implied in the
mere contrast between the true God and idols of wood
and stone. To us, at least, the title speaks not simply

of an intelligent and Almighty Being, as compared with the idol-work of our own hands graven by art and man's device, not simply of One who is above this world and the Creator of it, not simply of One whose power and presence pervades and sustains all things that He has made, but of One who is in the highest sense the Father of us all, and longs to recall us from our rebellion to His love; of One who has what we may almost call human sympathies, though far purer than those of man, who has infinite love, and pity, and compassion, and forgiveness for the erring creatures of His hand. It is not because of His Almighty power, but because we believe that He can really be touched with a feeling for our infirmities, that we venture to approach Him in the language and attitude of prayer. "The Lord is merciful and gracious, slow to anger and plenteous in mercy. He will not always chide, neither will He keep His anger for ever. For as the heaven is high above the earth, so great is His mercy toward them that fear Him. As far as the east is from the west, so far hath He removed our transgression from us. Like as a father pitieth his children, so the Lord pitieth them that fear Him. For He knoweth how we are made, He remembereth that we are but dust." And here we may notice how much wiser and truer is the natural instinct of simple minds than the questionings of idle speculations, and thank God that what has been hidden from the wise and prudent has been revealed unto babes. For no doubt very difficult questions may be asked about prayer, and this very attribute of God, "that He heareth prayer," may be set in a fancied opposition to other of His attributes, or at least to our conception of them. Can God, the All Wise, the All Good, in whom there is no variableness or shadow of turning, be turned or influenced by prayer? Might it not even seem to be derogatory to the Divine nature to be at all touched or moved by anything that man can urge upon Him? Even in the courts of human law the judge is deaf to prayer. He sits in his place as the representative and interpreter of law, and neither prayer or tears can alter the law or facts with which he has to deal. Shall prayers be thrown into the balance of Divine justice when they are excluded from the balance of human? Again, our hearts are narrow, and the very sense of weakness in ourselves, which is the basis of charity to others, tends to confine it within a very narrow range. We will relieve distress when it comes close home to us, but we require to have our interest excited and our feelings moved before we can be induced to take up a cause with which we have no immediate concern. But is it consistent with our ideas of the infinite benevolence of God to suppose that it can admit of any increase, that it can contract or expand in proportion to the absence and carelessness, or the frequency and urgency of our prayers. If His goodness is over all His works, are we to suppose that goodness to be in suspense because we do not importune Him with our prayers? Or shall we suppose Him to hear us, like the unjust judge, not from the goodness of our cause, or the greatness of our need, but because we trouble Him with our appeals?

And again, as to the wisdom of God. If He has ordered all things for the best, and governs the world, as far as we can see, by the fixed laws of His wisdom, are we to suppose those laws will be violated and the course of things changed to meet our personal necessities, or our ideas of them? It does not seem to be so in the natural world, from which philosophy falsely so-called is striving to banish the special providence of God. All that is necessary for our existence here seems to come to us in a natural way, and if we think so, it is reasonable to ask, and it will be asked, what grounds there are for supposing that God deals with the wants of our bodies on one system, and the wants of our souls upon another. If we deny special providence as the answer to prayer, it will be but a happy inconsistency if we still believe in special grace as an answer to prayer.

But all these are idle questions, and I have asked them not to perplex your minds by an attempt to answer them, but because I believe there is an answer ready for them in your hearts. I believe there is in the very bottom of your hearts a conviction, far deeper than any of these shallow questionings, that whatever may be said, God *is* after all a God that heareth prayer. We know it by an instinct, not of earth but of heaven, that leads us to fly from our distresses and our sins to the very bosom of our heavenly Father, as a child flies to its mother, or as a helpless, unreasoning youngling to its

dam. We know it far better, those at least who have
tried it by experience. No one who has prayed earnestly will deny that there is a real strength in prayer.
The bonds of sin are loosened, good resolutions confirmed, an unknown influence is poured in upon the
soul in the act of earnest supplication. It tells God
nothing of our wants, for He knows them all before,
but it opens the door of our hearts, and gives free
entry to His grace. Men may kneel down almost
in despair, and, as a last resort, lonely, friendless, and
deserted, but they will rise with the assurance that
they are not alone, that they have a real friend,
though they thought little of Him before, till other
friends and other help has failed them. But now
they can say in their hearts, " The Lord is my shep-
herd, therefore I will not fear."

You may remember that little more than a year
since, some hundred or more of our hard-working col-
liers were immured in a coal-mine, from which they
never came out again to see the light of day. The
horrors of that long and dark imprisonment, must be
left to our imagination, but one of the poor men, it appears, kept a brief journal of their life in that sad dungeon, and the last entry, made apparently just before
the fatal poison put out the lamp of life, was to the
effect that they held a meeting for united prayer.
There was no notice of anything that happened after
that, and one would gladly believe that the last
breath of life was breathed out in prayer. But this
we may surely believe, that when God gave them
the heart to pray He sent a ready answer to their

prayers, and all was not dark even in that valley of the shadow of death. Like Jonah, they cried out of the very belly of hell, and from the bottom of the mountains. The earth with her bars was about them for ever. Their soul fainted within them, and they remembered the Lord. Who can doubt that their prayer came in unto Him even unto His Holy Temple? But not more dark and dreary is the dungeon of sin, in which many a soul is confined, fast bound in misery and iron, nor less certain the deliverance if men will cry to God for help. It is, indeed, a hard thing to break the chain of confirmed sin, nor can it be expected that men can cast off in an hour or in a day the shackles of a bondage which they have spent a life in forging. Good resolutions are formed, but they speedily give way to bad habits; men's hearts sink within them; they begin to feel that holiness is not a state for them; the tempter whispers in their ear "too late," and they fall into despair. At last, perhaps, the conviction comes that He "who heareth prayer" will hear their prayer. He does hear them, and by His aid they work their way out of the dungeon in which their souls are cast.

"He brings them out of the horrible pit, out of the mire and clay; He sets their feet upon a rock, and ordereth their goings; He puts a new song into their mouth, even a thanksgiving to the Lord their God."

SERMON X.

On the Recovery of H.R.H the Prince of Wales.

JONAH iii. 10.

*" And God saw their works, that they turned
from their evil way."*

IN these words we have a short but powerful description of the effect of a single preacher's voice
upon an ancient and famous city. Nineveh was
the oldest city in the world. It dates from the
days of Asshur, and its vast and mysterious ruins
cover up the records of an antiquity in comparison
with which history itself is young, and tell us still
the story of an empire whose records have passed
away. The seat of power and the centre of civilization have drifted down the stream of time far
away to the west, and Nineveh, under the divine
judgment, lies deserted and desolate on the scene
of its former dominion; but in the time to which
the text carries us back, it was called "that great
city," the mightiest symbol of human magnificence
and grandeur that had yet established a dominion
over the subject world. The notice of its extent
which we have in the book of Jonah is singularly
verified both by the accounts of ancient authors,
and the discoveries of modern times. It is described

as a city of three days' journey, meaning, that is, the
circuit of its walls. Later historians speak of it
as being oblong, having two longer and two shorter
sides, making altogether sixty miles of wall. This
would correspond accurately with Jonah's description of it, as of "three days' journey." A traveller
of the seventeenth century gives us exactly the same
measurement. Modern travellers speak of its site
as at present occupied by four huge ruinous mounds.
No one of these corresponds at all to the historic
account of Nineveh, but supposing them to have
been connected together and enclosed we should
have an area of exactly the same dimensions. It
is not necessary to suppose that all this space was
densely occupied by houses, for we know that in
the rival city of Babylon there was room left for
extensive cultivation, and there is no reason to suppose that the population was anything like that of
our own capital, London. But the Lord in rebuking
the prophet who mourned over the withering of the
gourd, speaks of the city as containing more than
six score thousand persons that could not discern
their right hand from their left, and who were therefore innocent of the general corruption : and if by
this we are to understand children of three years
old and under, as has been reasonably supposed,
we should form a fair estimate of the population
by multiplying that number by five. But whatever
the greatness of the city, it was as pre-eminent in
wickedness as in power and multitude, and God
sent a special messenger to startle it into repentance.

"Arise," He said, "go to Nineveh and cry against it, for their wickedness is come up before Me." It came up before Him as the cry of Sodom and Gomorrah; as the wickedness of the world before the flood calling for vengeance. And the prophet, after the experience of his own deliverance, went to execute his mission. "He began," says the author of the book, "to enter into the city a day's journey, which would enable him, if I have given its dimensions rightly, to traverse its full length; so that the whole city might hear the purport of his message. It was a brief but it was an awful one—"Yet forty days and Nineveh shall be overthrown." It was a single monotonous cry constantly repeated. The great preacher of repentance, John the Baptist, filled the desert with the same deep sounding voice that this mysterious prophet made to echo in the streets and courts of Nineveh, "Repent ye for the kingdom of heaven is at hand." Our blessed Lord vouchsafed to begin His office with these self-same words. And among the civilized but savage inhabitants of Nineveh probably that one cry was more impressive than any lengthened appeal would have been. It is said that four years before the final siege of Jerusalem, while everything was in peace and quiet, a young man burst in upon the people at the Feast of Tabernacles with a similar cry. He repeated it day by day, and when scourged by the magistrates as a disturber of the peace he repeated it more and more, "Woe, Woe to Jerusalem," till a true instinct made itself felt that there was something unearthly in the warn-

ing. But it was too late for Jerusalem, because
she had filled up the measure of her sins. She knew
not the day of her visitation, and though all conversion is the work of the grace of God, that grace had
long since departed from her. Nineveh remains in
the history of mankind a signal instance of God's
overpowering grace. The people believed God, a
deep and solemn conviction took possession of their
hearts. The prophet was not only a preacher to
them but a sign, as his history became known; they
felt that as God had punished *his* disobedience, so
He was ready to take vengeance upon their sins. The
voice of authority was not necessary. The peril was
instant, and they could not wait for orders. One
impulse possessed them in the common danger. One
common cry rose out of one common terror, and the
same feeling ran through the hearts of all by an
irresistible contagion. "Proclaim a fast, put on
sackcloth from the greatest unto the least." The
king heard the news upon his throne, and was at
once carried away by the feeling of his people. He
laid aside his magnificence, put on sackcloth, and sat
in ashes; and with the consent of his nobles at once
issued a proclamation in answer to the voice of the
prophet. "Let neither man nor beast, herd nor flock,
taste anything; let them not feed nor drink water.
Let man and beast be covered with sackcloth, and cry
mightily unto God." Even the dumb and senseless
animals were made to share in the common fast, as
involved in the threatened destruction. He acted
according to the ideas of the time, which are not our

ideas, but there is an element of truth and reason in them. There was an indistinct consciousness of a communion between the lower orders of animals and man, their lord and master, and who will find fault with his conviction that God "cared for them also." The Psalmist looks on God's care of His creatures as a fresh ground for man's trust in Him. "O Lord, Thou preservest man and beast. How excellent is Thy loving-kindness. Therefore the children of men put their trust under the shadow of Thy wings." As our Lord teaches that God's care of the sparrows is a pledge to man of God's minute unceasing care for him, so the Ninevites felt truly that the cry of the poor brutes would be heard by Him. And God confirmed their judgments when He told Jonah of the "much cattle" as a ground for sparing Nineveh. The moanings and lowings of the animals and their voices of distress must have pierced man's heart also, and added to the sense of general misery. The pride of human nature alone could think that man's sorrow is not aided by these objects of sense, and nature was far more true in the king of Nineveh.

But outward demonstrations are of no value, and sackcloth and ashes are mere hypocrisy where they express no conversion of the heart. And the call for the fruits of repentance was as instant and urgent as for the external expressions of terror and woe. "Let them turn every one from his evil way and from the violence that is in their hands. Who can tell if God will turn and repent, and turn away from His

fierce anger that we perish not." And it was as effectual as it was urgent. God who knows the heart of
man, saw not only their sackcloth and their ashes,
but their works, that they turned from their evil
way. Their whole way and course of life was
changed, they broke off not this or that sin only,
but all their whole evil way. They were ashamed
of their sins, but they were not ashamed to confess
them. They published their guilt with groans, and
laid open their secret misdeeds. One cry was heard
along the city walls, along all the houses echoed the
piteous lament of the mourners; the earth bore the
confessions of the penitents, and the heaven itself
re-echoed to their voices. Then was fulfilled indeed
" the prayer of the penitent pierceth unto the clouds."
As soon as prayer took possession of them, it at once
conquered the habit of sin. It reformed the city at
once, and excluded profligacy and wickedness from
its home. It filled it with the spirit of heavenly
law, and brought with it temperance, loving-kindness, gentleness, and care for the poor. Had one
entered the city who had known it before, he would
hardly have known it then; so suddenly had it
passed into life out of death, into godliness out of
reprobation. The completeness of their repentance
not outward only, but inward—turning from their
evil way—is in its extent unexampled. The fact
rests on the authority of one greater than Jonah,
to whom all hearts are known. Our Lord bears
witness to it as a fact. He contrasts people with
people, penitent heathen with impenitent Jews, the

inferior messenger who prevailed, with Himself, whom His own received not. "The men of Nineveh shall rise up in judgment with this generation, and shall condemn it: because they repented at the preaching of Jonas; and, behold, a greater than Jonas is here."

As I looked along the countless multitudes that filled the streets of our own great city on Tuesday last, I could not help thinking whether some Jonah was not needed there, and what effect he would have if he came. If some great preacher were to traverse its length and breadth, with the same awful cry, "Yet forty days and London shall be destroyed," would they hear his voice? would they believe in God, and turn each of them from his evil ways? Perhaps they ought not to listen to the raving of a fanatic, and a true prophet might find himself within the walls of the prison, or the restraint of an asylum, as a disturber of the peace. But let the appeal be made in all calmness, and in accordance with established law and order, would it not be an awful sight to see London thronged with as many penitents seeking pardon and mercy by united supplication, as were brought together—some, no doubt, to see and be seen —but many, we may hope, to return hearty thanksgiving unto their God, for the restoration of their Prince to life and health by His marvellous mercy. And though it is of no use exaggerating the wickedness of great cities, or flattering ourselves that we who live in distant fields and a purer air, are holier than those who live in courts and alleys; and though God—thanks be to Him—has, no doubt, much people

in that great city, yet when one passed out of the
crowded thoroughfares into the narrow lanes which
hardly seemed to have cleared themselves of any of
their population; when one thought of the multitudes
to whom a church is unknown, and to whom the teachers
of this generation will make it almost a crime to impart the elements of a creed; when one saw the
visible tokens of their sordid, hopeless lives, and the
indifference of many who are raised above want, and
the hypocrisy of others who think it respectable to
pay some attention to religion; one could not help
reflecting whether if every heart could be softened
and every sinner reformed, and every one who
is on the broad way that leadeth to destruction
thoroughly alarmed, and conviction brought home to
the consciences of all,—there might not be as large
a crowd as was gathered together on an occasion of
great joy, and the riches of the west and the poverty
of the east, brought down to the common garb of
sackcloth, and ashes on their heads, from every
suburb that looks from every quarter of the heavens
to the great centre of St. Paul's.   It is true that the
nature of the occasion called for no demonstration of
sorrow, but was one of grateful overpowering joy.
The nation felt that it had been delivered from a
great calamity, the weight of which it had hardly
realized till it appeared imminent; and they had
full experience of the truth of the Psalmist's words,
that "it is a good and joyful thing to be thankful."
Few persons will object that our Queen and the
mother of our Prince, ought to have gone to present

herself before God with any other state than that
which becomes the dignity of her position. I have
indeed met with an opinion that the pageantry of
state by which she was surrounded tended rather
to the exaltation of the principal persons who took
part in the ceremony than to the glory of God whom
they were approaching in humble adoration; and
in whose presence all men are equal. This seems
to me a great mistake. If "the powers that be are
ordained of God," and kings and queens are, as we
believe, the fittest representatives of that power that
cometh from Him, then it is right that in all national
acts they should appear in their true character, and
with all the external tokens of their dignity. If they
do this in a right spirit, then their pomp and magnificence becomes part of their offering, for with
themselves they offer all that they have. God does
not value sackcloth and ashes, any more than the
royal robe of Solomon or Herod, but the humble and
faithful, and obedient and thankful heart that may
beat under either. Probably in all the vast throng
that crowded that high festival of last week there
was no heart more full of holy thoughts, more devoted, more thoroughly overpowered, by the sense
of the weakness and littleness of man, and the Majesty of Almighty God, than hers on whom the eyes
of all were fixed, and who, while she joined in the
thanksgiving of the nation for the restoration of its
Prince, had a joy peculiar to herself in the restoration of her son. Nor do we generally find many
tokens of a true humility, in the assertors of an in-

solent and presumptuous equality. But leaving this I will yet notice one more point. Our vast metropolis, and the whole country with it, in heart at least and spirit, if not in presence, was, for once, last week united in a religious act; and it came home to us as a real fact which the Archbishop insisted upon, that "we are members one of another." It was an act, I may say, and I am glad to say, totally inconsistent with the principles that are now assiduously preached, and find too much countenance from public men, and which tend, if they are not checked, to the certain severance of national life from all religion whatever. I do not find that any one regretted the existence of a national Church on that occasion, in which our Queen might pay her vows in the presence of all her people; and those who think it almost a crime to permit any portion of the national revenue to be devoted to the furtherance of any religious object, allowed a considerable sum to be expended in a service which they will be compelled to describe as denominational and sectarian, without a protest or a murmur. I do not know what account they will be able to give of their short-comings to those who placed them in a position to trouble the councils of the nation with their voices. Perhaps they were afraid to assert their principles on such an occasion; perhaps they themselves were carried away by the current of general feeling, and left them behind. At all events, it is a matter of satisfaction that in the hour of danger and in the day of deliverance the nation threw the lessons that have been so diligently forced upon it by those who call themselves the friends of the people to the winds, and joined, in spite of its teachers, in a religious action.

Oh that the spirit and feeling of that day would abide with us for ever. Oh that it might be impressed upon us that this country and this whole world is governed not by statesmen, or economists, or popular orators, or representatives, but by God; in whose hand are all our ways, without whom our power may crumble into ruins, and our numbers dwindle into insignificance, and all our riches make to themselves wings and fly away. The world has seen great changes, and may see more as great, and the time may come when Manchester will be a howling wilderness, and London, with its merchant princes, like deserted Tyre. We do not know the issues of things, but this we do know, " that righteousness exalteth a nation, but sin is a reproach to any people."

And we know this also, and I hope believe it, that the promises even of temporal well-doing are large and abundant to those who love and fear God. For them there will be " no captivity, and no complaining in their streets."

" Happy are the people that are in such a case, yea, blessed are the people who have the Lord for their God."

SERMON XI.

St. Mary Magdalen.

———◆———

ST. LUKE viii. 2.

" Mary called Magdalene."

IF you will look to the calendar of this month[a] in
your Prayer-Books, you will find yesterday distinguished as the Feast of St. Mary Magdalen, in
whose name the ancient church of this parish was
dedicated to Almighty God. But we gave you no
notice of her festival, and therefore you had no
opportunity of shewing that indifference to it with
which the notices of other festivals are usually
received. And the reason we did not do it is because, though the day is noted as hers, there is
no special service appropriated to her memory.   If
we had daily prayers here, there would be nothing
in the service to remind us of her. And if you
were to take the trouble to compare the different
forms that our Prayer-Book has assumed since the
Reformation you would find many other changes
connected with saints'-days.   Before that period
of history the calendar was crowded with saints, of
some of whom very little or nothing was known,
and that which was known of others was not always
edifying or worthy of imitation. In the first edition of the Prayer-Book our reformers made a clean

[a] July.

P 2

sweep of all but two in this month—St. Mary Magdalen, or Magdalen simply, as she is called, and James the Apostle, not even honouring him with the title of Saint. In the second edition even "Magdalen," disappeared, and the "Dog-days" came in instead of Saints'-days, with some other astronomical notices. But afterwards the Church began to recover from the shock, and to claim again its connection with antiquity. Accordingly, in the present month, you find on the second, the Visitation of the Blessed Virgin Mary; on the fourth, the translation of St. Martin; on the sixteenth, Swithun, Bishop, whose name is well known in connection with the weather; on the twentieth, Margaret, Virgin and Martyr of Antioch; on the twenty-second, St. Mary Magdalen; on the twenty-fifth, St. James the Apostle; on the twenty-sixth, St. Anne, mother of the Virgin Mary. It is well known that many of these names were restored for certain civil reasons, into which it is unnecessary to enter; but others are the names of holy persons, and commemorative of real events in connection with them, such, for instance, as the Visitation of the Blessed Virgin Mary, and if there is no special service for those days, that is no reason why they should be passed over without honour. Perhaps it was thought that sufficient honour was done to the Blessed Virgin in the festivals of the Purification and the Annunciation, especially as no other of her sex has a similar place in the Calendar. But if I had been alive in those days, and had a voice in the matter, I would certainly have put in a claim on behalf of St. Mary Magdalen. She is no legendary character, and what we know of her from Scripture is quite enough to make her name dear to our memories. The first notice of her is that of a woman who had endured an unequalled misery, and experienced an unequalled deliverance; seven devils had gone out of her—by whose command we know—and she is presented to us afterwards as following our Lord with grateful devotion, and with many other women ministering to Him of her substance. From that time forward she is never spoken of except in the closest connection with the person of our Lord. She was one of the many women which came up with Him to Jerusalem, and she stood by His Cross with Mary His mother, and Mary His mother's sister, wife of Cleophas—three Marys. And when the stone was rolled against the door of the sepulchre in which her Lord was laid, Mary Magdalen and the other Mary are left sitting over against it. The next morning they return with sweet spices to anoint His body, and the bright angel of the Lord announces to them the glad tidings: "He is not here, for He is risen, as He said. Come see the place where the Lord lay." If the details of our Lord's resurrection are not perfectly clear, it is certain from St. Mark that He appeared first to Mary Magdalen, out of whom He had cast seven devils; that he spoke to her as she was weeping over His loss, repelling her embrace by words of solemn mystery: "Touch Me not, for I am not yet ascended to My Father," and making her His mes-

senger to the disciples—"Go to My brethren, and
say unto them, I ascend unto My Father and your
Father, unto My God and your God." Confining
ourselves, therefore, strictly to the pages of Scripture,
we find sufficient reason for remembering the name
of St. Mary Magdalen, though it may be impossible
to fix upon any special event of her life as having
occurred on a particular day. But the name of
Mary, or Miriam, being so common among the Jews,
there seems to have arisen a good deal of confusion
as to the persons who bore it, and the Church of
Rome, on what grounds I know not, has identified
Mary Magdalen with Mary the sister of Martha
and Lazarus. Anything more unlikely it is impossible to conceive, and there is no event, nothing
whatever beyond the sameness of the name, to connect them together. Mary Magdalen followed our
Lord from Galilee, ministering to Him of her substance.   Mary and Martha had their home fixed
at Bethany; and St. John, in preparing us for the
resurrection of Lazarus, mentions of his sister, "that
she was that Mary which anointed the Lord with
ointment, and wiped His feet with her hair, whose
brother Lazarus was sick." But the confusion seems
to have arisen in this way. There is another woman
whose praise is in the Gospel, who is described as
anointing our Lord's feet, and kissing them, and
wiping them with the hairs of her head, in the
house of Simon the Pharisee. But though the act
is exactly similar, the conversation that follows
shews that the occasions and persons were different.

In this case the question was whether our Lord
could be a prophet when He allowed such a woman
to touch Him in ignorance of her character? And
you may remember those gracious words of our
Lord's, which are a message of love to the fallen
of her sex for ever: "Her sins, which are many,
are forgiven, for she loved much; but to whom
little is forgiven, the same loveth little." But in
the case of Mary, the sister of Lazarus, the question
raised by Judas is altogether one of wasting upon
our Lord's person that which might have been sold
for three hundred pence and given to the poor.

So that beyond the mere washing of the feet,
which was almost an act of common hospitality,
and might have been repeated on many occasions,
there is nothing in time, place, or circumstances,
to lead us to suppose that the same persons are
referred to. But what appears to have happened
is really this. This woman, who was a sinner, is
first supposed to be the same as Mary Magdalen,
out of whom had gone forth seven devils, mentioned
in the next chapter of St. Luke; and then a further
identification takes place with Mary the sister of
Lazarus, three distinct persons being thus combined
into one, and the Gospel narrative confused and
perplexed without a shadow of authority. I am
glad that our Church has avoided committing herself to this confusion, and am still more glad that
we can find nothing in our Prayer-Book corresponding to that which appears in the Romish Service
for this day, "Grant, O Lord, that we may be aided

by the prayers of St. Mary Magdalen, in answer
to whose prayers Thou didst raise from the dead
her brother Lazarus, after he had been dead four
days." Here you see the identity of the persons
is distinctly declared, but that is to my mind far
less objectionable than the spirit of the prayer.
If those who sleep in Jesus are still able, as members
of the Universal Church, to join in the sacrifice of
prayer, we may depend on it that we have the
benefit of it, and we know that our blessed Lord
heareth prayer; but to ask Him that we may be
aided by the prayers of a particular saint seems to
me to be a very circuitous method of obtaining
spiritual benefit, and to be casting doubts on His
willingness to hear us Himself as our Mediator and
Advocate, when we address our prayers to God
through Him. And the concluding prayer of the
same service, after the communion, "that we may
be delivered from all evils by the protection of
St. Mary Magdalen," is so alien to all that we
have been taught in Scripture, of the true source
of protection from all evils, that we may dismiss it
without further notice.

Now, in contrast with this let me repeat the collect
of our own Church in the first edition of our Prayer-
Book, which was unfortunately omitted in the second,
and you will feel as though you were breathing
a different atmosphere. It is a prayer that will do
you no harm if you use it every day: "Merciful
Father, give us grace that we may never presume
to sin through the example of any creature, but if it

shall chance to us at any time to offend Thy Divine
Majesty that then we may truly repent, after the
example of Mary Magdalene, and by lively faith
obtain remission of our sins, through the only merits
of Thy Son our Saviour Christ." The prayer is
beautiful both in words and spirit, and it contains
a wise and delicate caution against being encouraged
in the presumption of sinning in the same way, by
the complete forgiveness of one whose sins had been
so many and had fallen off her so easily. But you
will notice that it still assumes this woman, who was
a sinner, to have been St. Mary Magdalen, though
it disconnects her with Mary the sister of Lazarus.
But I still think this extremely doubtful. Mary
Magdalen is not mentioned till the next chapter,
and then not as the woman who had washed His
feet, and whose name is not known, but as " she out
of whom went seven devils," a mark that is not
of identification, but of distinction. And the idea
of demoniac possession, though frequently connected
with uncleanness, is something quite different from
the gross sensual sin of this forgiven woman. And
it may have been the sense of this inconsistency,
or at all events the uncertainty of that which is nowhere declared in Scripture, combined with other
causes, which induced our Church on the second
revision of the Prayer-Book to omit altogether St.
Mary Magdalen from the list of saints, to whose
days a special service is assigned.

Nevertheless, the name of St. Mary Magdalen
as the forgiven penitent has not been disestablished

among us, and her supposed example still holds its
place in our minds. Colleges, churches, hospitals,
still cherish and preserve the name. Institutions
for the rescue and restoration of the fallen still find
it a potent spell when they appeal to Christian hearts
for sympathy and support. The odour of the precious ointment that she lavished on her Saviour's
feet surrounds her own memory. When we see in
painting and in sculpture the long flowing hair,
the features that once invited men to sin, but are
now turned in purity to heaven, the tearful eye,
we ask no question, we want no information, we
know that it is a Magdalen. She teaches us that
vile and common as woman may be, foul as the
fairest may become, there is hope and pardon for
the sisters of the streets, a far better hope than for
the authors of their degradation, whose sin society
makes light of and condones, while it turns away
in virtuous indignation from their victims. And
let it not be thought that the possibility of recovery
makes the sin of those who cause the fall the less.
It would not do so if all who fell could be recovered.
But how many fall, how few are recovered! And
as one of the most eloquent of the prelates of the
Church of Ireland, which a statesman of this age has
robbed of its inheritance, says, "It is a hard and
weighty consideration what shall become of any one
of us, even though repentant, who have tempted our
brother or our sister to sin and death; for though
God hath spared our life, and they are dead, and
their debt-books are sealed up to the day of account,

yet the mischief of our sin is gone before us, and it is like a murder, only more execrable; the soul is dead in trespasses and sin, and sealed to an eternal sorrow, and thou shalt see at doomsday what damnable uncharitableness thou hast done. That soul that cries to the rocks to cover her might have followed the Lamb in a white robe, if it had not been for thy wicked temptation; that poor man who is clothed in shame and flames of fire, might have shone in glory if thou hadst not forced him to be a companion of thy baseness. A soul is lost by thy means, and who shall pay for this loss? what shall happen to thee by whom thy brother or thy sister dies eternally?"

The discarded service of the day gives us in the Gospel the entire history of the sinning and penitent woman from the seventh chapter of St. Luke. With what I will venture to call exquisite taste, it says nothing whatever about her past life, and avoids all mention or notice of the number and details of her sins. We do not know how she fell, or how long she had lived the life she was then living. He who told the woman of Samaria all things she had ever done, "knew thoroughly the history of this woman's life, and all her thought." But there is nothing in Scripture either to excite or satisfy any curiosity about her. An author not instructed by the Holy Spirit might probably have attempted to magnify her Saviour's mercy by enlarging the account of her sins. But Scripture says simply "a woman who was a sinner," words which we might have taken in a general sense, a sense, indeed, applicable to all men and women, if it had not been for the Pharisaic doubt whether He could really be a prophet who suffered such a person to wash His feet. It was a Pharisaic company, and they received a lesson suited to their class, "that the publicans and harlots might go before them into the kingdom of God."

But if we have no picture of a life of sin in the Gospel to stimulate our imaginations, we have a beautiful picture of the domestic life of a Jewish lady by way of contrast in the passage appointed for the Epistle, a lady of rank and position in her own lands, in those happy times, before the nation was divided, and the waves of invasion had begun to sweep over the inheritance of Israel. There were rich and poor even then, as there always will be; but while the rich had their large establishments, the poor dwelt under their vines and fig-trees, none making them afraid. The picture we have is evidently that of a lady who had to rule and provide for a large household, and we are told how she did it. Habits of life are of course different in different climates and centuries, but right principles of conduct are the same for all times and all places, and for the rich as well as for the poor. Those who have those principles will have no difficulty in adapting them to all times and all circumstances. Sarah calling her husband lord is the pattern of all faithful wives, and as all the faithful men are the children of Abraham, so all true wives are the daughters of Sarah. The Jewish lady contemplated in the book of Proverbs does not seem to have had any advanced views of woman's rights, but she had a very enlarged notion of a wife's duties, and as such she reigned as a queen in her own home, which is the true empire of a woman. But I will read you the whole passage from the book of Proverbs, and I think you will say nothing need be added to it. At least nothing shall be added by me.

"Whosoever findeth an honest faithful woman, she is much more worth than pearls. The heart of her husband may safely trust in her, so that he shall fall in no poverty. She will do him good and not evil all the days of his life. She occupieth wool and flax, and laboureth gladly with her hand. She is like a merchant-ship that bringeth her victuals from afar. She is up in the night season, to provide meat for her household and food for her maidens. She considereth land, and buyeth it, and with the fruit of her hands she planteth a vineyard. She girdeth her loins with strength, and courageth her arms. And if she perceive that her housewifery is good, her candle goeth not out by night. She layeth her fingers to the spindle, and her hand taketh hold of the distaff. She openeth her hand to the poor, yea, she stretcheth forth her hands to such as have need. She feareth not the cold of winter shall hurt her house, for all her household folks are clothed with scarlet. She maketh herself fair ornaments, her clothing is white silk and purple. She maketh cloth of silk and selleth it, and delivereth girdles unto the merchant. Her husband is much set by in the gates when he sitteth among the rulers of the land. She openeth her mouth with wisdom, and in her tongue is the law of grace. She looketh well to the ways of her household, and eateth not her bread with idleness. Her children shall arise and call her blessed, and her husband shall make much of her. Many daughters there be that gather riches together, but thou goest above them all."

"As for favour it is deceitful, and beauty is a vain thing, but a woman that feareth the Lord she is worthy to be praised.

"Give her of the fruit of her hands, and let her own works praise her in the gates."

SERMON XII.

Jesuitism.

ST. JOHN vii. 17.

*" If any man will do His will, he shall know of the doctrine,
whether it be of God."*

I THINK I have observed before this, as a matter
of my own experience, that it is one great advantage of reading Holy Scripture out loud in Church
in our own tongue, that we are more impressed with
its truth, and depth, and power, than when we
are reading it quietly in our room. I hope the
same may be said of the hearer as of the reader.
And I do not think this is due entirely to the
circumstance that in Church one is obliged to read
carefully, and with due attention to what one is
reading, so as to make oneself audible and intelligible to others, whereas in one's study one may read
carelessly and inattentively. I think something is
due to the influence of the place itself. "How
dreadful is this place. This is none other than the
House of God, and this is the gate of Heaven." That
is my feeling when I enter a church, and I hope
others are impressed with the same feeling. I was
very much struck with those words of our Lord
when I listened to them last Sunday, and I shall
make them the subject of my sermon this morning,

though other words might have been selected more
closely connected with the great festival of Whit-
sunday; yet they are not] inappropriate to a day
when we pray specifically that "we may have a right
judgment in all things," a judgment we can only
have by the aid of that Holy Spirit, which is the
special gift of this day. For the text refers directly
to the judgments which we are to form, and the
knowledge we are to seek on divine questions, and
divine things, and tells us under what condition
this knowledge is to be obtained. "If any man will
do His will, he shall know of the doctrine, whether
it be of God, or whether I speak of Myself." In commenting on these words I am afraid I may appear
to touch upon controversy. You are aware how
seldom I do so, and if I ever refer to opinions with
which I do not agree I hope I do it with charity.
I think the best thing you can do is simply to preach
the truth clearly and plainly according to the power
which God has given you, and leave it then to take
care of itself. I never could see the use of arguing
against persons who are not present to state their
own case or hear the arguments by which it is overthrown. And nothing is easier than to set up nine-
pins and knock them down again. But I shall never
shrink from noticing any applications of Scripture
which I think to be mistaken or injurious, though
in so doing I shall be careful as far as I can not
to mistake or misinterpret the opinions of those from
whom I differ. For I do think these words of our
Saviour have very often been used, and are used to

do violence to the consciences and scruples of sensitive persons, and force on them the acceptance of doctrines and even practices to which they have a natural and sometimes a proper repugnance.

If I am mistaken in this idea, then I have read a good many books that have made a wrong impression upon me. There are in the Church of Rome persons who are called *confessori*, spiritual guides and directors of consciences. These offices may not always be discharged by the same person, but they very much resemble each other, and can hardly be distinguished. We have no such persons professionally known in the Church of England, though no doubt many persons confess their sins to a priest, which they are at perfect liberty to do, and many open their griefs, and seek advice for their conduct, from those whom they think better able to judge than themselves. This is perfectly right and natural, and we are encouraged to do it in the Communion Service. And when those who require comfort and counsel come to the minister of God's Holy Word to receive the benefit of Absolution, together with ghostly counsel and advice, it is, I think, the duty of a minister not to discourage an anxious soul, but to give him the best advice and counsel he is able. But I do not think many persons in our communion place their conscience absolutely at the disposal of another, as part of the duty and privilege of their religious life. The degrees of influence which one person may have over another are of course infinitely various, and in giving or receiving counsel great

Q

regard must be had to those who watch over the souls of others, as they that must give account. But I am speaking of absolute surrender of the will and conscience, if such a thing is possible. For if we profess to do it nature will assert herself, and there rises a protest from time to time which must be overcome. Now these words of our Saviour are, I believe, used for this purpose, and as we read them they sound very well suited for it. Does any one revolt from any strange or extreme doctrine which is forced upon him. "How," he is asked, " can you expect to recognize the truth unless you conform yourself, as the first condition of knowledge, to the will of God? Do that first as I tell you, and then your eyes will be open and you will discern the truth. Right action is the way to true knowledge. So long as you refuse to do what is right, how can you expect to know what is true? Begin with implicit obedience, and knowledge will grow upon you out of your own action." I believe that consciences are constantly tortured and ruined by this insidious argument when men have once resigned them to the dictation of another. God, I believe, has intrusted our souls to our own keeping, and does not will us to give up our own judgments to others, but to acquire ourselves a right judgment in all things under the promised guidance of His Holy Spirit. It may be said, indeed, that you can only give up your judgment to another by an act of judgment of your own, and that you can do this just as you can make over the whole of your property to any

person you please. It is your own now, and you
can dispose of it in that way, but the act will be
your own. Just so, you can dispose of your judgment, and perhaps the best thing you can do is to
make it over to some one else, but this can only be
done by an act of final irrevocable judgment. But
I do not believe God requires this of any man. He
has given us reason and conscience, and He expects
us not to give them up once for all by a summary
act, but to cultivate and exercise them freely on
every occasion of life. To do otherwise is to act
in the very spirit of Jesuitism, and I am sorry to
say the Jesuit principle seems to me to be the
supreme power in the Church of Rome. Indeed,
I can hardly conceive a Roman Catholic who is not
a Jesuit at heart, though he may not have been
formally admitted into the body. The principle
of that body is unconditional obedience, and the
Church is very lenient and indulgent to those who
will at last render *that.* It will easily forgive scruples, resistance, opposition, if in the end men can be
brought down to silence and submission. It is known,
for instance, how many distinguished prelates and
laymen were opposed to the last new doctrine of the
infallibility of the Pope, but the decree was passed,
and they have accepted it in silence. They must
do so, or they could not continue members of the
Church of Rome, for it is now as much matter of
faith as the Doctrine of the Trinity. One pities
those who had this tremendous alternative placed
before them, and were obliged to choose. I read

Q 2

in the magnificent Church of St. Peter the names
of the prelates who were present at the Council,
some of whom were opposed to the Doctrine, and
now impose it upon their subordinates. No doubt
it must occur to them that, if it is true, there is
no need of any other article of faith, for it embraces
every one of them. Indeed, if I remember right,
Cardinal Newman, whose name I mention with the
greatest respect, maintains that a man may hold the
entire body of what is called Catholic truth, and not
be a true Catholic. He may hold it because he
thinks he finds it in Scripture, because it commends
itself to his reason, because it is supported by ancient authority, and the teaching of the primitive
Church. But such a person, if he could not read it
in Scripture, if his reason revolted from it, if he
found nothing like it in the belief of the early ages
of the Church, would clearly give it up. It would
slip from its foundations, he would hold it no longer.
Such a person, therefore, is no true Catholic, he is
only one by accident, holding the truth, but not
holding it rightly, he is little better than a heretic.
The actual voice of the present living Church is the
only safe basis of truth; to bring in Scripture or
history is to alloy its purity, and to sap its foundations. It was pretty well known that Dr. Newman
was opposed to the Doctrine of the infallibility of the
Pope. He has accepted it now, and in professing
and maintaining it he must derive some satisfaction
from feeling that he has discovered a principle which
enables him to do so consistently. But this is, as

I have said, the very principle of Jesuitism. The Jesuit is not to choose, or prefer, or object, but simply to obey. His obedience is not perfect if he thinks it reasonable, or unreasonable, or thinks of it at all. The aim of the system is to reduce all its members to automatons and marionettes, set in motion by one controlling power. Family affections, natural tastes, moral choice, are to be suppressed; they bring a human element into the machine which is inconsistent with perfect obedience.

In most cases a man may love his work, and his work will be perfected by his love, but a Jesuit must not admit that feeling. He must do his work with indifference, for perhaps he will be called upon to do the contrary to-morrow, and he must do that with equal indifference if he is perfect in obedience. It has produced wonderful instances of endurance and self-denial and heroism; and yet those terms can hardly be applied to it, for they bring in human nature, which the tendency of the discipline is to destroy. In speaking of Roman Catholics, I do not mean to say that all of them are Jesuits or Jesuitical, and some, no doubt, would protest against the imputation of being so, but after all that is the real principle of the Church growing in power and intensity every day. If I were asked the real distinction between us and Roman Catholics I should say it was this, that we claim for ourselves the right and the duty of judging what is right and true; they refer all such questions to the Church, that is to say, to the particular priest or director of con-

sciences to whom they have entrusted the care of
their souls.   I do not mean to say that we have
cast aside the authority of the Church where it has
clearly spoken, as, for instance, in the creeds, nor
that we might not with great advantage have more
frequent recourse to those who are set over us in
the Lord; still this great difference exists, and
is a characteristic mark.   For myself, I should be
glad if some one would think and judge for me,
and tell me what I ought to do on all occasions.
It would be a great relief, if instead of acting for
myself I could throw the onus of responsibility on
some one else; I would rather obey than choose,
and I rather envy the simple duty of the soldier,
to whom it is said, "Go, and he goeth, do this, and
he doeth it."   And if you enter on that line of
action, that which is a restraint and a burthen at
first soon becomes easy and comfortable.   This is
a very proper thing in an army, which cannot exist
without strict discipline, and in which, a heathen
author says, "the soldier has no right to ask anything."   But I do not believe it is the line of duty
in which it is intended that the soldier of Christ
should walk; I believe it to be the duty of Christians to think and choose, and to do this constantly;
to think what is true, and to choose what is right,
and the Spirit of God will help us to do both.   As
to some acts of choice, they should be final.   "As
for me and my house, we will serve the Lord."
There need be no revision, and therefore no repetition of that choice, only constancy in holding to

it. And some professions of faith should be final. We are not to waver in them, and if an angel from heaven teaches anything contradictory to them we are not to listen to him. But the occasions of choice are as frequent as the occasions of action, and the precept, "Try all things, hold fast that which is good," will apply to opinions which are brought before us every day. "Choose life" does not imply that any one would be likely to choose death directly, but it means choose the things tending and pertaining to life, about which people are constantly mistaken, choosing death instead, so that the people of God are asked, as if it were a strange thing, "Why will ye die, O house of Israel?"

One would have expected that the right and the duty of private judgment would have brought with it a feeling of responsibility and almost of fear, but it does not seem to have had that general effect. We are advised to "work out our own salvation with fear and trembling, for it is God that worketh in us, both to will and to do according to His good pleasure." In one respect this should be a cause of confidence, but it is clearly implied that we may be found to be working against God. For though God is omnipotent, it is part of His omnipotence to be able to leave us free while He is working in us. And one would think that the duty of personal judgment of what is true and right would make us fearful lest we should judge wrongly. And it should also make us very careful to use every assistance in informing and correcting our judgments, such as prayer, study of Holy Scripture, deference to those who are better informed than ourselves, especially those who are set over us, and the general opinion and concurrence of holy men in all ages, who have adorned their doctrine with their lives. You would expect to find modesty and reserve in judgment, willingness to hear, and not over-readiness or haste to speak. You find the exact contrary. Everybody is ready with an opinion on every subject, without information or any attempt to obtain. Everybody's opinion is worth as much as anybody else's, or rather more in the man's own estimate. There is no question so difficult, so awful, so unrevealed, but what you find somebody, and perhaps many, to answer it off-hand. Those who do not exercise their judgment in any other way will exercise it by resigning it to some other person, who will rule them more absolutely than any pope ever thought of. Men are either popes themselves, or they select their popes and obey them.

I perceive that I am wandering from my subject, and therefore I will return to my text. I said that it was a passage which has been much misinterpreted and abused, and therefore, after repeating it, I will state briefly what I mean. "If a man will do His will, he shall know of the doctrine, whether it be of God." It is almost impossible to read the verse without putting the stress on the word *do*. That is accordingly the case, and men are told, "you must *do* the will of God, i.e.

what *I* tell you is the will of God, and then the
truth will be brought home to your mind. You
cannot expect to know it till you have done that
well." Now any one who is worth listening to
will tell you that this is entirely a misinterpre-
tation of the actual words. The true meaning is
this. If a man has a real will and a wish and
a desire to do the will of God, then he shall know
of the doctrine, whether it be of God. The em-
phasis in the sentence is changed. It does not
rest on the word *do*, but on the word *will*. This
is what we should expect. It is in accordance with
what we know by experience of human nature,
and have a right to expect from Divine grace.
Those whose real earnest wish is to do the will of
God, who love His law, as David loved it, to whom
it is more precious than gold, and sweeter than
honey and the honeycomb, will not be suffered to remain in ignorance by Him. "They shall all be taught
of God" is one of the most gracious and general
promises to the people of God, and here is the
condition of *learning*, that they *wish* to do His
will. They may, perhaps, be mistaken as to His
will in particulars, but that is of small importance
if they *wish* to do it; though I do not think they will
go far wrong under that condition. Law, word, commandment, statute, ordinance, truth, are words constantly interchanged, and it is difficult to distinguish
them, but they are all summed up in truth. "Sanc-
tify them by Thy truth, Thy Word is truth." God
promises to each one of us truth, not as a rule de-

rived from an external standard, but as a treasure abiding in our own hearts. It is the spirit of Truth whose gift we are celebrating to-day. He is expressly so called. If we wish to discriminate the gift more particularly, let us ask Him to be to us a spirit of wisdom and understanding, a spirit of counsel and ghostly strength, a spirit of knowledge and true godliness. Yea, let Him fill us with the spirit of His holy fear, now and for ever.

SERMON XIII.

Calbinism.

ST. MATT. vi. 33.

" Seek ye first the kingdom of God and His righteousness."

THE word *first* here seems to me to be susceptible
of two meanings. It may mean either first in
order of time, or first in respect of importance.
And these two things are not always coincident,
though in practice we generally do that which is
of most importance first, and that which is of less
importance afterwards. Sometimes, however, the
order of action is reversed, and we clear away small
matters on the instant, in order that our hands and
time may be free for greater ones, or for the greatest
of all. But I believe that our Saviour here means
simply *first* in order of time, which is its natural
meaning, and that He impresses this precept upon
us with earnestness which is so peculiarly His own,
because it implies the very contrary to the practice
which the world is in the habit of following. For
assuming that the Kingdom of God and His righteousness, in relation to ourselves, is identical with
the good of our immortal souls, I think all persons
will allow that that is a matter of much more importance to us than anything that can happen to

our bodies and estates. All persons will allow that it would profit us nothing at all if we were to gain the whole world and lose our own souls. So that as regards the relative estimate of our souls, compared with anything else, there is a general agreement. The bad agree with the good on this point. They do not wish or intend to throw their souls away, though in fact they are doing it. I do not mean to say that there are no men so vile and lost as to care nothing for their eternal destiny, for the majority of irreligious men certainly do care something for it, only they put off the thought of it; they intend to give their minds to it, and to do something better at some future time. Our blessed Saviour seems to me to be addressing all men, but especially those who are just entering life. And as regards their duties and interests, He seems to me to insist pointedly on the "order of time." He is speaking not of corrupt men and hardened consciences, but to men of good intentions and principles, who are anxious to know what they shall do first. Let us suppose the case of a young man or young woman, such as I am thinking of, mapping out the course of life on which he or she is entering, and endeavouring to lay it down and trace it out the to end. The man intends to do right, and to do good, which is a matter of far less importance than doing right. Say that he is going into business; he will be regular and honest, he will do whatever his hand findeth to do with all his might. He sees others who have done the same before him, and he will follow their

example. They have prospered, they have retired
in the evening of life, everybody speaks well of
them, and they seem to be employed in doing good.
Their lives have not been very heroic, but they have
brought them to comfort and competence ; they have
found honesty the best policy, though they were
never so base as to be honest on that calculation,
and they seem now to be making God some return
for the prosperity by which their lives have been
crowned. People observe "that they have become
quite religious," and their religion is thought to
be quite natural and proper. They would be ungrateful if they were not so ; and their lives are
held up as examples. See what good men of business they were, how steady, how punctual, how
sober ; and now what good men they are, how
happy they make everybody around them, what
good they are doing !

Now our blessed Saviour never said that good
habits were not likely to lead to prosperity and comfort, nor would He be likely to reject the intention to
do what is right at any period of life, or any service
offered to Him however late, but I think He would
say that such persons had not observed the order of
action commended in His precept. They have not
sought " the Kingdom of God and His righteousness "
first but *last*, if they have found it now. Be religious
men and women from the first. Start in life with
the resolve that you will be so. It is nothing, or
worse than nothing, it is a vain delusion to intend
to be so when you have served your apprentice-

ship to the world. Begin a religious life, soberly and seriously, now. Consider its duties to yourself, to man, to God. You owe something to yourself, in fact any duty to another is also one to yourself. But some belong to yourself particularly, as chastity and temperance; others to your neighbour, as honesty and kindliness; others to God, as faith, hope, and charity. We need not be particular in classifying these duties, in fact they all run into each other; and to these I might add what may be called ecclesiastical duties, such as not forsaking assembling yourselves together, hearing the Word, partaking the Holy Sacrament, doing consistently all things which shew that you are a member of Christ's Church, and of that branch of the Church in which, happily for you, as I think, it is the will of God that you have been born. Make up your minds on these points now and act accordingly, and—I will not hold it out as a bribe to you, that you will therefore at once prosper in this world, but I will venture to say you will suffer no injury or inconvenience from it; nay, I will simply repeat our Lord's own words, "Seek ye first the kingdom of God and His righteousness, and all these things which the Gentiles seek shall be added unto you."

Now what I have said about Christian life generally will apply closely enough to the particular duties of this season. It is our duty, and it is also our interest, to devote some part of the season of Lent, more than any other season, to serious thought, taking, as it were, stock of our lives; and to repentance, which must be the result of anything like serious thought. Nothing can be more formal and hollow than general confessions of sinfulness which cost· us nothing and promise us nothing, if no remembrance and sense of actual sins come home to our consciences. We have all sinned abundantly during the last year, and those are the things we ought to remember, and in respect of which we ought to aim at amendment. If along with that we confess and deplore the sinfulness of our nature, not as an excuse for sin, or at all events a palliation of it, which I fear it is frequently thought to be, but as a continuous fuel and encouragement of it, then I think we may hope that God will not only blot out all our iniquities, but will create a clean heart, and renew a right spirit within us. And I believe few persons enter upon the season of Lent without some weary feeling about their sins, and some intention of getting rid of them. Perhaps they say to themselves, "Our clergyman will tell us the same things that he did last year; we know what he will say already. If they are not verbally the same sermons, they will amount to the same. He will invite us to be more regular at church, and perhaps have some special service, which, we hope, it will do our neighbours good to attend. He is a good sort of man, and it will be unpolite and disrespectful if they do not. Besides that, he is only doing his duty. It is his duty to tell us such things, and we can take to ourselves the credit of never denying that they are true.

Only there is no hurry; we heard the same last year, and shall hear the same next. We really believe that there is a great deal in what he says. He does not say it simply professionally, but believes it himself. It is worth our consideration, and we shall give our serious attention to it some day. At present we are engaged, and as it is as certain to come round again next year as spring and summer, we can surely afford to wait.

Alas! you are very inconsistent here! You do not defer the duties and works of this spring because next year also will have a spring of its own; but you put off the duties and opportunities of this Lent, though none of you can be certain that you will ever live to see another. Still I believe what is said and done in Lent—and the very word *Lent*—makes many persons weary and uncomfortable. They have been told so often that they have certain duties regarding it, that they cannot help thinking there is something in it; they have heard so much about repentance, that they will make some effort and go on if they find any encouragement. They ask how they are to begin, and they do as they are told. Perhaps they attend church one or two times, or at services where they were never seen before; they try to be attentive and serious, they listen and endeavour to think of what they are hearing. But the interest they would wish to feel is never created. The service is dull and unprofitable. The preacher never touches their heart, or fans the spark of piety into a flame. They find no fault with him, for all he says seems to them to be sincere and true, only that is the fact. They give up the effort as a failure, and throw themselves into the world again, which is quite ready to receive them on the old terms. But it is quite possible that they may receive very different advice; they may be told that they can do nothing for themselves, that all that they can do is to wait; that conversion will come when it is intended to come, or not at all, and that anything they can do to invite God's grace will only have the effect of repelling it. I do not know whether any of you are familiar with the poems of that thoroughly English poet and clergyman, Crabbe.

There is the story of one "Abel Keene," which I shall use in illustration of what I mean [a]. It is not an uncommon story. Abel Keene is a man of humble birth, but of sound principles and sufficient education. Through the influence of a kind friend he is placed in a merchant's house in London, at a more advanced age than is usual in that situation, where his position in respect of pay and prospects greatly improved. But he is thrown into the society of dissolute and irreligious men, much younger than himself, among whom he is soon accustomed to hear the truths and principles which he once held in reverence spoken of with contempt and derision. Being a weak man, he cannot resist the evil influence, and becomes in conversation, dress, and life, such as they

[a] "The Borough," Letter XXI. Vol. iv. of Murray's edition of Crabbe's works, in 8 volumes. Cf. vol. iii. Letter IV. p. 89, where the same subject is treated of, with illustrations.

R

are, feeling himself a coward all the time for being so. He has a sister who, hearing of his change of life, expostulates with him in language which would do you good to read, and with a power which few preachers possess; but as her expostulations are unheeded they only make him worse. He flies into worse excesses, and is plunged in them when his employer dies suddenly, and leaves him in his waning years a mere wreck in character and prospects, "Now lost to fortune as before to grace." Thus he returns to his native place, to contempt, beggary, and misery—and his sister died.

> " His sister died with such serene delight,
> He once again began to think her right.
> Poor like himself the happy spinster lay,
> And sweet assurance blessed her dying day.
> Poor like the spinster he, when death was nigh,
> Assured of nothing, felt afraid to die."

At length he is found in a shed, having hanged himself in despair. But he has left behind him a paper giving the spiritual history of his life. The whole of it is well worth reading, but I shall quote only a part of it. It is where his conscience being alarmed, he tells us how he sought advice from one who had a great reputation as a physician of souls. He tells him all his miseries, and is told in answer that "he is just an object meet for saving grace."

> " No merit thine, no virtue, hope, belief,
> Nothing hast thou but misery, sin, and grief,
> The best, the only titles to relief."

But, like the Philippian jailor—

> " ' What must I do,' I said, 'my soul to free?'
> ' Do nothing, man—it will be done for thee.'
> ' But must I not, my reverend guide, believe?'
> ' If thou art called, thou wilt the faith receive.'
> ' But I *repent* not;' angry he replied,
> ' If thou art called, thou needest nought beside.
> Attend on us, and if 'tis Heaven's decree
> The call will come—if not, ah ! woe for thee.' "

Thus advised, the wretched man attends exciting sermons, he sees others in transports and ecstasies, but nothing comes to himself :—

> " They wept and they rejoiced, but there was I
> Hard as a flint, and as a desert dry ;
> To me no tokens of the call would come,
> I felt my sentence and received my doom.
> But I complained. 'Let thy repinings cease,
> Oh man of sin, for they thy guilt increase ;
> It bloweth where it listeth—die in peace.'
> ' In peace—and perish,' I replied. 'Impart
> Some better comfort to a burthened heart.'
> Alas, the priest returned, 'Can I direct
> The heavenly call ? Do I proclaim the elect ?
> Raise not thy voice against the Eternal will,
> But take thy part with sinners, and be still.' "

This terrible story was much commented on at the time, and denounced as a perversion and misrepresentation of a certain style of religious appeal, which was more common fifty years ago than now. It is no doubt the representation of an extreme case, and it is the gift of men of imagination and clear powers of reason to represent and illustrate principles in their extreme exhibitions, but I am much mistaken if this is very far removed from the doctrine which is preached and insisted upon in many of the meeting-houses of our land without any distortion whatever, (I am bound to say that I have heard the same preached by excellent men in our own Church, who did not see clearly the tendency of what they were saying); and I find this supported by a pamphlet published about that time, entitled "A Cordial for a Sin-despairing Soul," in which the writer informs us "that after he had full assurance of his salvation the Spirit entered particularly into the subject with him," and among other matters of like nature assured him "that his sins were fully and freely forgiven, as if they had never been committed." (That happily we may learn from better authority than our own heart); but he goes on with a strange mixture of truth and error, "Not for any act done by him—whether believing in Christ, or repenting of sin—(there faith and repentance are got rid of at once, and I think I observed that when Moody and Sankey were disturbing men's minds here, the word 're-pentance' was never uttered by either of them);—nor yet for the sorrow and misery he endured, nor for any service he should be called upon to do in his militant state, but for His own name and for His glory's sake," and so on.

For the whole drift and tenor of the book is to the same purpose, viz. the uselessness of all religious duties, such as prayer, contrition, fasting, and good works. The author shews the evil done by reading such books as the "Whole Duty of Man;" he com-

plains of an Irish bishop who wanted him to join in
family prayer; he considers all attendance upon the
ministers of the Gospel unnecessary and even injurious. In fact his principle is to let *ill* alone; his
talents are not to be employed; and the hopes of
glory are rather extinguished than raised by any
application of the means of grace. This I will allow
is very extreme doctrine, but it is the consistent development of doctrine that in other cases is not extreme, and let me ask you whether it is not some
idea or feeling of this sort which keeps you away
from the means of grace which are offered you in
this place, to which you never come?—You wait for
an impulse that you cannot resist—you think it unnecessary to form any resolution of your own.

Let me not be supposed to deny the possibility of
such an instant conversion as Abel Keene is represented as waiting for, but which never came. I am
not the man to deny or limit the miracles of divine
grace; and if I had time this morning, and possessed the book in which the history is contained, I
should read to you the account of the conversion
of Col. Gardiner, as narrated by himself. He was
a most dissolute and profligate infidel in a dissolute
age. As far as I remember he was visited by a spirit
or angel—I am not sure that it was not in the image
of our Lord Himself—who spoke to him awful words,
which I wish I had at heart to repeat[b]. Such a

[b] He believed that he saw "before him, as it were suspended in
the air, a visible representation of the Lord Jesus Christ upon the
Cross, surrounded on all sides with a glory, and was impressed as

dream or fancy, if it were a dream or fancy, might turn a man into a madman or fanatic. But the reality of the vision was attested by a total and consistent change of life from that hour. Out of the materials of the vilest sinner there was re-created one who passed the rest of his life, humanly speaking, as a perfect saint. He brought forth works meet for repentance, and no one doubted that he had fled from the wrath to come. The account of his end is written, and he passed his last hours in prayer, and giving advice and exhortation to others on the eve of the battle of Prestonpans, in which he fell. The case, though extraordinary, proves nothing, as a general rule, beyond the power of divine grace, which I should think nobody would deny; and from what I remember of Col. Gardiner's life, and its influence on others, he did not advise them to expect or wait for the same sudden conversion and illumination which he had himself experienced. It must have been a constant wonder and amazement to him that he of all men should have been the object of this mercy, but the effect of it was to make him exhort all men over whom he had any influence to take immediate steps to depart from all iniquity lest it should be their ruin, to think seri-

if a voice, or something equivalent to a voice, had come to him to this effect (for he was not confident as to the words), ' Oh, sinner! did I suffer this for thee, and are these thy returns?' "—From " Some remarkable Passages in the Life of Col. James Gardiner, by P. Doddridge, D.D."

The reader will find the account of the Conversion and Death of Colonel Gardiner in notes to Chapters vii. and xlvii. of " Waverley," marked by the letters C and V, in the Centenary Edition.

ously and repent, and strive to return to the paths of
holiness and peace, in which he did not doubt they
would be assisted by God's grace. And I think
a very wrong use is made of those words, "The Spirit
bloweth where it listeth," so wonderfully illustrated
by that particular case, when a reason is found in
them for waiting and doing nothing towards returning unto God, till the Spirit lays hold of us irre-
sistibly, and we cannot help being saints any more
than we can now help being sinners. And it is they
who so force the words, who are practically limiting
and defining this power of "blowing where it listeth"
of which they seem to make so much. They deny
Him real freedom, they say "He must and shall work
in this particular way, or else He shall not and cannot be allowed to work at all." They deny His
power and working unless, as we may say, they can
actually "hear the sound thereof." If there is any
vile and hardened heart anywhere, I recognize the
power of the Spirit in purifying and softening that
heart under any circumstances, for nothing but that
can have such virtue and effect. Nor do I tie down
the actions of the Spirit to the means of grace that
Christ Himself has ordained. But I have no reason
to doubt that God answers prayer, that He blesses
the ministry of the Word, that He regenerates by
water, that He gives the grace of His body and
blood in the Holy Communion, that He gives more
grace by laying on of hands, that He looks with com-
placency at our weak and feeble attempts to forsake
sin and amend our lives, and if we do what we can

for ourselves, He is mighty and ready to do more for us.

And if the sinner prays, "Create in me a clean heart, and renew a right spirit within me," God seems to turn the words of the prayer back upon the sinner, "Make you a new heart and a new spirit— Why will ye die, O house of Israel? Wherefore turn yourselves and live ye."

SERMON XIV.

Christianity — what?

ROM. viii. 34.

" It is Christ that died, yea rather, that is risen again, who is even at the right hand of God, who also maketh intercession for us."

IT is worthy of remark that the word Christianity is never found in the pages of Holy Scripture. If it had been found there, of course it would have been as a new word; but the writers of Holy Scripture did not invent new words, but took those which they found in daily use, and stamped them with a new value to serve new purposes. Most of their words, which have now almost exclusively a Christian sense, were very ordinary and common words when they were adopted and appropriated by the Apostles. "The Gospel," for instance, speaks for itself as a Christian word, but it is the translation of a word that might have been used by any pagan author for a message of good tidings, which in fact it is. *The word* itself is, as we may expect, one of the most common words in the language in which Scripture is written. When we hear of the *Church*, we at once think of the whole body of Christians, or of a particular congregation of them; but when the Apostles took it up it meant merely a "meeting of the people in their ordinary place of assembly."

Now these words constantly occur in the Acts and Epistles of the Apostles. We hear that in one place they preached the Gospel, in another that the word of God grew and prevailed mightily, in another that the Lord added daily to the Church such as should be saved, and so forth, in instances without number. And it is said that the disciples were called Christians first at Antioch, whether by themselves, or by Jews or heathen we cannot say, but we know that they accepted the title willingly, and gave themselves up to death or torture rather than renounce the name. But the word Christianity itself, and such expressions as the progress, and practice, and principles of Christianity, are nowhere to be found. Nor is this any objection to the word, or difficult to be accounted for as a fact. It is a word that was the produce of reflexion when the Gospel had asserted its position in the world, and men were bound to take notice of it. When Christians had become a large and important body of men, living under a certain rule, holding certain principles, paying a manifest obedience to laws, which were not those of the outward political world, and looking up to a common head, then it was time for such a word as Christianity to be invented. The system had come into existence, and a word was needed to represent it, so that it might be compared with other systems, as, e.g., with Judaism, Heathenism, and Mahometanism, and many other *isms* which modern times have produced in more or less close connexion with it. And now men can talk freely of Christianity, and acknowledge what great things the genius or spirit of Christianity has done for the progress and improvement of the world. And all persons who are more or less under the influence of that spirit, or who are members of a society which has not repudiated it, are conventionally supposed to be Christians, unless, indeed—which is a portent not altogether unknown in these days—they positively and for themselves repudiate the name. We would not of course call a man a Christian in the face of his own denial that he was one, but such few cases excepted, we assume, as a matter of course, that all the persons that we meet are Christians. I am speaking of course of our own and other civilized countries, the day may yet be far distant before we can speak in the same terms of the whole world. And as Christianity may cover whole nations with the breadth of its name, so the effects or influence of Christianity may be seen all over the world, and he need not be a Christian himself who acknowledges them. These effects are undoubted, though they have in some cases, perhaps, been exaggerated. The Church has in many of its branches, from time to time, sunk into the corruptions of Heathenism, yet all will allow that Christianity has raised the general tone of morality, wherever it has prevailed. It has brought virtues to light which were little thought of before, it has condemned vices that were almost sanctioned by public opinion. It has raised woman to her true position of honour and dignity in relation to man, though the present tendency in some quarters seems to be to displace her

from it, under pretence of raising her to a more complete equality. It has struck the fetters off the slave,
and perhaps doomed him to extinction in the presence of a superior race. Twenty years ago it was
thought that it had, or was going to, put an end to
war, because people of all nations were brought
together to exhibit their commodities under a glass
roof. It is true that since then the ingenuity of men
has been mainly employed in improving implements
of destruction for their horrible work, and blood has
been poured out in every quarter of the world like
water, so that if exhibitions are of any use in this
respect, we wonder how things could have been
much worse without them. But Christian charity
has yet found a field for herself on the plain of
battle, and it is some mitigation of the horrors of
war, that it is considered inhuman to destroy an
enemy with an explosive bullet of less than a certain
size. Again, Christianity has been credited with the
general extension of intercourse between nations, and
I remember a distinguished statesman saying that
the Gospel meant, or rather *was*, free trade. No
doubt the Gospel, by teaching that " God hath made
of one blood all nations of men to dwell on all the
face of the earth," has done much to remove the
barriers to free intercourse between people and
people, and the lines that separated Jew, and Greek,
and Barbarian, and bond and free, disappear under
the Gospel; and the sense of union in one common
nature, though this is denied by some, must tend
towards the increase both of commercial inter-

course and every other form of communion between man and man. But I should myself rather look for the fruit of Christianity in fair dealing, and just measures, and in the conferring of mutual benefits, than in the simple extension of trade, which may after all only make the most successful trader liable to the curse of St. James: "Go to now ye rich men, weep and howl for your miseries that shall come upon you. Your riches are corrupted and your garments are moth eaten. Your gold and silver is cankered, and the rust of them shall be a witness against you, and shall eat your flesh as it were. Ye have indeed heaped treasure together for the last days." However, I am the last person to deny what Christianity, or rather Christian man, is believed to have done for the improvement of the world, and the belief itself may be accepted as a witness of the life and power of Christianity.

On the other hand, those who go along with the influences that tend to the improvement of the world, and which undoubtedly belong to Christianity, and possibly throw themselves into the movement, are liable to be called and considered, perhaps to consider themselves, Christians without Christ. For it is not with Christ our Lord as it is with other reformers and benefactors of mankind. There have been others before and after Him to whom we owe a debt of gratitude, though their names may be to many of you unknown. And it is not necessary that they should be known. You reap all the benefit of their labours, their genius, their industry, and their devotion, without knowing the persons to whom you are indebted. All persons share in the great inheritance of civilization, of material comfort, and of thought, that has been accumulated during the successive generations of their fathers.

Some have passed away, having simply enjoyed this inheritance as most do, others have enlarged and enriched it for those who should be born hereafter. Educated persons may properly think it a duty of gratitude to preserve the memory of those without whom they would never have been what they are; and antiquarian curiosity may hunt out details of the lives and histories of such persons that seem to be of small importance. Sometimes party or political feeling will take up a name as representative of a particular cause, and place the bearer of it on a pedestal made for the occasion. Sometimes local or professional feeling will fasten on some forgotten worthy, and make or find a convenient niche for a figure that will soon be forgotten again. But on the whole we are content to enjoy, and we do enjoy, whatever comes ready to our hands, without troubling ourselves about the names of those who have thus provided for us. But it is far different as regards Him, whom we look to as the object of our faith. By common consent Jesus Christ has wrought a greater change in the world than any who have attempted to reform or benefit it, before or since. And we cannot avoid falling under the influence of what He has done, and sharing in the benefits He has conferred, whether we will or no. In that

senso we must all of us be Christians, for the inheritance of Christianity has descended to us, and
we cannot repudiate it. But the true nature of
Christianity consists in this, that it connects us
directly, not with any system, or principles of conduct, or even doctrine, but with the person of its
founder, with Christ Himself. Men may be good
men, men of charity and virtue, given to good works,
leading lives of purity, a blessing to all around them,
and may reap the reward of all this, as I have no
doubt many heathens will do ;—but they are no true
Christians unless they attach themselves consciously
and really to the very person of Christ. The Apostles did not preach Christianity as a plan or system,
but Christ Jesus Himself. And herein they only
followed His own example. If it is true in one
sense that He did not bear witness of Himself, save by
the works that the Father had given Him to finish,
it is emphatically true that he did *preach* Himself,
and Himself alone. "Come unto Me," He said,
"all that labour and are heavy laden, and *I* will
give you rest. Take My yoke upon you, and learn
of Me ; for I am meek and lowly of heart, and ye
shall find rest for your souls." "I am the resurrection and the life ; he that believeth in Me, though he
were dead, yet shall he live. And whosoever liveth
and believeth in Me shall never die." The preaching of the Apostles is variously described, as, e.g., that
they preached the Word or the Gospel, but it all
amounts to the same thing. The substance of what
they really preached was the person of Christ. Christ

is Christianity, or rather Christianity is Christ, though this present age is not disposed to view it in that light. Christianity is not related to Christ, as any philosophy or system of doctrine to the person who invented it and then launched it upon the world, leaving it from thenceforth to rest upon its own merits, and implying no necessary relation, beyond that of history, between its author and those who may hereafter accept it. It is true that devotion to the memory of one who has done great things for us, must be a natural sentiment in the minds of those who have an intelligent apprehension of what has been done for them. But this, though part, is a small part of the tie which must unite the Christian to his Lord and Master. It belongs to Christianity, that day by day, and hour by hour, the Christian lives in conscious self-sustained communion with Him who is the ever-living and ever-present Author of his creed and life. Take away Christ and Christianity perishes, whatever moral or social good may incidentally remain. It is not a doctrine bequeathed by Him to a world, with which He has now ceased personally to have any dealings; it becomes extinct directly men begin to abstract it from the person of its Founder. He is felt by His people to be their ever-living Lord, present with them now and for ever, even to the end of the world. Christians form a distinct society, but how different from any other society, for there are other societies besides Christians. Men are bound together by various ties, and are formed into various groups. They are united both by natural and voluntary associations. Localities of birth and nationality both separate and combine men into different families; kindred pursuits are the bond of union between many. Whatever object it is possible for men to pursue—pleasure, profit, or instruction—may become the basis of an association. But all these combinations are of a temporary and superficial character; they exist mainly during our own pleasure, and may be broken off at an instant. They do not go to the heart and life of our being; we can sever ourselves from them as we will, and enter into new combinations, without really being affected by them as men. But Christians are one body, and cannot be otherwise; one, not by act and will of their own, or by power of flesh and blood, but by a marvellous union with Christ the Head, "from which all the body, by joints and bands, having nourishment ministered, and knit together, increaseth with the increase of God."

And so it is our office and our duty to preach Christ. Faithful are we in the discharge of our duty if we do in fact preach Him. If we go into topics which do not seem to be necessarily connected with Him; if we speak to you of repentance, of good works, of righteous living, of charity, of temperance, of the practical duties of life, our preaching is vain, if the end is not to bring you round to Him. We have just passed over a great day of the year, and one which I wish was more observed among you. We have been brought round to the last act and the final close of Christ's mission upon earth. There is nothing more to be done, nothing beyond to be commemorated. That which is to follow has no memory in our minds, we can only dwell upon it in anticipation. "Ought not Christ to have suffered these things, and to enter into His glory?" It was decreed in the mystery of God's eternal counsels that He should so suffer. All things that were written in the law of Moses, and in the Prophets, and in the Psalms concerning Him have been fulfilled, and He has therefore entered into His glory. And we, if we are His, may on this day ask with something like the manifest exultation of St. Paul, "Who shall lay anything to the charge of God's elect? It is God that justifieth. Who is he that condemneth? It is Christ that died, yea rather, that is risen again, who is even at the right hand of God, who also maketh intercession for us." He died as man, because for this purpose He came into the world. He rose again for our justification, as He had Himself foretold, and to that sign He appealed, by which men might know His real claim to their homage. His resurrection is but the prelude to His ascension into heaven; and there He sits to complete, in the presence of the Father, the work which it was given Him to do on earth. His intercession is omnipotent; He intercedes by His very presence, but not as any human intercessor. He is no suppliant before the majesty of God; He is a Priest, but a Priest allpowerful upon a throne. All power is given Him in heaven and in earth. All things are put in subjection under His feet. To be a Christian is not to be a philosopher, or a moralist, or a philanthropist, but to look to Him as our Lord and God, the object of our faith, the receiver of our prayer, the source of our life.

"Who shall separate us from the love of Him?" asks the Apostle in the sequel of my text. "I am persuaded that neither death, nor life, nor angels, nor principalities, nor powers, nor things present, nor things to come ; nor height, nor depth, nor any other creature, shall be able to separate us from the love of God which is in Christ Jesus our Lord."

SERMON XV.

What Rizpah, the daughter of Aiah, did.

———◆———

2 SAM. xxi. 14.

" And after that God was intreated for the land."

THE chapter which you have heard this morning as
the first lesson of the day contains an episode or
isolated event in the history of David, to which it is
difficult to assign any definite place in the history of
his reign. It commemorates one of the many judgments and deliverances of his people by which his
reign was marked, but we are unable to say why it
was introduced in this particular place. Neither
need we maintain that it is the most instructive passage of his history that could be offered for our consideration, but such as it is, I do not think the short
time generally allotted to a sermon will be wasted
by the attention which I propose to pay unto it. It
is a history of punishment long deferred, but in the
end certain to be inflicted, for a cruel and a grievous
sin, and that not on the author of the sin himself,
but on those who owed to him the gift of their existence; and it will be well worth our while to consider it, if it only serve to impress upon our minds
that the evil which we do does not always end with
ourselves, but tends to propagate itself, and involve
in the penalties due to us those who are personally

innocent of our sins. The Gibeonites were among
the ancient inhabitants of Canaan, and you may remember how it was that they were exempted from
the general sentence of extermination that was passed
upon that unhappy race. It seems that they saw
further into the future than the other nations of the
guilty land, and while the other peoples and their
kings gathered themselves to resist the invaders by
arms, a certain presentiment of their utter destruction,
warned them to seek safety by submission, accompanied by what we should consider a very pardonable
act of fraud. They sent an embassy to Joshua, with
old sacks upon their asses, old and patched-up wine
bottles, worn-out garments and shoes, and every mark
of a long and tedious travel. They represented that
they had come from a distance, where the report of
the prowess of the army of Israel had reached them,
and were anxious for terms of peace with the mighty
nation whose host at that time filled the camp at
Gilgal.

To Joshua they were as strangers, and he professed that he had never heard of them; but when
they offered voluntary submission and vassalage he
received them under his protection, and engaged to
them that they should live without molestation; and
the princes of the congregation entered into a solemn
covenant with them on these terms. They had not
been too quick in their movement, for only three
days after, Joshua learned the deceit that had been
practised upon him, and that the men whom he had
engaged to preserve were of the race which he was

commissioned to destroy. The people, when they
knew the truth, were clamorous for their destruction,
and it required all the firmness of Joshua and the
princes to resist the popular feeling, and maintain an
engagement which had been wrested from him by
deceit, but the terms of which nevertheless he felt
bound by the sanctity of an oath to observe. But
he had sworn only that their lives should be spared,
and they had no other claim upon him; they were
an humble and submissive people, their spirits were
utterly subdued, and they were well satisfied with
the condition allotted to them. They became a kind
of inferior caste, though with a kind of dignity
attached to their degradation. For "Joshua made
them that day hewers of wood and drawers of water
for the congregation, and for the altar of the Lord,
even unto this day in the place which the Lord shall
choose."

Now this was four hundred years and more before
the time of Saul, and one might have thought that
a people so usefully and humbly employed, with
a prescription of four hundred years' forbearance in
their favour, might have been safe from the fury, if
they could not escape the notice, of the capricious and
violent king. Yet for some cause or other they fell
under his wrath, and we may conjecture from the
language of Scripture that the result was a general
if not an universal massacre of the helpless and un-
offending tribe. One expression gives us a clue to
the king's motive: he did it in "his zeal to and for
the children of Israel and Judah." He acted for the

good of his people, and thought it was for their interest that the feeble remnants of these ancient
nations should no longer be permitted to exist among
them. And we can hardly help contrasting and connecting his cruelty toward this helpless tribe with
his disobedient mercy toward Agag and the Amalekites. By his wilful disobedience, then, he lost the
throne to his family for ever, and it is possible that
by his equally wilful severity here he might have
thought of repairing the loss, and atoning for his sin.
The great fault in the character of Saul was that he
would not submit himself to the direction of God,
and do the work for which he was appointed in the
way in which it was commanded to be done. He
could not resign himself to be a mere instrument,
but must act upon his own judgment, and take his
own course. Having been brought to a true sense of
his sin in his treatment of Amalek, it would belong
to the same temper of mind to offend in the other
direction by slaying those whom he was under a
solemn covenant to spare. Were they not of the
same blood as the nations that he was commanded to
destroy utterly? and were they to continue for ever
to enjoy the advantages of a fraud, and the protection of an oath that ought never to have been given
them? If he had spared Amalek, and thereby lost
his high position, might it not be accepted as a compensation, and be set down to his credit on the other
side, that he had massacred Gibeon? and would not
his zeal for Israel and Judah be a sufficient justification for the deed? We are speaking of times when

men were familiar with deeds of blood and slaughter, but the tendency of human nature, in its self-defence, to set one thing thus against another, and our will and choice against our positive duty, is the same in all times, under every possible difference of circumstance. Saul had yet to learn—and few of us are there who have not yet to learn—the lesson that "to obey is better than sacrifice, and to hearken than the fat of rams." His act of mistaken zeal, so far from being acceptable to God, became a sin and a curse, bringing evil to his people, and destruction to his family.

In the reign of his great successor a famine arose in Israel. For two years it was endured in silence, and no doubt attributed to natural causes. Perhaps there was nothing extraordinary in two years' drought or unfruitful harvests, but in the third year things began to look serious, and David enquired of the Lord. Then the truth became known that God was angry with His people, and that they were suffering the penalties of their sovereign's crime. When David knew the cause he at once proceeded to offer such satisfaction as the nature of the case allowed. As the Gibeonites were the injured parties, he placed himself in their hands to do whatever they required; "What shall I do for you, and wherewith shall I make atonement that ye may bless the inheritance of the Lord?" Their answer was in accordance with the ideas and temper of the times, and shews a nobleness of spirit and a sense of justice which four centuries of oppression had not destroyed.

They might have asked for some sordid compensation for themselves, for some relief from their burthens, or improvement in their social or political position; but their demands, if cruel and bloody, were at least unselfish; they asked for neither liberty, nor gold and silver, nor the death of any other Israelite. It was the house of Saul that had outraged them, and the vengeance shall be confined to the house of Saul. I think we may almost acquit them of any feeling of personal vengeance, they thought rather of justice, and what was due to God. They were placed in the position of judges, and they considered, according to their own ideas, what justice required. The law of God was before them, "He that sheddeth man's blood, by man shall his blood be shed," and it was open to their very eyes that God was " visiting the sins of the fathers upon the children;" and it was in accordance with the measure which God was dealing to His people that they demanded in exchange for their own sons the lives of seven of Saul's sons. The strong sense of justice in the mind of David, and his affection that must have been deeply wounded by the terrible demand, did not shrink from the sacrifice, and he delivered unto death two of Saul's own children by Rizpah, and five grandchildren, who are described as "the sons of Michal, the daughter of Saul, whom she brought up for Adriel, the son of Barzillai, the Meholathite."

There is some difficulty in the history here, for you may remember that David himself was married to Michal. But we learn from the same history that

Merab her sister, who was first offered to David, was married to Adriel, and it would seem probable, on the supposition of her death, that her children were adopted by Michal, and brought up by her for their father. If this were so, and it entirely agrees with the language of Scripture in this place, they must have been almost as children to David himself, but he could not bring himself to give up Mephibosheth, the son of Jonathan, for the oath's sake, and the love that had bound him to his father. But the number was made complete, the seven were given up, and hanged before the Lord, as an offering to Him, and not to human vengeance, in Gibeah of Saul. Saul's own city was the scene of the execution. Those possibly who had witnessed the crime were made witnesses to the punishment. They were hanged upon *the hill* before the Lord, that all men might see their doom, for a warning to those who had aided or been present at the oppression of the helpless. And here is narrated a very affecting incident, which gives a colour of tenderness and human feeling to what we might otherwise consider, and rightly should consider, if enacted in our own days, a picture of ruthless barbarity. It was the beginning of barley harvest, and from that time till the rain fell—we know not how long—the bodies of the slaughtered victims were kept hanging in their place of punishment. Not till the seasonable rain gave tokens of the Lord's reconciliation were they removed from their gibbets, and the people of Gibeah had the ghastly memorial before their eyes. It may be presumed that they averted their looks and turned their steps another way from the revolting spectacle of the putrifying corpses. But all that terrible time Rizpah, the daughter of Aiah, lay upon her bed of sackcloth upon the rock, and kept daily and nightly watch over the festering remains of her slaughtered sons. She was not entirely alone in her melancholy vigil, for the beasts of the field roamed round her by night, and the birds of prey wheeled round her during the day. Those who have been in countries that lie under the keener influence of the sun know very well what that implies. "Where the carcass is, there shall the eagles be gathered together." You see them, if any animal has died, or beast of burthen has fallen by the way, mustering at once from every quarter of heaven. You cannot tell where they come from, or what secret attraction is drawing them to their prey. It cannot be sight, for they seem to rise from far below the visible horizon. It can hardly be scent, for they come from the direction of every wind that blows. But an unerring instinct guides or impels them, and you see them in long lines traversing the breadth of sky, and all converging to the point where nature summons them to their loathsome feast. Such creatures, probably of the vulture rather than of the eagle kind, kept screaming and croaking round the unhappy Rizpah on her sackcloth bed. But she kept her enemies at bay, and maintained her guard, "from the beginning of harvest until water dropped upon them out of heaven. She suffered neither the birds of

the air to rest upon them by day, nor the beasts
of the field by night." And when the atonement
was complete, and the rain from heaven gave evidence that the wrath had passed away from Israel,
we are glad to find in David also a return to the
feelings and manners of humanity. He had given
up the children and descendants of Saul, because
he believed that the sacrifice was demanded by the
God of justice; but now that the sacrifice was completed and accepted, he treated their remains with
all the honour due to the corrupting relics of mor-
tality. They were accursed in their death, but
the curse had passed away, and they were reinstated
in honour by their burial. He gathered the bones
of the men that were hanged, and buried them with
the bones of Saul and his own beloved Jonathan,
in the sepulchre of Kish their father. He that
lamented the lamentation which we have read in
the beginning of this book, who spoke of Saul as
the beauty of Israel, slain in its high places, of
Saul and Jonathan as pleasant and lovely in their
lives, and undivided in their death, who called upon
all the daughters of Israel to mourn, and the dew to
cease from the mountains of Gilboa, for the disgrace
and death of their king could offer them no higher
honour. They lie together, the offender and those
who paid the penalty of his sin, their bones ming-
ling in the country of Benjamin, their common patriarch, in Zolah, their souls waiting the award which
God will judge to every man in that day according
to his work.

I hope I may not be thought to have wasted time
over a story the like of which can never be enacted
again. It is impossible that such a series of events
could take place in our own days and in this our
land. But the tragedy is instructive to us by its
very contrast. Few men now think of enquiring of
the Lord concerning any evil that comes to us, as
we say, in the course of nature. Drought and rain,
storm and tempest, are natural events, and men look
for the account of them in the laws that are ascertained to regulate the course of nature. And it is
perfectly right to search thus into the causes of
things—our reasoning powers were given us for
this very purpose—but if we are not to carry the
search backwards to infinity it would seem certain
that the chain of causes must begin somewhere,
and that that beginning must be found in a personal, omnipotent, over-ruling will. In earlier times
men looked for this will immediately behind the
event which moved their gratitude, or excited their
alarm; and it is possible that as God spoke then
in a more personal manner to His people, so His
personal action on the very material elements of
the world was more immediate and definite. Let
not us, who are in so many respects better informed,
turn the knowledge, which like every other good
gift comes down to us from the Father of Light,
against the truth of His over-ruling Providence.

But this is too large a subject to enter upon now.
I have thought the facts of the history well worthy
of a morning's attention, and I can only leave

them now to the reflections of those who are thoughtful among you.   But it will be well if it serve
to remind us that in this world the innocent often
suffer with and for the guilty; the guilty are often
saved from the consequences of their sin at the
cost of the innocent.   They may declaim against
the justice of the dispensation, but they cannot
deny the fact.   It is illustrated by the ordinary
experience of life, and it is sanctioned by the highest
possible example.

"Christ suffered once for all for sins, the just
for the unjust, to bring us unto God;" nay, "He
was made sin for us who knew no sin, that we might
be made the righteousness of God in Him."

SERMON XVI.

Our Cross.

—◆—

GAL. vi. 14.

*" The cross of our Lord Jesus Christ, by whom the world
is crucified unto Me, and I unto the world."*

WISELY does the Church bring before us year
after year the great facts of our Lord's life,
by which our salvation was worked out. And not
only are these facts brought annually to our remembrance by the words of the holy Evangelists, and many of them by holy days and commemorative festivals, but we are called upon to imitate
and reproduce them after a manner in our own lives.
The Christian life is indeed, and is intended to be,
an exhibition of the Divine life of our Lord upon
earth, cast as it were in the same mould, and pre-
senting the same essential features, as far as can be,
in a grosser material. We find this to be the case
from the date of its commencement. His earthly
course began with His birth into the world, so our
heavenward course begins with our second birth. As
in the assumption of our nature He was born of a pure
virgin, and thereby became "the Son of Man," so
did He give to as many as received Him power "to
become the sons of God, even to them that believe
on His name: which were born, not of blood, nor of

the will of the flesh, nor of the will of man, but of God." And as He thus, born among the children of men, grew and waxed strong in spirit filled with wisdom, so it is our prayer when thus received in the family of God, "that all things belonging to the Spirit may live and grow in us, and that we being regenerate may be daily renewed by the same Holy Spirit; which God gave Him not by measure; and of whose fulness we have all received, even grace for grace." The first step, therefore, of the Son of Man earthwards corresponds to our first step heavenwards, and so it is all through. As He in fact was made like unto us in all things, so it is our duty to be conformed to His image, and to be like Him in all things, even to the exclusion of sin; and He has given us the power to be so when He gave us the power to become the sons of God. There is even a communion, a fellowship of suffering, between us and Him. In some mysterious mode His sufferings are ours, and ours are His. He bore our sorrows and they became His own. We are not His, unless His sorrows, too, are ours. St. Paul speaks constantly of our being dead: "We are buried with Him by baptism unto death." "Ye are dead, and your life is hid with Christ in God." He argues upon this death as a fact that was beyond dispute, and that carried certain consequences with it, "If ye be dead with Christ, why, as though living in the world, are ye subject to ordinances?" Nay, we are dead by the very instrument of His death: "Our old man is crucified with Him." "They that are Christ's

have crucified the flesh with the affections thereof."
"The cross of Christ, whereby the world is crucified to
Me and I unto the world." We do not stop even here.
If we are buried with Him by baptism unto death,
in baptism, too, we are risen with Him. We have
passed through the grave and door of death not into
nothingness, but into a new and spiritual life derived
from Him who has life in Himself: "If ye *be* risen
with Christ seek those things that are above." Nay,
while we look hereafter for the glory that shall be
revealed, and the earnest expectation of the creature
waiteth for the manifestation of the sons of God, even
here we are in a manner glorified, and the Father of
our Lord Jesus Christ "hath blessed us with all spiritual blessings in heavenly places in Christ."

Now the meaning of all these and other passages,
though we may not be able to exhaust its fulness, is
at the very least this, that the Christian life runs, and
is intended to run, parallel in all its stages and
in all its circumstances to the life of our great example and Redeemer. And this is true not only of
our life, taken as a whole, but of each part of it, as
it is divided into years. The mysteries of redemption recur, and their recurrence brings with it both
the remembrance of old and the accession of new
grace to the Christian soul. If our spiritual birth
cannot be repeated, if once born again we cannot be
born again a second time, any more than a man can
enter his mother's womb and be born again when he
is old, there is no reason why there should not be
a sensible strengthening, a new spring of life on

T

each feast of the Nativity. It may be a date not
simply in our calendars, but to mark a sensible progress and a point gained in grace. Man, it is true,
grows imperceptibly, and nature's growth, too, is
mostly imperceptible. After a considerable interval
we find our stature greater than it was, we see the
result, but the process was too slow to note; and so
in nature. We see the blade, the ear, the full corn
in the ear, and then we put in the sickle, but no eye
can see, no measurement mark, the change that takes
place from hour to hour, or even from day to day.
So as to our spiritual growth; if we are really
making progress we can look back upon the past,
and compare ourselves as we are with what we were.
Happy are we if we see the bonds of sin loosened,
our old follies left behind; wonder at the temptations
by which we were once led astray, and the seduc-
tions to which we yielded; find our resolutions
stronger and better kept, our thoughts more on God,
and our minds set on things above; but we cannot
always trace each particular action of grace upon our
hearts, or every motion of the Holy Spirit by which
we were moved. We cannot, I say, always do this,
but it will be strange if no trace of hard conflicts
with Satan and of Divine aid, no victory over ourselves, no sense of special weakness and of strength
renewed, no instance of the sufficiency of God's grace
has any place in our recollections of the past. These
were the critical points of our lives, and there are
few men who cannot remember occasions when their
fate seemed almost to be trembling in the balance.

Yet it is possible to measure the years of our spiritual as we do of our natural life, and we may find ourselves growing better as we know that we are growing older. And holy seasons like that on which we are just entering give us an opportunity of taking a survey of the past, comparing our present with our former stature, and ascertaining whether this is the case or no. Are the things belonging to the world and the flesh growing weaker in us, and the things belonging to the spirit growing stronger? and what can we do towards crucifying the world and the flesh that claim dominion over us? This is a fit enquiry and a fit employment for the season of Lent. It is a fast of forty days, and in keeping it we are following the example of our Lord, who for our sake suffered being tempted, and is able to succour those who are tempted. There is indeed a difference between our temptations, and there is a mystery in His which we in vain attempt to solve. Every *man* is tempted when he is drawn away by his own lusts and enticed. Our own nature is our temptation, or if Satan tempts us directly it is through our nature. It is hard to see how his temptations could reach us if there were not in our nature lust, or pride, or some form of evil to which he could appeal. There must be some correspondence or affinity between the temptation that is outside and the evil tendency within. We could not be tempted by our bodily appetites if we were not susceptible of hunger and thirst; objects of desire would have no influence upon us if there were no feelings of sensuality to be irri-

T 2

tated by them; and the pomps and vanities of this world would have no attraction for us if there were no feelings of pride and ambition to be gratified by them. An old philosopher says that temptation assails those who have no understanding from every side. Every sense, and every feeling, and every power may be the avenue or vehicle of its approach, if it is not barred by the stern resolve of our higher powers; our necessary employments, our tastes, our business, our pleasures, all of them may be the sources or encouragements of temptation. In our blessed Lord there was no trace of evil, no tendency to sin; He took our nature on Him, but it was that pure, unspotted nature in which our first father was created, and which God pronounced good. The temptation, therefore, of Adam was external, we trace it not to himself, or his own appetites, but to the tempter. The serpent beguiled Eve and she did eat, and gave it to Adam, and thus they both fell. They were free from sin, and yet not beyond its power; they were in a state of probation, free to obey or disobey, free to choose life or death, not in that state in which the souls of the just made perfect live for ever beyond the possibility of misery. We can barely conceive how Adam was tempted and how he fell, but it is beyond our power to conceive how the force of temptation acted upon the pure soul of Him who was altogether holy, harmless, undefiled, and separate from sinners. But in all things it behoved Him to be made like unto His brethren, and Divine wisdom found a way for that which passeth human understanding. It is possible, though it may seem a contradiction to say, that though He could not sin, though His divine purity repelled the very thought of evil, that the temptation itself and the nearness of sin was a sorer trial—a trial that we cannot conceive—to His perfect innocence than it can possibly be to us who are conceived in iniquity, and whose imaginations are evil from our youth upward. But if for our sake He was tempted in a way that man cannot understand, He resisted and conquered; by the same arms that are put into our hands, and which are mighty now as then to pull down the strongholds of the enemy, by the spiritual armoury that is provided for us, and by the word of God which is the very sword of the Spirit, leaving us His example as an encouragement, that if we have the boldness to say to the tempter, " Get thee behind me, Satan," he will depart and leave us.

And now the Church calls upon us, in imitation of Him, to keep the fast of forty days, as a preparation for the great day of atonement that we annually keep. How shall we keep this holy time to our profit, devoted as it is to the work of repentance and the mortification of our sins? It would be mere affectation to pretend to be ignorant that the idea, and still more the practice, of fasting in the literal sense, as part of a religious discipline, is almost lost in this country. Yet it is strange that we who above all other Churches profess to reverence the Bible, and to understand it, and to draw each one of us our faith and practice from it, overlook or ex-

plain away the many plain passages in Scripture
which commend this practice to us, if they do not
impose it on us. And I would suggest to you to
consider when you meet with such passages whether
there is not a reality and meaning in them which has
hitherto escaped your notice? Is it to be supposed
that our Lord would have given directions about our
demeanour when we fast, as was read in the Gospel
of this day, if it was intended that we should never
fast at all? and were prayer and fasting united by
His word and by the practice of the Apostles simply
in order that we might sever them in ours? When
our Saviour said "This kind goeth not out save
by prayer and fasting," what could He mean, except
that some evil spirits might yield to the two together, who could resist prayer alone? And if there
are no set fasts resting on the authority of our Lord,
and if our own Church, though it has appointed fasts,
or rather received those that have ever been observed
in the Church, has prescribed no fixed mode of observing them, this is done not that the practice might
be neglected among us, but that each member might
look to his own edification, and the mortifying of
his own particular lusts.

The question, How shall we keep Lent to our
advantage? is therefore still a practical one, and
it concerns you all not to neglect it. Speaking to
the poor it would be a mockery to urge them to
abstain from the food so hardly earned by the labour
of their hands, and necessary to enable them to
sustain that labour. I would that your earnings

were more ample, and such as to justify me in calling
upon you to deny yourselves some little of what
might be called the luxuries and superfluities of life.
But I know that it would be an idle and a cruel
thing to tell the poor that they ought to live on
a harder or a scantier fare than is generally their
portion. Yet surely if there is any indulgence that
you feel to be unnecessary, or perhaps hurtful; that
brings no good upon your families, but rather ruin
into what might be a happy home; that draws you
on the Lord's day far from the House of God into
the haunts of sin, that unfits you for the duties of
your place, and degrades you in your own esteem,
and in the sight of other men, this is the time to
cast off the evil habit, and abjure the miserable
thraldom, and crucify the evil lust that is leading
you into perdition. And if we have any taste or
any pursuit that is drawing us away further and
further from God, any pleasure, however innocent
in itself, that is getting a dangerous hold upon
us, surely it is a wise institution of the Church
which fixes a time when our thoughts may be turned
backward on ourselves, and so directed upwards
unto Him who claims the service of our hearts. In
the Commination service of this morning you might
have heard the curses pronounced by God's authority
upon heinous sinners; but after the mention of
various crimes and sins, punished by human law,
or at least condemned by human law, we come to
a curse which seems to me far more dreadful than
those that have gone before, because we know not

how far it will reach, who will be affected by it,
or how near we may be to it ourselves: "Cursed
is every one that putteth his trust in man; and maketh man his defence, and in his heart goeth from
the Lord." For if we fall not under the curse pronounced against the unmerciful fornicators and adulterers, covetous persons, idolaters, slanderers, drunkards, extortioners, it is so far well; but it will avail
us nothing for our salvation if our hearts have departed from the Lord, if we are living without the
love of Him, or even without the fear, caring only
for the world without its grosser sins, and fixing
our affections upon earthly things. Here, then, is
an employment for Lent, or rather the end of our
employment, whatever form it takes, to tear away
our hearts from the world, and bind them closer
unto God. What is the world to a man who is
dying on the Cross? Behold it is fading away in
the night that is falling upon his eyes. Or what
is the world to him whose *life* is hid with Christ
in God? It is a dead world crucified; it hangs
lifeless and worthless on the cross, and has no attraction for him. Therefore St. Paul speaks of the
"Cross of Christ, by whom the world is crucified
to Me, and I unto the world."

Happy those who in heart and soul, by endurance and self-denial, by faith and prayer, make that
cross their portion here, as it will be their strength
and their salvation in the world to come.

SERMON XVII.

Calling and Election.

ST. MATT. xxii. 14.

" For many are called, but few are chosen."

THESE words are what may be called the moral of two parables, but I think it may be said that they do not give what seems to be the *natural* moral in either case. It is not at least the moral that strikes us at first sight, and we must look deeper than the surface to see how it is inherent in the substance of the parable. You must remember the impressive parable of the labourers called to work in the vineyard at the different hours of the day. How some went early in the morning, some at the third, the sixth, and ninth, some at the eleventh hour, after which there was no further call. You must remember how at the close of the day all were called together to receive their wages; the last called receiving their wages first, and the others in like order, till the first came in their turn. And how these then murmured that they received no more, dissatisfied, not because their pay was insufficient, but because the others' pay was equal to it. "These last have wrought but one hour, and Thou hast made them equal unto us, which have borne the burden and heat of the day." And you must remember, too,

the answer to these murmurers: "Friend, I do thee
no wrong; didst thou not agree with Me for a penny?
Take that thine is and go thy way. I will give to
this last as even unto thee. Is it not lawful for Me
to do what I will with Mine own? Is thine eye evil,
because I am good?" And the conclusion of all is,
"The last shall be first, and the first last; for many
be called, but few chosen." Now the parables of
our Lord have this divine peculiarity, that while
the simplest minds can hardly fail to catch at once
the practical meaning of them, there is a depth of
inner wisdom in them that the spirit of man seems
hardly able to fathom. They are at the same time
the easiest and yet the most refined method of teaching, equally suited to the elementary lessons of child-
hood, and the instruction of the perfect man of God.
What power of learning anything can that man or
child possess who does not feel that this parable
is an appeal made personally to himself, to leave
the idle haunt of the market-place, and go and do
the work that is waiting for him in the vineyard
of the Lord? and yet how difficult it is to see the
entire bearing of it upon the solemn and alarming
conclusion by which it is wound up. For previously
there has been no hint as to the relative numbers
of those who were called at the various hours, no
comparison of them as few or many. We are left
in ignorance again as to the number of the murmurers; whether all who commenced their labours
early in the morning or only some of them. The
parable speaks of them in general terms, but our

Saviour addresses one of them individually, perhaps the spokesman or ringleader of the rest: "Friend, I do thee no wrong;" but we only gather incidentally from the last words of the parable that he was the representative of the majority. And what I have said on this subject applies still more strongly to the parable with which we are now immediately concerned as the Gospel of the day. For here one person only is mentioned at all, one person only in the whole assembly found without a wedding garment, without a word to suggest that there was any other in the same state; and yet the warning meets us again that practically his was no exceptional case, but a type of many among which we ourselves may be found: "For many be called, but few chosen."

The words are alarming, and fill us with the dread of exclusion while we count ourselves within the pale of safety. Let us endeavour to determine how they are intended to affect ourselves. Now I think there may be many calls and many *choosings* before we come to the final and irreversible election. Speaking generally, any presentation of truth or duty to the mind and heart of man is a call to those whom it reaches to embrace that truth and take up and follow out that line of duty. But what we mean by a call in a true religious sense is the opportunity of hearing, and the consequent duty of receiving, the Gospel of Jesus Christ. There can be no doubt that all men to whom that Gospel is preached have in a general sense received a call. A call that does not necessarily reach the ears of all with the same clearness and distinctness of tone, nor lay all under the same guilt for rejecting it; God alone is judge of that, whose ears are closed by dulness, whose heart is shut against the truth by wilfulness; some cannot understand the things that belong to their peace, and are to be pitied; others will not, and are to be condemned; "but the sound that is gone out into all lands" is surely a call of some kind, in whatever land its vibrations have made themselves felt. And those who are called in this way are, so far as they obey the call, and in fact whether they obey or not, *elect,* chosen that is, out of the rest of the world, as the recipients of a blessing not shared by others, distinguished by God's favour, and entrusted with the deposit of His truth, whether they will hear or whether they will forbear. Thus St. Paul writes to the Romans generally as "called" to be *saints,* sanctified i.e. by the Holy Ghost, that had been given them. And we find this and similar titles constantly used by St. Paul in his epistles to the other Churches. The Corinthians, for instance, are spoken of as "sanctified in Christ Jesus," called to be saints. And writing to the Ephesians he speaks of himself, with other members of the body of Christ, as "chosen in Him before the foundation of the world; to be holy and without blame before Him in love. Having predestinated us unto the adoption of children by Jesus Christ to Himself, according to the good pleasure of His will." It is clear, therefore, that a call is to those whom it reaches an election, or selection, to some particular favour which is not extended to the world at large. A call in fact includes an election, just as the greater and more general includes the lesser and more special. All who are elected are called, but all who are called are not elected. And if it is asked wherein is the ground and basis of the distinction, it seems to me to lie in this. That whereas the call lies entirely outside our own act and concurrence, we cannot be elect without the consent and agreement of our own wills. It is said in our Articles that we *through grace* obey the calling, and he must know little of his own heart who imagines that he can raise himself from earth to heaven without the aid of Divine Grace at each successive step. Nor will we perplex ourselves here with endeavouring to determine the action of Divine Grace upon the will of man. It is enough to know, and a practical answer to all questions to feel, within ourselves that God is working with us both to will and to do according to His pleasure, and they that obey the call will be conscious to themselves that it is by grace that they obey it. Anyhow they obey it, and by that act they rise from the lower rank of the "called" to the higher order of the elect. But this is, after all, the first degree of election, and they cannot rest on the first stage of their ascent. All Christian life is indeed but a series of calls, and there is a sifting and election on each successive call. We are called out of darkness into light, out of ignorance into knowledge, from worldly into spiritual duties and relations, from a low and sensual life into a high and heavenly one, from the shadows and vanities of this world into the truth and realities of a better. Wherever we are there is an onward call to us to be something better than we are, more pure, more holy, more self-denying, more like Him that has called us out of darkness into His marvellous light, and wills that where He is, there we should be also.

But this election to the higher implies of necessity the rejection of those who are content with the lower. It is a process continually going on, God is perpetually inviting us to higher privileges and a fuller portion of His love. His Holy Spirit is ever striving with us to raise our thoughts and purify our hearts, and conform our will entirely to His Will. It is ours to choose, and thereby we shew that we are chosen. It is ours to reject, and thereby we shew that we are rejected by Him. The work of refinement, clearing off the grosser elements and separating the higher ones, is constantly in progress. "Many are called but few are chosen." These words are intended not to depress or discourage us, but to make us what we must needs be here, diligent and careful, working out our own salvation in fear and trembling, for the very reason that it is God who worketh with us and in us. What was the case of this man of whom we have just been hearing in the Gospel? He was called, and he obeyed the call. He was not among those who made light of the

message, or pleaded their pleasure or their business,
or who entreated spitefully and slew the messengers
who came to call them. He was found at the marriage supper of the King, and surely it was no uncertain sign of election, and no small degree of favour
to be admitted to the royal feast. Good and bad
were there, for the wedding was prepared for both.
Good men such as Cornelius, whose prayers and alms
had already gone up as a memorial to God. Gentiles,
who having not the law, yet shewed the work of it
written in their hearts, and were a law unto themselves ; others far gone in moral depravity, sinners
of the worst class, which St. Paul enumerates, adding
of the Corinthians "and such were some of you."
This man was amongst them, but he was without the
wedding garment. It is idle to enquire, how could
it have been otherwise ? How, gathered in hastily,
unsummoned, from the highways, could he have provided himself with one ? The difficulty belongs simply to the earthly details of the parable, and does
not attach to the spiritual truth. It would not have
been inconsistent with the custom of a royal banquet,
prepared with the magnificence due to the marriage
of a king's son, that all the guests were provided
with garments for the occasion. There are traces of
such a custom existing in the East in former times.
At all events the gift of costly garments on a great
occasion was considered to be a gift worthy of
a king, and the rejection of the gift could not be
taken otherwise than as a marked affront. Had this
man no opportunity of dressing himself as the other

guests, it is clear that a great wrong was done unto him. But whatever others may say or think on his behalf he himself had nothing to say, he was speechless, his mouth stopped, actually gagged, with no plea of inability, no defence for his contemptuous behaviour; he was self-condemned, and judgment immediately was pronounced against him: "Bind him hand and foot and take him away, and cast him into outer darkness. There shall be weeping and gnashing of teeth."

There is something very striking in the circumstance that no one seems to have observed the state of this man till " the King Himself came in to see the guests." None had seen him before, or at least ventured to remove him. It was the servants' work to gather in the guests, and they had discharged it faithfully, but, as in the parable of the wheat and tares, there could be no separation of the worthy and unworthy till He whose ministers they were appeared. And most fit it was that this office should be reserved for Him. For the outer garment which all may see and judge is but the figure; the real garment for the marriage-feast is the clothing of the inner man, which is seen and known not of man, but of God.

It is idle to be over curious in enquiring what that grace was in which he was wanting, when we know what God requires us to be. God requires us to believe in Him, to obey Him, and to love Him. Shall we say that his faith was evident from his being there at all, when like others he might have refused to come, and therefore say that he had faith, but was lacking in charity? There is no advantage in thus setting up one grace against another, as though it were possible for them to be independent of each other. If his faith went no further than to bring him to the feast, because he believed there would be a feast, without any regard to his own fitness to appear there, it was that faith which is pronounced *dead*, not that which worketh by, or rather is made active and energetic by, love; that faith which is less than charity, not because charity is without it or distinct from it, but because charity is its flower and crown. He had not, according to the language of St. Paul, *put on Christ*, clothed himself with His righteousness, faith being the power that is put on, righteousness the robe that is worn, a robe not of our weaving, not made with hands, and yet akin to us, fitting and adorning our natures, though far above them, freely offered to all, and received by those who will receive it; the righteousness which is in Christ, who is indeed the "Lord our Righteousness."

When our blessed Lord was asked, "Are there few that be saved?" as a speculative question, He did not care to give a direct answer to it, but evaded it, as we say, by a solemn and practical warning: "Strive to enter in at the strait gate," but He added, "For many, I say unto you, will seek to enter in, and shall not be able." There were then, and there are now, many obstacles between men and the kingdom of Heaven. It was, as our Saviour says, suffering violence, and the strong men were taking it by force. There was the barrier of Jewish prejudices to be broken, and the conceit of Jewish pride to be humiliated, the folly of ages, inveterate in the human mind, and miscalled wisdom, to be convinced, human nature itself to be overcome, persecution promised and sure to ensue, to be encountered and endured. Nothing but a strong purpose and a resolute will, divinely formed and strengthened, could be expected to embrace a religion with such requirements and such prospects. A dilatory wish and a feeble sentiment under such circumstances would lead to nothing. Most of these difficulties have disappeared, the material obstacles that could keep men out of the kingdom of Heaven are less than nothing. The difficulties and obstacles that remain are simply those that arise from the state of our own hearts. It is still a strife and a struggle to enter in, and maintain our place there when we have entered. It is according to that state that we shall be judged by the Discerner of all hearts when He shall come in to see the guests. Let the knowledge that if there be but one in the furnished room unworthy to sit there the eye of the King will be on him in an instant, and detect and condemn his unworthiness, make us give heed. But let us not, on the strength of our Saviour's words of caution, narrow the breadth of God's kingdom, either to the exclusion of others or our own despair. Let us rather think of His large and liberal words of invitation, of God's unbounded mercy, of the Saviour's own assurance, " that whoso-

ever cometh unto Him, He will in no wise cast out."
Be sure there is a place for us among those that
shall come from the east and from the west, and
from the north and from the south, and sit down
in the kingdom; among that great multitude which
no man can number, of all nations, and kindreds,
and people, and tongues, who, after the sealed of
Israel, will stand before the throne and the Lamb,
clothed with white robes and palms in their hands,
crying with a loud voice, "Salvation to our God and
unto the Lamb."

SERMON XVIII.

Conbersion.

————◆————

ROM. vi. 21.

" What fruit had ye then in those things whereof
ye are now ashamed ?"

ST. PAUL makes an appeal here to the experience
of those to whom he is writing. He had not
drawn from his imagination such attractive and
repulsive pictures of two different modes of life
as might come from the pen of a philosopher, or
moralist, or poet, and then asked them which they
preferred, as to its pleasures, or troubles, or results,
but he writes to them as men who in their own
persons had already, so to speak, passed through
one state of existence, and had now entered upon
another. Pictures of happiness or misery as resulting from this or that line of conduct may have
their influence on our hearts, and we may be drawn
onward in our heavenly course by the idea of " things
which the eye hath never seen, nor the ear heard,
nor hath it entered into the heart of man to conceive;" but there is no teacher like experience,
and he that has passed through that ordeal can give
an answer to the question that is asked him, as to
what the real state of things is which no amount of
mere thought or imagination can supply. St. Paul,

therefore, puts this plain question to the experience of the Romans, "What fruit had ye then in those things whereof ye are now ashamed?" They had lived one life, and they were now living another, and they could compare the two together. If we want to know what life they had lived, it is described in few but very significant words: "They had been servants, or rather slaves, of sin,— their affections had been given up to sin,—and righteousness had no share in them." And as in all natural motion there must be a point *from* which, and a point *to* which, and a space *through* which the motion takes place, so is it with regard to moral and spiritual change. *Servants of sin,* that was their fixed and normal state, their starting-point, so to speak. "But they had obeyed from the heart that form of doctrine that was delivered to them." Here was the change or motion of the inner man, and it is worth noticing how it is described. We should be disposed to connect a form of doctrine, i.e. a system of truth, rather with the understanding than with the heart, and should speak of a man rather as assenting to it, and believing in it, than as obeying it. Thus if I were able to teach an ignorant person the laws of astronomy, or any other laws of the material universe, and bring them home to his comprehension, I should say that he took them in—or made himself master of them—rather than that he obeyed them. The natural world goes on the same, whether we know its laws or are ignorant of them; and the man of science

deals with tangible things in very much the same
way as the practical man who has no pretensions
to science. People formerly thought, and very ignorant persons may even now think, that the sun moves
daily round the earth, and each glorious morning
recalls to us the idea of " this ruler of the day coming forth as a bridegroom out of his chamber, and
rejoicing as a giant to run his course." But if
we know how to distinguish between appearances
and reality, the daily routine of our lives does not
seem to be in any way affected by the knowledge.
"Man goeth forth to his work and to his labour
until the evening," without thinking how it is that
day succeeds to night, and night to day. I am far
from saying that science is of no use to life, but that
men live a great part of their lives without conscious
obedience to it. The laws of the material world
do not necessarily become laws of their conduct.
And this is the great difference between natural
and religious truth. Religious truth, the form of
sound doctrine, once received and believed, becomes
at once a power within ourselves, a new form of
conscience which will be respected and obeyed. It
may be expressed in words, and those words may be
learned like any other lesson, the intellect may even
be impressed and convinced of them, and yet, by the
constitution of human nature, they may never reach
the heart. This is in fact degrading religious truth
to the level of natural truth; it is what may be
called " having the form of godliness without its
power." But St. Paul thanked God for the converts

at Rome, not that they had embraced the "form of doctrine" which he had delivered to them, in this sense, but "that they had obeyed it from the heart." It had become a rule of their conduct, in thought, word, and deed, not reducing it to order and system according to the word of command, and a moral drill, but determining it from within, by its own essential force and constraining motives, bringing every thought into captivity to the law of Christ, and yet emancipating them into the glorious liberty of the Sons of God. This was the change or space through which they had passed, and here is the point at which they had now arrived — *Servants of God.* Let me repeat again the whole process. They had been slaves of sin; they had obeyed from the heart the form of doctrine delivered to them; they were now slaves of God.

Now observe that St. Paul is speaking here simply of facts—of the actual circumstances, that is, of the persons to whom he is writing—respecting which he appeals to their own experience whether the account he gives of them is not true. These Romans were such, and he thanks God for it; but he by no means tells us that all persons ought to live such lives as to oblige them to confess "that they had ever been servants of sin;" for this would be in effect to deny that God had ever given unto those whom He has adopted into His family, and taken into the arms of His mercy, such a measure of grace as to preserve them from sin; it would be in effect to declare that the prayer which we offer over every new-born child

that is brought to the laver of regeneration—"that
he may lead the rest of his life according to that beginning "—is a mere profane mockery of idle words,
breathed in no spirit of faith, and therefore powerless
to obtain any spiritual blessing; it would be to declare that it is by God's appointment, and not by our
despite of His long-suffering and goodness, by the
failure of His gifts, and not by our neglect and wasting of them, that "men continue in sin, in order that
grace may abound." There is the same cause as
ever to give thanks for the restoration of the lost,
and the recovery of the sinner; but who in the
very heart of God's Church, and with His Word and
Ordinances, will contend that it is necessary that all
men should have been *sinners*—I mean in the sense
of "servants of sin?" for no one will suppose that those
whom St. Paul now calls "servants of God" were
absolutely free from all stain of sin. The ways of God
are mysterious, and past finding out. The Spirit
moveth where He listeth, and we know not the laws
of His motion, and nothing is more presumptuous than
either to say or deny how He may or may not act
upon the heart of man. Therefore while we may
yield hearty thanks to Almighty God that it hath
pleased Him to regenerate with His Holy Spirit each
infant that is brought unto Him in Baptism—to receive him as His own child by adoption, and to in-
corporate him into His holy Church—there is nothing
to hinder us from believing—and when we look to the
irreligious lives of many who are sealed with the
name of Christ we may find comfort in believing—that

He may act also with power and efficacy, and in a more sensible way, upon those who have hitherto not known Him, at a later hour of their day, or when the shades of evening are closing thick around them. To use the familiar word, what I deny is not the reality of *conversion* in particular cases, but its necessity in all. I deny its necessity, because I deny the necessity of all persons ever having been in any part of their lives " the slaves of sin." I believe God's grace to be sufficient for men in any part of their lives, and growth in grace, just as much as growth in stature, to be the proper law of their lives. St. Paul gives a fearful list of persons who shall not inherit the kingdom of God, among whom thieves, covetous, drunkards, are not the most abominable. Such were some of the Corinthians, but what higher language can be used than that in which he now speaks of these same persons: " Ye are washed, ye are sanctified, ye are justified in the name of the Lord Jesus and by the Spirit of our God?" but is it necessary that any baptized Christian should ever have classed himself with such persons? There are such persons now, but when he that steals learns to steal no more, when the man of profligate and abandoned life manifestly forsakes his sins, and alters his ways, when the obdurate heart is broken down, and yields to influences of which it was never sensible before, when there is a manifest improvement, and a struggle upwards—though it be a painful one and with many falls—then I see a good work beginning, and there is ground to hope that He who has begun that good work will carry it on unto perfection. Such a man is passing, if he has not passed already, from death unto life; old things are passing away, and all things are becoming new. He is really crucifying *the old man*, though late, and putting on the *new*. We will not differ about words; let it be called, if you please, conversion, or even a new birth; for it is in effect a new birth unto righteousness, and we may say truly of such a person, " He was dead, and is alive, he was lost, and is found."

But it may be said, though all men need not have been thieves and drunkards and extortioners, and therefore need not the change that such persons are capable of, yet that there is even among persons of irreproachable lives a worldliness and a deadness to spiritual things, out of which we must pass before we can call ourselves the true children of God, and that some persons are sensible of this change coming over them at some particular period or even moment of their lives—it has come upon some we know in their beds, and a heavenly influence has filled the darkness and silence of the night, and that this is that *conversion* of which our Saviour speaks as necessary to those who would enter into the kingdom of Heaven; —let them give thanks to Him who has so mysteriously called them, and be careful to date a really new life from the impression which their memory records. And if by insisting on the necessity of some such change as this they merely mean to say that men in general give little evidence of the life of God within them, and that a great and sensible

change is needed before they can call themselves
true children of God, so far, unhappily, we are compelled to agree; but let them not deny the possibility in other cases of a growth of grace from the
first stirring of Christian life, more closely resem-
bling that growth of natural stature by which the
helpless infant is advanced to the full measure of
a man. In the years of our growth we cannot
measure ourselves, or estimate the increase of our
strength from day to day; the change is too gradual
to be perceived: we cannot say, this day I ceased
to be an infant and began to be a child, on such
another day I counted myself to be a man; but after
intervals we feel that we are taller, stronger than
before; and though our growth has been continuous,
circumstances may have impressed it upon us at particular times, so that we can distinguish its stages.
Just so in looking back upon our spiritual life we
may remember critical periods: times of special
experience, moments of refreshment by God's Holy
Spirit, hours of deep and solemn thought, days of
protracted struggling, how we strove successfully
with some besetting sin which has left us for ever,
how we formed some good resolution which we have
consistently kept. These are the red-letter days
of our calendar; on each of these we made a sensible
advance towards heaven, but it does not follow that
our whole course has not been upwards, though we
only felt its weariness; and if all this and much
more should be compressed into one moment, so that
we seemed rather to be borne on the wings of a

dove than to be creeping on the feeble limbs of
a man, and to be caught up into the third heaven,
yet God may be drawing others to Himself by another, and perhaps a safer way, not of transports
and ecstasies, but of humble faith, and patient labour,
and ordinary means of grace, and consistent continu-
ance, through His aid, in well-doing. It is possible,
too, that a man's sins, or some sin, may drop off him
all at once, like a discarded garment, while they
may cling closely to others, so that they cry in
agony, "Who shall deliver me from the body
of this death?" But let those who feel that it is so
with them, and that they can now speak of the
service of sin as a thing that is passed, remember
how St. Paul writes to them whom he yet calls
"servants of God:" "They are free from sin," yet
they are warned not "to let sin reign in their
mortal bodies," which implies that they are still
under its influence. They are to yield their members servants to righteousness as they once did
unto iniquity, which implies that they may still
"by reason of the infirmity of their flesh," even
if their will be good, do otherwise, and if there is
no condemnation for them which are in Christ Jesus,
it is with this provision, "who *walk* not after the
flesh, but after the Spirit." They who feel that
the bonds of sin are really loosening from them,
and the burden that hinders them from running
their course freely is becoming daily lighter, have
every encouragement to persevere; but when men
profess to have undergone a thorough change, and

to have passed at once from the condition of "servants of sin" to that of "servants of God," it is time to warn them against self-deceit, and to bid them take heed lest they fall. The Apostle who used the strongest language on the perfection of Christian obedience,—who tells us not only that he "that abideth in God sinneth not, that whosoever sinneth hath not seen Him, neither known Him;" nay more, that "whosoever is born of God doth not commit sin; for His seed remaineth in him: and he cannot sin, because he is born of God. He keepeth himself, and that wicked one toucheth him not,"—writes also in terms that are familiar to all: "If we say that we have no sin, we deceive ourselves, and the truth is not in us. But if we confess our sins, He is faithful and just to forgive us our sins, and to cleanse us from all unrighteousness." And while he tells his little children that he writes to them "that they sin not," he almost assumes that they will, for he adds, "And if any man sin, we have an Advocate with the Father, Jesus Christ the righteous, and He is the propitiation for our sins: and not for ours only, but also for the sins of the whole world." So that while it is a disgrace and a reproach to us to have to confess that we were ever "servants of sin," we may not boast ourselves to be free from sin, even in professing ourselves "servants of God." And I fear there are few of us to whom the question of St. Paul may not be put with more or less of fitness—"What fruit had ye then in those things whereof ye are now ashamed?"

Which of us can unroll the record of his past life
and find nothing there that is occasion of shame?
A great deal might be said of this feeling of shame.
It is a sense of dishonour, of vileness, of degradation
here.   It is a painful trouble and disturbance of
mind when we are grieved and cast down by the
remembrance of sin against God.   It may be the beginning of repentance when we resolve that we will
no more dishonour and defile ourselves, and rise
again to the dignity of our nature, and the standard
of our call.   And so far it is a good affection, though
it may bring an agony with it; but if it is not that,
then in bad men it becomes part of the tortures of
hell.   There are those who are ashamed of "the Son
of Man and of His words here, and of whom He shall
be ashamed when He cometh in the glory of His
Father with the holy angels."   And then, perhaps, just
so much of a reprobate conscience will be left us as
to make us feel the ignominy of being objects of contempt, not to men only, but to those higher beings,
who might have ministered to us as heirs of salvation, or rejoiced over us as repentant sinners.   Let
the shame which surrounds the memory of past mis-
deed quicken us to a resolution to forsake all things
that put us to shame, and bring shame on us.   "For
the end of these things is death," death of the body,
even when renounced and repented of, otherwise
death, i.e. infinite misery of body and soul together.
"The wages of sin is death."   What a lamentable
consideration.   By the labour of a whole life to
have brought upon ourselves not only reproach and

shame, but to have ensured remorse and torment without interval or limit. And that, too, not from adverse circumstances out of our control, which have confounded our plans, and disappointed our hopes, but from sheer wilfulness, because we would not receive a blessing prepared for us, because life and death were set before us, and we chose death; for if "the wages of sin is death, the gift of God is eternal life, through Jesus Christ our Lord."

SERMON XIX.

Power maketh Man.—American Presidents.

———◆———

1 SAM. x. 6.

" And the Spirit of the Lord will come upon thee, and thou shalt prophesy with them, and shall be turned into another man."

I KNOW no character in Scripture, except Saul the son of Kish, of whom these words, or anything like them, are used; and virtually they are explained by what is said a few verses lower—that " God gave him another heart." They may remind some of us, perhaps, of the change which was promised by our Lord to the Apostles, and realized on the day of Pentecost, " Ye shall receive power after that the Holy Ghost is come upon you." But, whereas the Apostles became what we call in popular language "different men "—in respect of their ideas, knowledge, and action—we cannot help feeling that Saul was very much the same man before and after the " Spirit of God came upon him, and he prophesied among the prophets," and this notwithstanding the change which was so great as to be almost inconceivable among those who knew him, so that it became a kind of proverb, which was used familiarly, " Is Saul also among the prophets?" By saying that Saul continued to be very much the same man, I do not of course mean to deny that the Spirit wrought a great change in him, I mean that his moral qualities and character do not seem to have been materially altered. These qualities, as we infer from his history in Scripture, were partly good and partly bad. We have no reason to suppose that the first were wanting before the Spirit of God came upon him, and no one would think of attributing the second to that source. Every man is a mystery even to himself, he has an individuality which belongs to no one else, he is not an unit of a large number, but stands absolutely alone. Hereafter he will not be counted in but judged. The character of Saul has an individuality of its own, mysterious beyond that of all other persons. We cannot say whether a jury of the present day would have pronounced him mad or sane if he had committed the crime which he persistently attempted of the murder of David. The strange influence of music upon his wilful and passionate nature belongs to those secret things which it is impossible to account for even in oneself, yet I think we can all feel that there is something real in this influence, and that it is not altogether strange to our experience. "It came to pass, when the evil spirit from God was upon Saul, that David took an harp and played with his hand: so Saul was refreshed, and was well, and the evil spirit departed from him."

If we look to the good features of Saul as a natural man I think we shall find these to be among them; he was generous and magnanimous, he had energy and decision in action. When his elevation to the

x

kingdom was announced to him he was not unsettled, but kept the matter secret. When the divine lot fell upon him he hid himself, as though he shrank from the high position. When the children of Belial asked, "How shall this man save us?" and "despised him," he shewed no resentment, and simply held his peace. After his victory over the Ammonites the popular cry arose, "Who is he that said, Shall Saul reign over us? bring the men, that we may put them to death;" but he set himself against the cry, "There shall not a man be put to death this day: for to-day the Lord hath wrought salvation in Israel." We seem here to find noble traits of natural character; on the other hand they are closely associated with other qualities of reserve, wilfulness, pride, and self-will, which are at the same time symptoms of mental aberration, and, in another point of view, not inconsistent with magnanimity. The persons who were raised to high places in the commonwealth of Israel were, above all other persons in the world, expected to be passive agents of the Divine will, they were to do exactly what they were told without discretion. This is a hard place to occupy, requiring an entire sacrifice of one's own will, and Saul would not consent to it. He shewed this on two occasions, and both occasions terminated in his deliberate fall. When sent to inflict judgment on the Amalekites, he spared those whom he was ordered to slay; he preferred his own ways to those which God had determined; his obedience was not refused, but it was limited and discretionary, and it called forth words which are

a warning to all men to the end of time : " Hath the
Lord as great delight in burnt offerings and sacrifices,
as in obeying the voice of the Lord ? Behold, to obey
is better than sacrifice, and to hearken than the fat
of rams. For rebellion is as the sin of witchcraft,
and stubbornness is as iniquity and idolatry."

It is, I say, difficult to define what is exactly meant
by "Saul being turned into another man."   But it is
well pointed out that the word which we translate
"heart" in x. 9 points rather to the intellect and
courage than to the affections and conscience. He
was endowed at once by the special gift of God with
those gifts of courage and intellect which fitted him
to be a king and ruler of the people whose destinies
were committed to him. That people wanted a king
to lead them into battle, and his gigantic stature and
majesty was endowed with a capacity for ruling a
nation; the humble searcher after his father's asses
found himself suddenly an anointed king, and no less
suddenly made fit for it. Surely if such dignity was
thrust upon us we must be other men if it did not
crush us; and let us not here diminish the force of
the words of Scripture. Undoubtedly they imply
that a special divine gift and illumination was conferred upon him, by which he became capable of being what the old Greek poet calls in his grand and
simple language a "king of men." And here we are
not to confound the special action of the Spirit of
God with that development of unknown and unsus-
pected powers, which is sometimes found in persons
who are elevated to a high station. An eminent

x 2

person told me once that he thought any one had wit
enough for any office if he had wit enough to get it.
It seemed a quaint way of stating what has really a
great deal of truth in it. A man is not without
strong reason to decline any office of which other
persons think him worthy, because he feels himself
unequal to it. If he has sought a position by dis-
honest means that is of course a different thing. But
if he has won it by means not to be ashamed of, or
not sought it at all, then it seems to come to him by
way of providence, and to be his duty to accept it;
and it seems to me matter of experience that in many
such cases men's powers are enlarged, and they become different men from what they were supposed to
be. I would mention in illustration of this the case
of the Presidents of the great American Republic, the
last of whom is lying between life and death from the
bullet of an assassin, from which I fear neither absolute power nor popular election can secure the ruler
of a country who has enemies. And I am sure that
if it please God to preserve that valuable life, there
will go forth to the great daughter from the great
parent country, not perhaps a formal message of con-
gratulation, which must needs be cold and dry, but
a general effusion of sympathy and joy which will go
far to draw still closer the ties that bind them in a
happy union of interest and affection. The Greeks
had a peculiar word to express the feeling between
parents and children, which the Latins called " piety,"
and it was extended to the feeling between parent
states and their offshoots, and I trust this feeling

exists between us though we have lost the word.
But it is the word used by St. Paul, where it is mentioned as one of the darkest characters of heathen
immorality, that they were "without natural affection." But as regards these American Presidents, I
think the elevation of some of them to their high
position is quite as extraordinary as that of Saul,
who went out to look for his father's asses and found
the destiny of a king secured to him before he came
back. The election of a President in America is the
result of four years' intrigue, combination, wire pulling, and caucus holding. It is of course a party
affair, and people are able beforehand to form an
opinion as to which is the strongest party. But the
strongest party do not always choose their best man.
They are rather afraid of pre-eminent ability; they
want a man whom they can use and control, and
are rather afraid of one who is likely to rule them;
a country does not seem likely to prosper which is
afraid of its best citizens. But I think we may say
that in America, if there is any person pre-eminent
in virtue, principle, and power he would not be likely
to be President[a].

[a] Upon this point an American writer (Mr. George Ticknor
Curtis), in discussing the mode of electing American Presidents,
makes the following remarks:—"A certain number of throws
from two dice-boxes will inevitably give a major number of points
to one or the other of the persons playing: but a bystander might
as well undertake to predict what is to come out of a given number
of casts of dice as to pronounce beforehand who will receive the
nomination of a party convention for the great office of President
of the United States. Eminent talent, long public service, high
character, statesmanlike accomplishments, which would seem to be

In England we can forecast with some confidence
of the future who is likely to be Lord Chancellor or
Prime Minister some years hence, but who in the world
can mention the name of the next President of the
United States, or half-a-dozen names out of which he
will be chosen? Nevertheless, it must be allowed
that the Presidents of the United States are a series
of most remarkable men, and that no one of them,
not even of those who seem to have been placed in
their high position by chance rather than by choice,
has been found unequal to its duties. It was said
by a great historian of Rome that one of its emperors, in the judgment of all, would have been deemed
worthy of empire if he had not been emperor. But
we may say of some of these emperors (for the position
is imperial) that they would have been deemed unfit
for it if they had never occupied it. The inference
I draw from this is, not that anybody will do for
the President of the United States, but that these
men had ruling and imperial powers in them, which
were drawn out and developed by and in the high
office to which they were providentially called.
They were in fact "turned into other men," but

sure elements of calculation, are the least potent of all the factors
which bring about the result; and of those factors which really
produce the result there is no calculation possible, they are so
diverse, contradictory, and inappreciable. The only tangible one
of all those factors is money, or its equivalent in the shape of promises of future preferment. But somehow a nomination is made.
Thereupon, instantly, all over the land, throughout all the adhe-
rents of the party, if white has not become black, and black white,
it has become inexpedient to speak of the difference."—*Century
Magazine*, November, 1884.

I should be sorry you should suppose that this is
all that is meant by what is said in such a striking
way of Saul. "Power will shew the man" is a very
old saying, i.e. it will shew what a man really is
when he has liberty to display himself, and it has
shewn it in the case of these men; it has not brought
them any gifts of character which they had not before; it has simply brought out into activity those
which were already in them. And you must not
suppose this is the interpretation which I put on the
words of Scripture as regards Saul. I believe, on
the contrary, that he had real gifts, and was "turned
into another man." But what I infer from this history is that there are real gifts of power in the
dispensation of the Spirit which cannot be called
graces, because they do not touch the heart. In
the case of Samson there was a gift of supernatural
strength, and if this was combined with the grace
of faith by which he waxed valiant in fight, and
turned to flight the armies of the aliens, I do not think
that we can mention any other grace that is united
with it. In the New Testament, of course, we expect to find more about the gifts of the Spirit which
were to be poured out upon all flesh than in the Old,
and we are not disappointed. We have in fact a spe-
cification and catalogue of the powers and gifts of
the Spirit in more places than one, e.g. "To one is
given by the Spirit the word of wisdom, to another
the word of knowledge by the same Spirit, to another
faith by the same Spirit, to another the gifts of healing by the same Spirit. To another the working

of miracles, to another prophecy, to another discern-
ing of Spirits, to another divers kinds of tongues,
to another the interpretation of tongues," and we have
no reason to suppose that the list is thus completed.
But I will just point out to you that no one of these,
except faith, touches the spirit of the inner man.
They are really gifts, not graces, "given to every
man to profit withal by the self-same Spirit divid-
ing to every man severally as He will," but clearly
to profit not the man himself but the Church. Some
of them might even be occasions of confusion, of
unseemly rivalry, of evil rather than good to the
Church, and of falling to the man himself. Would
a man be a better man, and nearer to salvation,
because he had the gift of healing? or would the
gift of prophecy imply any sanctification of the heart?
We know that it did not in old time. It left its
possessor sordid and profane as he was before, and
he sold his soul for the wages of iniquity, as Judas
did. St. Peter would not allow a miracle which
he wrought, to be attributed to any holiness of his
own. And St. Paul seems to refer to his own enumeration of the gifts of the Spirit, and almost to
set them aside, in that beautiful passage with which
you must be familiar—"Though I speak with the
tongues of men and of angels, and have not charity,
I am become as sounding brass or a tinkling cymbal.
And though I have the gift of prophecy, and understand all mysteries, and all knowledge; and
though I have all faith, so that I could remove mountains, and have not charity, I am nothing. And

though I bestow all my goods to feed the poor, and though I give my body to be burned, and have not charity, it profiteth me nothing." And in the same way, in speaking of the various persons given unto the Church, Apostles, Prophets, Evangelists, Pastors, Teachers, he tells us that they were given " for the perfecting of the saints, for the work of the ministry, for the edifying of the body of Christ." But none of these persons, as such, has any guarantee of salvation, nor any security for it, beyond that which the humblest Christian who is not called to such high office may claim for himself. These particular gifts are, in fact, very much the same as the particular endowments which we recognize among other men. Such are wealth, position, power, learning or the opportunities of obtaining it, eloquence, temper. All these tend to make a man eminent among his fellows, they mark him out as a person from whom more and better things may be expected than from other men. They are God's gifts, and they are good. But they are dangerous, because " to whom much is given, of him shall be much required," and we may be condemned for the use or misuse of talents which a wise man would not earnestly covet, but which he must accept if they are offered him. We must not confuse doing good with becoming better ourselves. It is a blessed thing to be able to do good, but it is far more blessed to do right, and to grow in grace. And if in looking back on the histories of men who had those special powers which we read of in the Old and New Testaments we feel that we do not exercise them now, we are not to suppose that God regards us with less favour than the men of old, or is less liberal of His mercies. God may restore those powers to His Church at any moment, and it seems to me presumptuous to say that the time for them is gone. That they are not *now* necessary for the Church is a pious opinion, because we do not possess them; but if a spirit of prayer and supplication were poured out upon it, if we could all be brought again to the unity of the Faith in the Son of God, who can say that we should not see and do "greater things" than those which the world will hardly believe were ever done? Meanwhile, we are supplied with everything necessary for life and godliness. And the one gift of sanctification that tends to the salvation of its possessor is guaranteed to all who are admitted to the Fellowship of Christ's Church. It is more than guaranteed; it is stamped upon us; we are already sealed by the Holy Spirit of promise; we are sealed by Him to the day of Redemption, when God will recognize His own seal, and claim us for His own.

When we read how the Spirit came upon Saul, and he was "turned into another man," we cannot but be reminded that we also "must be born again," and that Christ Himself has told us how this is to be, and instituted the sacrament of regeneration. I might carry on the parallel further if I had time. Even this gift, though it places us in the way of salvation, will not save us if we misuse or dishonour it. The Spirit of Grace will not help those who do despite to it. And the Spirit of God may depart

from us, as it did from Saul, and our last end will be
worse than our first. And though we have undergone the new birth and God's gifts are without repentance, yet the temper and spirit of the flesh, and all
that St. Paul calls the old man—whom we ought to
crucify and abolish—may revive and get the upper
hand, and then what good will even the grace of
sanctification do us? For even this grace is given us
to be used, and we are on our trial in respect of it.
It is not omnipotent in us, and will not force us into
holiness and heaven against our will or without
our will. Abstract questions of grace and nature
may employ idle disputants, or they may engage
the thoughts of the holiest men.

It is easy to get into verbal contradiction, and
to quote Scripture against Scripture. Practically
there is no difficulty which a holy life will not sweep
away. *Solvitur ambulando.* Walk worthy of your
calling and your walk will be straight and plain.
The best man knows by his own experience that
it is possible to grow in grace and the knowledge
of our Lord and Saviour Jesus Christ. He knows
that the Spirit of God guides, comforts, supports,
and helps him. He knows that he is led by the
Spirit, and he is therefore careful and fearful because he also knows his own weakness. He knows
that he is being *drawn* into the kingdom of God.
He feels that he has been "turned into another man,"
that he is consciously a "son of God" even now,
though "it doth not yet appear what he shall be."

SERMON XX.

An old Man's Reason.

———◆———

1 PETER iii. 15.

" Be ready always to give an answer to every man that asketh you a reason of the hope that is in you with meekness and fear."

THIS wise and liberal precept of St. Peter could not be better illustrated than by the conduct of the Apostles themselves towards the various classes of men with whom they were brought into contact or collision. And it is laid down here with the greatest possible breadth and precision—"Be ready *always* and to *every man*,"—as though no exception need be taken into account. Christians were in exclusive possession of the truth, and it would have been a false humility of mind on their part to have allowed it to be made a question of; but unlike some societies and mysteries of ancient, and we may add even of modern, times, they were not to keep it as a treasure that could only be communicated to the initiated, but to proclaim it boldly, and set forth the reasons on which their hopes and convictions rested. " With the heart man believeth unto right-eousness," but, like David, they were not to *hide* it within their hearts, but to publish it in the great congregation of the world which they were sent to convert. And in the precept to be ready to give a reason for the hope that is in them it is of course implied that the hope is reasonable. And what is said of our hope may, I think, be equally said of our *faith*. Indeed in this passage faith and hope may be considered as one, for our hope is reasonable only so far as our faith is, and if either of them is given up as not being so, it would be extremely difficult to maintain the other. If indeed there is anything reasonable in the world I would maintain that our faith is eminently so, and not the least so in those parts of it which transcend and surpass reason. I am speaking of it of course as revealed to us by God, and not discovered by the action of our minds. Now a revelation is the uncovering of what is unknown and beyond the range of ordinary knowledge, and it is, I say, highly reasonable that it should be partial, incomplete, and imperfect, just as our minds and faculties, however excellent, are imperfect; and those who think most deeply on religious subjects have always been most ready to confess this. "We cannot by searching find out God," and "we see through a glass darkly," are confessions that appeal to the consciences of Christians in proportion to the seriousness of their thoughts, and the light that they have. And as the truth is reasonable—otherwise it would be impossible to give a reason of it—so in the commandment, that we should do so when asked, it is implied that men generally also are reasonable, i.e. that they are willing to hear and capable of understanding a reason. Men are creatures endowed with reason, and it is therefore part of the honour due to all men to deal with them as such; and it is our duty in endeavouring to impart to them that truth which we possess to appeal to their reason. Indeed, we need not fear to say that it is one of the marks of the truth which we hold that it does not shrink from the appeal to reason. It challenges all that is best and noblest in man, either in his affections or in his faculties and powers. The Jews of Berœa were more noble than those of Thessalonica, in that they received the word with all readiness of mind, and searched the Scriptures whether these things were so—i.e. that they applied their reason freely and without prejudice to the question before them—and the natural consequence was that "many of them believed." Remember that I am not going myself now to give a reason for the hope that is in me, but am only speaking of the general duty of doing so when asked. But I must not misquote the Apostle, for he does not tell us actually to do so, but only to be ready to do it. And there is clearly a difference, for we do not always do what we are perfectly ready to do, unless we judge the time and the occasion suitable. And if people ask us for a reason, it must of course be assumed that they ask us in sincerity, and with a real wish to be informed. And though we are not to be suspicious of men's motives, but rather give them all possible credit for honesty, yet it is necessary to exercise great discretion in dealing with them. Different persons came to our Saviour with their questions, prompted by widely different motives, some simply with the hope of entangling Him, others to inform themselves of the truth. If He saw through the wickedness and hypocrisy of one, He was able to tell another, from His knowledge of what is in man and each man, that "he was not far from the kingdom of God." If we cannot see into the dark secrets of the heart as He could, we must use such powers as we have, in charity, of discovering the characters of those with whom we have to do. If we are not to sit in judgment upon men it is impossible to avoid receiving some impression of their motives, and by that impression our conduct must needs be influenced; otherwise we should have to treat all men in the same way, casting, perhaps, our pearls before swine, or throwing what is holy unto the dogs. I do not think St. Peter meant that you should introduce and discuss the truths of your religion with all persons, or in all places and times. And I would not advise you to be drawn lightly into argument with men of whom you know nothing, and whose object may simply be to perplex your understandings and to weaken your faith. Our reason is to be given, as St. Peter says, with meekness and fear, not with arrogance and presumption. For we may well feel humble in taking upon us to defend the truth of God, and even fearful lest we should injure it by our weak and faulty maintenance. All persons can give a reason for their faith and hope by simply stating it,

which is certainly one part of St. Peter's meaning,
though not the whole of it; and it will be a powerful
argument to commend our faith and hope to the minds
of men, if it is clear that we live according to them.
But to suppose that each of us is in full possession of
all that can be said in their defence would be to
court assaults, and expose our own faith to overthrow.
Depend upon it a great many difficulties may be
raised about the Gospel, and religion generally,
which it is very hard to solve; and we must be
content to hold our own, leaving them unsolved, for
we have here to live and walk, not to hesitate and
stand still. The activity of unbelievers in endeavouring to make other men like themselves was never
greater than at the present time; but you may take
my word for it that there is nothing new in their
cavils and objections, nothing that wise men in every
age have not thrown away as worthless, and lived
on according to the hope that is in them, as though
such things had never been presented to their minds.
When our convictions are fixed and solid we are
not much occupied or troubled by ingenious problems.
We have too much pressing business on hand to
give ourselves to them, and we have faithful sayings
to rest upon and the words of eternal life. Never
enter into argument with any one, except on the
understanding that the faith with you is not a matter
of argument at all, but of unshakeable conviction.
It is quite possible that you may be beaten in an
argument by a more subtle and ingenious dispu-
tant; but if you cannot hold your faith, notwith-

standing, it is better not to be drawn into an argument at all. As a man is not to allow himself to be tempted out of his faith by his passions and interests, so neither should he allow it to be wrested from him by arguments. Though reason is our highest gift, yet he is but a weak and feeble creature who allows himself to be turned and twisted about by various and inconsistent appeals to it. For though reason in itself is an absolute standard, our own particular reason may be weak and ill-informed; and in mistrusting it we do in fact mistrust ourselves, which most wise men do; and the word reason must be taken in the widest sense.

Man is not a calculating machine, to be carried on to a conclusion by the rules of arithmetic, where, if the process is correct, the result must necessarily be accepted, however contrary to what he supposed before; he is a creature of affections, and hopes, and fears, by which his actions are frequently guided, and even his judgments determined. "Knowing the terrors of the law," says St. Paul, "we persuade men." And this mode of persuasion is just as legitimate, and in truth as reasonable, as the appeal to his pure reason. Hope and fear are parts of our nature, and it is intended that we should be moved by them, just as much as by those arguments of pure reason that take no account of them. If we have within us the fear of judgment to come or the hope of immortality, that profession of truth which would move us to repentance and a better life by the action of the one, and lead us onward in it by strengthening

Y

the other, is worthy of our regard and acceptance on that very account. Whatever satisfies the wants of human nature or gives its energies a steadier and more worthy aim, has in that very satisfaction and effect upon us a strong argument in its favour. "The Spirit bearing witness with our spirit that we are sons of God" cannot be brought into court, or into the arena of dispute, as an evidence to other men, but it speaks to those who have it with a power and clearness which no other testimony can have; nay, it speaks by them to the world in a language and with an authority that will not be denied a hearing. The Gospel has had its defenders and apologists (*apology* is the word in the original, which we translate *answer* in the text), who have done good service to the Church, by stating its truths in form, clearing it of the false opinions which surrounded it, marshalling its evidences, and calling its witnesses into court as by a legal procedure, and have done well in giving a reason in public for the hope that was in them, and submitting to be tried before the public tribunal of the world, though not accepting its verdict. But however valuable their labours, it was not they who converted the world. "For God chose rather the foolish things of the world to confound the wise, and the weak things of the world to confound the mighty. And base things of the world, and things which are despised hath God chosen, yea, and things which are not, to bring to nought things that are." The faith and constancy of martyrs, men, women, and children, who gave up their lives for

the truth not accepting deliverance, that was the
victory that overcame the world, and won over the
persecutor many times at the altar and on the arena
Many of those who yielded their souls unto death
and their body to the flames, would have been found
very feeble in argument if brought into conflict with
disputers of this world, and the philosophers who
thought to destroy those whom they could not convince, and who held what they called their obstinacy,
and we call their faith, itself as a sin that deserved to
be visited with punishment. Even tender children
were known to defy the utmost efforts of their perse-
cutors, and they had no account to give of themselves
except the simple fact that they were Christians.
That confession was their strength, and the repetition
of it their comfort. If they gave up *that* they were
nothing, but holding fast *this* they had strength
to fight and overcome the world, the flesh, and the
devil. "Out of the mouths of babes and sucklings
hast Thou *ordained* strength, or perfected praise,"
read it which way you will as the strength of a firm
purpose, and the praise of a true confession, and "the
enemy and avenger" was stilled.

Men, whether so disposed or not, will at last judge
the tree by its fruit, and it was forced upon men's
minds by what they saw, that the Gospel was not
a curious device, nor a speculation, nor a philosophy,
but a vital power, filling those who embraced it with
a Spirit that could not be overcome, and that must
go forth to the end of the world conquering and
to conquer. If we are not called upon to shew our

constancy, and convince men's minds in the same way, our constancy need not therefore be the less, nor the argument of our Christian conduct less effectual. At all events, if we cannot answer objections to our faith we may at least vindicate its character, " Having a good conscience; that, whereas they speak evil of you, as of evildoers, they may be ashamed that falsely accuse your good conversation in Christ." Or, as St. Paul writes to Titus, each of you " in all things shewing thyself a pattern of good works, in doctrine shewing uncorruptness, gravity, sincerity, that he that is of the contrary part may be ashamed having no evil thing to say of you." Not, however, that the firmest conviction of our own minds and the most consistent conduct will always have their due effect. St. Paul, while in his treatment of men he addresses them uniformly as reasonable creatures, as having a right to ask questions and to expect answers, notes especially some persons as unreasonable, and prays to be delivered from them. Their minds are obstinately and incurably warped against the truth; they can neither be approached by argument, nor touched in their feelings, nor influenced by what they see with their eyes. Unreasonable men can only be left alone, we cannot stay to argue with them, and must go on our own way leaving them to theirs. They are not of those of whom St. Peter speaks, as asking a reason; for what they want is not a reason but a dispute and a wrangle, and therefore they are not of those to whom we owe an answer though ready to give one. Never dispute with known unbelievers and scoffers, and be careful generally with whom you do. But it is a good thing for all of you to know the grounds of your own faith, and the depth and solidity of its foundations, and if the question arises in your minds from time to time, "Why am I a Christian?" to be able to give at all events an answer to yourself. I have lately seen an answer to this question by an old man who has seen much of the world, and taken a leading part in some of its most important transactions for half a century. Having lived much in foreign lands, among Christians of various sects, and aliens from the name of Christ, it has occurred to him in the evening of his days to ask himself and to answer this very question. It is not to be supposed that his answer would satisfy all persons, for the truth is laid hold of in our minds variously—one person rests on this evidence, another on that—but the closing words of the wise and thoughtful old man will commend themselves to all: "What we designate as spots upon the sun are ascertained by astronomers to be vast tracts of inferior lustre or of downright opacity, yet do we not the less acknowledge that glorious orb to be the centre of light in our system, a nurse of life and source of vivifying heat, the extinction of which would plunge us in irrevocable destruction. Suppose a brighter light—the sun of salvation—extinguished in our minds, where should we turn for hope—however small—for a glimmer of hopeful light beyond the cold, dark goal of our earthly existence? If we reject that series of evidences, some single portions

of which go far to settle a Christian's belief, and the
whole of which leaves infidelity without excuse, what
can the unbeliever offer to make up for so immense
a sacrifice? Senses, faculties, affections, obliterated
for ever, our nature degraded to a level of the beasts
that perish, our motives of action reduced to vanities,
appetites, and earthly interests, a forfeiture of every
promise for which saints have toiled, crusaders fought,
the hermit courted poverty, the martyr died in tortures. No other substitutes he would have us to
accept for all the consolations, the spiritual supports,
the ennobling convictions, and the prospective glories
of our faith. He would renew the fall, and annul
the redemption of our race. The exchange he pro-
poses has too much the stamp of loss to engage my
assent. The evidences adduced satisfy my reason,
the hopes they warrant sustain my spirit. In them
I find a comfort and a strength, which in Christ's
name, and with God's assistance, I would fain hold
fast unto the end."

SERMON XXI.

Sir W. Hayter and Mr. Delane.

[The following notices of two men eminent in different walks of public life are inserted by desire of some who heard the Addresses delivered.]

* * *

ISAIAH xl. 1.

" Comfort ye My people."

OF him of whom I am about to speak my words will not be many. I miss, and you will long miss with me, that venerable face which I have seen turned towards me with attentive ear for so many years in this pulpit. And as what I say is entirely personal, I do not propose to touch upon what belongs to the political history of the times, or his connection with it, which has been already taken up by abler hands. It is known, however, to you all that he filled a very important place in the government of this country. A place, it is true, not of the highest rank, but one which required peculiar qualities, which no man possessed in a higher degree than himself[a]. I have often wondered that he never occupied the position of a cabinet minister, but I think the only reason must be that he thought

---

[a] Sir W. Hayter held the post of Political Secretary to the Treasury for many years.

he could serve his country better in a lower room. In the situation which he filled he gained the respect, and more than the respect, of all friends and opponents; and when on leaving the House he was asked to receive a magnificent testimonial from those with whom he had acted, a much more magnificent one would have been offered if it had been resolved to include in the list of his friends those who were opposed to him in parliamentary life. In the course of the duties of his office he must have had more experience of men than falls to the lot of most persons, and we shall not be accusing any party or class of men of corruption, if we think it possible that he may often have had to do with men not actuated by the highest order of motives, men of selfish objects, seekers of place, or honour, or gain. Such persons hang about all governments, and all persons in authority who are able to be of use to others; and the constant intercourse with such persons is apt to make others hard-hearted, cynical, and distrustful. Some persons display a perverse ingenuity in dissecting the motives of others, and getting to the bottom of them when they are two and three deep. They are proud to be thought men of the world, not to be taken in, and it generally happens that they are taken in more than other people whom they despise. It was a great charm in Sir W. Hayter that he had not one trace of this in his character. He was as free, open-hearted, and generously-minded as a high-born boy, who has not yet learned that there is such a thing as selfishness

or imposture in the world. A Greek philosopher
tells us how men are made misanthropes: it is by
a succession of misplaced confidences, by the experience of trusts betrayed, till at last you have lost
all faith in men, and begun to hate your kind. The
friend whom we have lost had, no doubt, his ex-
periences, but they led him on, not to misan-
thropy, but in the direction of greater kindness, geni-
ality, and charity. Fairness, equity, and kindliness,
were among the marks of our friend's character;
they were stamped upon his features, you felt the
warmth of them in his manner before he expressed
them in words. His virtues were not only true
virtues, but they were amiable and attractive virtues. The virtues of some persons are so severe
in form that they almost repel you from their presence. There is a temper that rejoices in iniquity, and is jubilant when it has found it, or thinks
it has, as though there were an "endowment of re-
search" in that direction. Sir W. Hayter was of a
temper the very reverse of this. He was incapable
of a base or sordid insinuation to account for conduct that was not base or sordid. He judged men
kindly and favourably, and I believe he therefore
judged them truly; and yet I should say few men
have been less deceived in life, and that not from
any extraordinary insight into character, though
in that he was not wanting, but from the simple
straightforwardness and honesty of his own ways.
You would not like to deceive him, for you would
feel sure you would be found out; there was some-

thing in his countenance that told you the attempt would not succeed. But besides this, honesty not only supposes but creates honesty; you actually make men better by thinking better of them. Even the criminal classes are some evidence of this. They are raised in their own esteem when they know there is anything trusted to their honour, and they will not sink again below the level to which they are raised by their new estimate of self. This idea is in fact the beginning of all moral reformation. Men feel that they have a hope of a better future directly they know that any one has a better opinion of them. I am sure that a prudent confidence in humanity is not folly, and life would be intolerable to me if I could not entertain it. The misanthrope is the most miserable of men.

Sir W. Hayter told me not long since that he had been reading a good deal of diplomacy, and that he thought that after all diplomatists were honest men, and endeavoured to do their best for their countries. I was delighted to hear him say so; for I do not pretend to understand their language, and their tortuous and technical phraseology requires a man to be well educated in the art before he can understand its meaning. No doubt every phrase has its value and significance, and is dealt out when occasion requires it, as if it were a coin, at its current value. But the kindly and equitable judgment of the old man belonged to his character. It was a weighty and deliberate judgment, formed by a most competent and conscientious judge, which

I am sure must rest on good grounds, and I have thought better of diplomatists, though I do not pretend to understand them, ever since in consequence.

I have said, perhaps, more than I ought upon this particular feature of his character, because I have always been much struck by it, and, in forming my judgment of others, perhaps improved by it; neither is it necessary to speak of deeds of kindness and generosity of which many of you are sensible. There are those here who know that he would not only *do* a kindness, but how he would labour and persevere in doing it, at the expense of great trouble and personal exertion, even in his extreme old age and declining health. And his attachment to this church, which would not have been built as it is, if it had not been for him, and of which he was proud to be Churchwarden, is also well known to you. And you know how, too, while his health lasted, and even after it gave evident signs of failing, no engagement, no weather, kept him from his accustomed seat. Even last Sunday he was thinking seriously of coming, and would no doubt have come if the weather had permitted; but he is gone for ever from us, and we shall see his face no more.

We should not have been surprised if we had heard any day that, full of years and full of honours, he had died peaceably in his bed. His wife, whose life has been bound up with his for so many years, would not have repined—I know not that she will now—for she knew well the time was coming. She would have watched him over the dark stream, waiting in confidence and peace for the messenger to summon her to meet him again in the light that is on the other shore; and his children and grandchildren around his bed would have learned how the way of life lies through the valley of the shadow of death.

It has not pleased Providence that this grand and good old man should be taken from us in this way. It pleased God in His inscrutable wisdom,—for I doubt not His wisdom—to prolong his days till that calm, equitable, and true-judging, practical mind was off its balance, and he became haunted by the idea of imaginary evils which pressed upon his brain. We simply know the fact of his end and the mode of it. It may have been a pure accident. We are fearfully and wonderfully made, both in body and soul, and when I consider how closely reason is connected with our bodily functions, though distinct from them, I am surprised that it is not oftener and sooner dethroned. It is, I think, permissible to pray that we may be called away before such a thing happens to ourselves. If it is permissible to pray for deliverance from sudden death, much more may we pray for deliverance from the sudden derangement or the gradual failure of the regulating powers. Such a death of such a man increases our sorrow but does not alter our opinions of, nor our affections for, him, and still less our hopes of his eternal future. I committed his honoured remains to the earth with the same confidence in the mercy of Almighty God, with the same trust in the saving virtue of the blood of Jesus Christ, with the same sure and certain hope of a resurrection to eternal life as if instead of dying alone, in the cold water, and under the chill covering of a wintry sky, he had died calmly in his bed, surrounded by all the comforts of home to the last, and by all that were dear to him to catch his dying breath, and with the words of humble resignation, or rather triumphant hope, upon his lips, "Lord, now lettest Thou Thy servant depart in peace."

Beside this striking portrait of a distinguished public servant let the companion picture of Mr. Delane, late Editor of the "Times," take its place.

THE last person whose mortal remains I committed to the keeping of the grave in this churchyard had not even attained to the inferior limit of the ages fixed by the Psalmist. He was still several years short of threescore years and ten, and therefore, as regards the fruits of experience and full maturity of mental power, in the very prime of life for action and counsel. I am not going to add to or repeat what so many papers have said, justly and truly as far as they went, but in my opinion inadequately, as regards Mr. Delane; but I cannot let his memory pass away without saying something of him as my own valued [friend, and as a lover and benefactor of this parish. He was born in it, and his affections were centred in it; he visited it constantly, and with pleasure. When in the midst of overwhelming work it was the best part of a chance holiday to ride over to it. In the last days, or rather years, of his long illness it was his habit and refreshment to drive into it. In fact, at last, as long as he was able to drive out, I think he never drove in any other direction. You do not know all his munificence. As an owner of a very small property here I might have expected and asked a little from him for such parish purposes as I have been able to accomplish, but I never asked him. He anticipated and surpassed everything I could have thought of. If he were alive he would be able to tell you that I was obliged to check and limit his munificence where I thought that in doing his part with others he was doing injustice to himself. While acknowledging the liberality of you, my parishioners, and the assistance of many friends, which I have great pleasure in doing, I do not think this church would ever have been built as it has been but for him and for his family. If it had not been for them certainly it would not have been so adorned. I am reminded of him weekly as I have that beautiful window of the parables and miracles of our Lord before my eyes, and the one to which your backs are turned in the tower, when I address you from this place. And I rejoice that his mortal remains are still under my keeping, with those of his father, mother, and brother, in the churchyard which he loved so well.

There is much in the position which our friend held, as editor of a paper which, under his hands, was for years without a rival, to absorb all his thoughts and feelings as well as his time, leaving no room in his heart for anything else. It is

a position or profession which belongs to modern
times; there was nothing like it in ancient days.
If it requires and encourages peculiar virtues and
qualities, discretion, reserve, quickness of observation, decision, almost intuition; if it calls into action
various mental gifts and powers, it cannot be said
that it encourages the more refined graces of character in the same degree. The tendency of those
who have most to do with men in the way of prob-
ing their motives and divining their intentions is to
become hard, and dry, and cynical. They become
like the persons they have to deal with. It does not
improve any one to become a hanger-on of great
people, and yet such people must be approached and
got at if possible by those who would occupy the
position of our friend. It is to his honour that no
one ever accused him of being the sycophant of any
man or party. He was sought out by others rather
than sought any person's favour or intimacy himself.
He received and preserved the confidences entrusted
to him in perfect independence. His great position
enabled him to do many acts of kindness to many
persons, and I should be much surprised if I were
told that when any appeal was made to him he was
ever found wanting. Kindness and generosity, and a
free and open hand, are not *all* the virtues which we
would like to see in a Christian man, nor when these
are mentioned is the list of those by which my friend
was adorned exhausted. It is comforting and con-
soling to hear the confession of Christ's faith and
fear from the lips of those who are dear to us. We

would gladly carry the echo of those last words, "Lord, now lettest Thou Thy servant depart in peace," as a perpetual music in our ears. But death-beds are not always or even generally what one might expect, when one considers the tremendous change to those who are passing from life into death. It very commonly happens that the mind and the body are enfeebled together. The body cannot move or act, and the mind cannot think. There is no power of reflection in it to make it feel anxiety. The sleep of peace cannot always be distinguished from the coma of insensibility; nature at once is motionless and dumb. Some of the most religious men I have known have been most reserved and un-communicative in their lives, and have passed away without a sign or with a slight movement of their lips from which we could only hope that they were breathing a prayer. We are glad of any evidence of joy and peace in believing where it is evinced, but it does not follow that belief is wanting, where such evidence is wanting, and our own hope and belief is not to wax faint because it derives no solid support from the hope and belief of others. No man know-eth the mind of a man, but the spirit of a man that is within him. But God is greater than our hearts, and to His love and keeping we can commit our-selves and those who are dear to us.

The death of friends, old and young, the dull-toned bell, that reminds us that another soul has taken its flight, do but add to the warnings of this solemn season. They warn us to "cast away the works of darkness, and to put on the armour of light, now in the time of this mortal life." We repeat the words from the first day of Advent unto Christmas Eve, and to-day we pray that we may embrace and hold fast the blessed hope of everlasting life which is given us in our Lord Jesus Christ. Let us be sure that this hope will not fail, will not deceive us, will not make us ashamed, when the truth and falsehood of everything shall be tried and known. And the God of all peace fill us with all joy and peace in believing, through the power of the Holy Ghost.

SERMON XXII.

Trinity in Unity[a].

REV. iv. 8.

" Holy, Holy, Holy, Lord God Almighty."

THE great festival of Trinity Sunday is different from any other by which the course of the Christian year is marked. Other festivals either commemorate what I will call historical events, or are intended to bring before us particular men whose names are held in honour among us, as apostles, evangelists, confessors, or martyrs. By historical events I mean things that happened, and the truth of which may be established by such evidence as is generally held to be sufficient to establish the truth of events of like nature. Thus, for instance, the birth of our blessed Saviour at Bethlehem is an event, the evidence of which is of the same character as that which establishes the birth of any other child. His death upon the cross was attested by the same witnesses, and by the same kind of proof as the death of the two thieves who were crucified with Him. St. Paul marshals the witnesses of the resurrection just as he would do if he were called to produce them in a court of justice. Any person would have been competent to give evidence of the Ascension if he had been present on the mountain where it took

---

[a] This Sermon was preached by Mr. Gordon on Trinity Sunday, May 20, 1883 : he died on the Friday following, May 25.

place, though the actual witnessing was committed to the Apostles. Any of the devout men who were then dwelling at Jerusalem, and possibly the scoffers also, were competent witnesses of what they saw and heard upon the day of Pentecost. And therefore I say that these were historical events, and we commemorate them as such on Christmas Day, Good Friday, Easter, and Whitsunday. That they were miraculous and momentous above any other events in the world does not deprive them of their historical character, or distinguish them in that respect from events of the most ordinary kind. Of course the Divine character of the Person concerned in these events is a matter of faith, but the events themselves are purely historical. A person might have witnessed the Crucifixion with the idea that our Lord was simply one of three criminals, and the worst of them, but that would not discredit his testimony as a witness of the Crucifixion. On the other hand, if an unbeliever had been permitted to be present at the Ascension it would have been difficult for him to have avoided the impression that He whom he saw received up into the clouds before his eyes was something more than a man of human flesh and blood. Thus you understand what I mean by saying that these are historical events, and you must be aware that the statement of these events makes up the substance of the creed with which you are familiar from your infancy. He that does not believe these statements, and holds them as undoubted truths, is no Christian, whatever else may be said of him.

z 2

There is a strange tendency now to undervalue creeds, and to think that we can get on as well, or even better, without them; and Christianity is supposed to consist not in the maintenance of definite articles of faith, but in a certain temper and habit of mind which is called Christian after Him who is a perfect example of it. It is thought that "men may have the mind which was in Christ Jesus," without troubling themselves to know or ask who Christ Jesus was, and in fact be very good Christians without Christ. It is true that anything like the mind of Christ Jesus is lovely wherever it is found, whether in believers or unbelievers, and they who have that mind without His faith will condemn those who have His faith without His mind. We do not separate those things which God hath joined together, and the Church in her prophetic wisdom sets before us first what we ought to believe, and then what we ought to be and do; holding that the one ought to follow directly from the other, nothing doubting but that her most faithful sons will celebrate with increasing joy and profit, as they grow older and wiser, these recurring festivals of the great events of our Lord's sojourn in the flesh. But other festivals are in commemoration not of events but of persons. The Annunciation, and the Purification of the Virgin, and the Conversion of St. Paul, may certainly be called events, but if you look over the list of festivals in general you will find that their object is to commend to us the services and characters of *persons*, doing honour to them as soldiers who have fought the good fight

of faith, and shewn us by example, how, being followers of them we may be followers of our blessed
Lord. That the services appointed for these days
should bring before us passages illustrative of their
character, or scenes in which they bore a prominent
part, is but natural, the object of these festivals still
being to commemorate not events but persons. And
though we pay so little attention to these days that
if the observance of them were omitted altogether
few of you would notice it, yet the Church at large
is more faithful than we her members, and it is well
that the names of her saints should continue on her
calendar, to remind us of what we owe them, and
possibly to rekindle from time to time the love and
zeal of some cold and sluggish heart, till it shall
please God to pour out a spirit of prayer and supplication, when the glorious company of the Apostles,
and the goodly fellowship of the Prophets, and the
noble army of Martyrs, will receive from her members that honour which the Church claims as their
due.

But the festival of Trinity cannot escape our notice
in the same way, for it is fixed to a Sunday, and we
are reminded of it every week for more than half the
year. And it is, as I said, different from other festivals, for it commemorates nothing that can be called
an event, and does honour to no created being however high. It sets before us for our adoration the
most inscrutable and glorious mystery of our religion.
It calls upon us to steady our minds in and by the
profession of a true faith, and to lay our souls pros-

trate in the contemplation of God Almighty as He
has revealed Himself unto us, one in substance
but three in person, in whose name we are baptized,
Father, Son, and Holy Ghost. Now if we are asked
for any warrant in Holy Scripture for the truth of
this doctrine, I do not think we could refer to anything more to the point than this formula of baptism
with which you are familiar. Or you might refer
to the blessing of St. Paul to the Corinthians, which
must be scarcely less familiar: "The grace of our
Lord Jesus Christ, and the love of God, and the
fellowship of the Holy Ghost, be with you all." We
should be rendering a sufficient account of the faith
and hope that is in us if we were to say that we commenced our Christian life in the name of these three
Persons, and that our highest prayer is that we may
spend it under their protection, living in the grace,
love, and communion of each. But you must be
aware that no such clear doctrinal statements as these
are to be found in the pages of the Old Testament.
God deals with His children as children, giving
them from time to time such lessons of truth and
intimations of His will as are suitable to their age,
and they are able to receive. The education of the
Apostles under their divine Master was progressive,
and He had to tell them in the course of it, " I have
many things to say unto you, but ye cannot bear
them now." St. Paul says, " When I was a child
I thought as a child, I spake as a child, but when
I became a man I put away childish things." But
any one who will read the passage will see that so

far from claiming to be a man in divine knowledge
he still professed to be a child, and only looked forward to becoming a man hereafter, when he should
no longer see through a glass darkly. Some persons
fret, and become impatient under this condition of
knowledge, and are disposed at once to reject all
knowledge that is offered them, which they are unable to understand. Yet it seems to me reasonable to ask, who would wish nothing to be true except
what he knows to be? who would wish his own
experience to be the ultimate test of facts; who
would wish the range of his own ideas to determine
the possibilities of truth? Is it a wide or a narrow
view that forbids the exercise, or condemns the
reachings out of faith after the unseen, and regards
it a vanity or presumption to dwell on the prospect
of things "which the eye hath not seen, nor the ear
heard, neither hath it entered into the heart of man
to conceive?"

Imagination is one of the endowments of our
nature, and therefore has its proper office and function, as our other gifts have, and if its wanderings
have to be kept within the lines of truth there is
enough within those lines to exercise and satisfy it.
Now it appears to me that those who lived under the
old dispensations could hardly have read many passages of their own Scriptures without deriving thence
some imagining of a truth that was hidden from
them. Many learned Jews, for instance, have observed what does not appear in our translations, that
the word *God* is really *Gods*, though the verb which

follows is in the singular number. Again, they observe forms of consultation, as though several persons were taking counsel together, with a view to united action, as "Let us make man in our image." "The man is become as one of us." "Let us go down and confound their speech." The Jews allow that were it not thus written it would not be lawful so to write. Again, those passages which name God as sustaining several capacities at the same time, as that by which our Saviour perplexed the Scribes and Pharisees: "The Lord said unto my Lord, Sit thou on My right hand, till I make thine enemies thy footstool. If David then call Him Lord, how is He his Son?" or where the name Jehovah, incommunicable to any but the true God, is used twice, clearly not of the same person, "The Lord rained fire upon Sodom from the Lord out of Heaven." And there are other passages in which the name of God or His Attributes is repeated thrice, which are not a little remarkable: the hymn of praise, for instance, in the vision of Isaiah, which is repeated in the epistle of the day, "Holy, Holy, Holy, Lord God of Hosts, the whole earth is full of His glory." Indeed that vision itself is perhaps the clearest in the whole volume of the Old Testament. The prophet felt that he had seen the King, the Lord of Hosts; he had seen God as no mortal eye had seen Him, and lived; a man of unclean lips, and living among a people of unclean lips, he felt himself undone, and woe upon him. But a seraph flew to him with a live coal from the altar, and touched his lips. Thus his iniquity was taken away and his sin was purged, and he was able to hear and undertake the mission with which he was charged, and which he received from the voice of the Lord. It was the final judgment of the faithless people that he had to declare, "Hear ye indeed, but understand not; and see ye indeed, but perceive not. Make the heart of this people fat, and make their ears heavy, and shut their eyes; lest they see with their eyes, and hear with their ears, and understand with their heart, and convert, and be healed,"—a judgment so true that it is repeated by each of the Evangelists. But St. John refers the words and the whole verse directly to Christ Himself. "These things said Isaiah, when he saw His glory, and spake of Him." The Apostle, like Isaiah, had seen the glory of Christ, and testified to what he had seen. But St. Paul, quoting the same judgment against his countrymen, brings in another Person: "Well spake the Holy Ghost by Esaias the prophet unto our fathers:" and thus we are able to account for the three Holies—Holy, Holy, Holy—both of the prophet and of St. John, and for the single Lord God Almighty; for "they are not three Eternals, but one Eternal; not three Almighties, but one Almighty; not three Lords, but one Lord." For "like as we are compelled by the Christian verity, to acknowledge every Person by Himself to be God and Lord, so are we forbidden by the Catholic religion to say there be three Gods or three Lords."

No person would, however, think of basing a doctrine on such passages as these if there were nothing

clearer revealed. Nor are we at liberty to frame
doctrines for ourselves, to account for or explain
passages in Scripture, because without such explanation they would be difficult to understand. But
when a key opens a lock it is a strong presumption
that it was made for that lock, and the more complicated the lock the stronger the presumption. And
when learned Jews allow that God is spoken of in Scripture in such terms as it would not be lawful to use
of Him without that authority, this itself is an argument that that doctrine which explains and accounts
for the expressions used is hidden beneath them
and is true. It is in this way that the Old and New
Testament,—the first sending our thoughts beyond
itself for the full understanding of its words, the
second taking up and carrying out the obscure intimations of the first,—lend support to each other as the
mutually involved parts of a consistent and gradu-
ated revelation.

The doctrine of the Trinity in Unity is of the very
essence and life of our religion. It was declared in
the very terms of the Annunciation: "The Holy
Ghost shall come upon thee, and the power of the
Highest shall overshadow thee. Therefore that Holy
Thing that shall be born of thee shall be called the
Son of God." The Persons are clearly distinguished
from each other: The Highest, the Holy Ghost,
the Son of God. It was revealed to the eye and ear
at our Lord's Baptism. The Spirit of God descended
like a dove, and was seen by St. John; a voice from
heaven was heard, the voice of the Father, for He

bore witness to His own beloved Son, who was there in His own Person. Our Saviour engages to pray the Father to send us another Comforter, who shall abide with us for ever, and He declares that this Comforter is the Holy Ghost. The three Holy Persons are engaged again in promoting the salvation of those who have been baptized in their name. Here again we find acts, and persons, and capacities, distinct.

The Father, from whom the Spirit proceeds, whom the Son prays, and by whom the Comforter is given.

The Son praying the Father, sending the Comforter from the Father, and testified of by the Spirit so sent.

The Spirit prayed for, given by the Father, sent from the Father by the Son, testifying of the Son, and abiding for ever with those disciples when the Son had departed.

Allowing for the imperfection of human language which belongs to things and relations of earth, and is only borrowed when it is applied to the things and relations of heaven, it seems impossible to conceive a distinction of persons more clearly set forth, just as in countless other passages of Scripture nothing can be more clear than the declaration that the Lord our God is one Lord. And we may conceive that in a future state, and among the spirits of just men made perfect, there will be powers of understanding developed in us, of which at present we have only the germ : so there will be a language more suitable to the realities of divine things than that which we are here

compelled to employ. At present the doctrine of
the Unity is guarded by the Trinity and the Trinity
by the Unity; and it is a great protection to us to
be taught how he that will be saved must not
only think, but even speak of the Trinity. Words
fashion and consolidate thoughts, and they that have
learned to speak in the same language will not be
likely to think very differently. It is not to be
wondered at if the wild speculations of presumptuous
men in various ages have driven the Church to
strict definitions and stringent formularies, which
are irksome to some as checks upon their liberty,
but are thankfully received by the wise as guaran-
tees of their safety.

But what is required of us here is not strictness
of thought or accuracy of language—though both
have their value—but reverence and adoration; and
if the will of God may be done on earth as it is
in heaven, we may anticipate here some of the employments of heaven, to which indeed we are excited by the portion of Scripture appointed for the
Epistle, wherein the blessed angels and spirits that
are about the throne of the Majesty on High are
represented to St. John as with most awful and profound reverence acknowledging and worshipping the
three Holies, who are one eternal and Almighty
Lord: a fit example for the Church Militant on earth
to follow, because in so doing we not only copy but
even anticipate the constant employment of the
Church Triumphant in heaven.

And so with all humility and reverence, with all

the angels and all the heavenly powers, with Cherubin and Seraphin, with apostles, and prophets, and martyrs, with the holy Church throughout all the world, we unite in praising and acknowledging this "Holy, Holy, Holy, Lord God of Sabaoth:" even the Father, of an infinite Majesty; His honourable true and only Son; also the Holy Ghost the Comforter; living and reigning one God world without end.

EXTRACTS FROM UNPUBLISHED SERMONS.

THE following Extracts from Sermons which cannot be printed entire for want of room, are intended to throw light upon Mr. Gordon's opinions respecting several subjects in which he took particular interest. He was always strongly opposed to the exclusion of religious doctrine from Public Elementary Schools established under the Act of 1870. His views have been made known during his lifetime in several publications; but he constantly recurs to a measure which seemed to him little short of a national abrogation of duty, as in the two following out of many passages :—

I. You can exclude Christianity and all religion from schools, but admitting it, you cannot exclude Christian dogma, for every precept carries us directly into it. Christ is at the same time our authority and our example, for He alone entirely fulfilled every precept which His lips delivered. To take these precepts without His authority and His example, is to rob them of their vitality and power, but directly you touch either you are in the region of dogma.

The law was of old a schoolmaster to bring men unto Christ the true Teacher. That will be a miserable law that does not bring them still to Him. Consider for a moment yourselves. In three weeks' time the Cross of Christ will be again lifted up before your eyes. It is the sight of sights, the subject of subjects, to draw to itself all eyes, to engage all hearts. Yet there are legislators of a Christian country who tell us that this of all subjects in the world shall never be mentioned in the schools to which the poor shall be compelled by fine and imprisonment to send their children. It shall be a crime to speak of it; it shall be banished, if possible, from their thoughts.

"These things which I command thee shall be in thine heart. And thou shalt teach them diligently to thy children, and thou shalt talk of them when thou sittest in thine house, and when thou walkest by the way, when thou liest down and risest up."

This was the law of a Jewish parent. Take the negation of each part and you will have the law which it is sought to impose upon every schoolmaster in a land that calls itself Christian. Will you not join with me when I say "God forbid?"

II. I have already spoken to you on the efforts that are now being made to proscribe and exclude all religion from the education to which your children shall be condemned, and it is impossible to say to what extent these efforts may succeed [a]. No doubt many compromises will be proposed, and one in particular—that the Bible shall be read in schools but no definite instruction given—has so plausible and taking a sound that some persons may regard it as a valuable con-

[a] These apprehensions were not wholly groundless. In many Board Schools no doubt the best is done that can be under a law which forbids any teaching of definite religious doctrine, though it imposes no restriction as regards the opposite extreme. From a Parliamentary Return it appears that in November last there were 45 Board Schools, chiefly in Wales, in which no religious instruction whatever was given. In some, such instruction was permitted twice a week between 1 and 2 o'clock (the dinner-hour).

In one Board School an attempt was made to introduce a hymn from a School Board Hymn-book, with the Lord's Prayer, at the opening of school. But a member of the Board opposed the motion on the ground that though he had no objections himself to the Lord's Prayer, many of the ratepayers had, and so the motion was lost; and similarly elsewhere.

cession. From what I have said you will not suppose that I undervalue the sacred volume, holding it to be in reality, and not simply to contain, somewhere in its bulk, the true Word of God. But if the reading of it is to be considered the sum and substance of a religious education, I must pronounce it to be a snare and a delusion. Are children of from six to twelve years of age supposed to be capable of framing for themselves an intelligible idea of religious truth, out of selections made we know not on what principle, or possibly on no principle at all? It may be said that Christian teachers would of course select such passages as are suited to the intelligence of children, and would lead them on naturally to the simple truths of the Gospel, and the duties connected with them. But what security will there be that teachers will be Christians? and if they are not so, it is a mere profanation of Scripture that such persons should read it as part of their day's work, with unbelief in their hearts, and possibly contempt in their voices. And if they are Christians, and select such passages for reading as will direct their pupils towards such truths as they think fundamental, then they will be simply doing in an indirect and ineffectual way that which the law forbids them to do in a more direct and effectual method; for a selection and arrangement of Scripture is in effect an explanation and commentary and summary of Scripture. Only this summary will not be that which the Church has received in all ages, but something that commends itself to the individual teacher. The truths of Christianity can be very simply stated, and the Church, under the pressure of necessity, but under the guidance of God's Spirit, has thrown them into such a form that they can be learned and understood by children; while they are held as a precious treasure and deposit by the wise. And Catechisms, though they have not the authority of the undivided Church, are the natural mode of stamping the impressions of truth upon the infant, and even upon the adult mind. St. Luke wrote his Gospel for the benefit of Theophilus, that he might know the certainty of those things wherein he had been instructed, or catechized, as the word is in the original. And in the Epistles of St. Paul we find traces of a regular system of instruction proceeding from principles to perfection. "I delivered unto you first of all that which I also received, how that Christ died for our sins according to the Scriptures, and that He was buried, and that He rose again according to the Scriptures." Here we are almost brought to the very language of the Apostles' Creed, as far as concerns one article of faith, and we do not know that the Apostles' Creed was not then used in its complete form. And in the Epistle to the Hebrews, repentance and faith, and the doctrine of baptisms, and of laying on of hands, and the resurrection of the dead, and eternal judgment, are spoken of as the principles of the doctrine of Christ. Are children to be left to pick out these principles for themselves out of the sacred volume, or such portions of it as may be selected for their reading? or shall we not follow the Apostles' example, and put them in possession of them from the first?

The Scriptures are able to make us wise unto salvation, not through their history, not through their study as a literary work, not even through their morality, but "through faith which is in Jesus Christ."

We baptize your children into that faith, and we endeavour to give them the substance of it in that form of sound words which has been delivered to us, that thus they may grow in faith, and, we hope, in grace. And we can send them freely to the Word of God, without fear and without reserve, holding with the Apostle that "All Scripture is given by inspiration of God, and is profitable for doctrine, for reproof, for correction, for instruction in righteousness," that under its guidance and comfort the child may grow up into the man.

A a

"And the man of God may be perfect, throughly furnished unto all good works."

His view of the relations which ought to subsist between masters and dependents is shewn in the following passage, possessing a peculiar interest from the circumstance referred to in p. 57, as affecting his own household.

III. "If thou have a servant, let him be as thyself. If thou have a servant entreat him as a brother," says the author of the book of Ecclesiasticus, and he, like St. Paul, is speaking of a bought servant. Let me give you an account of a lady in Israel, the head of a large household, and living in great splendour. "Who," asks Solomon, "can find a virtuous woman? her price is far above rubies. The heart of her husband doth safely trust in her." She is industrious and careful. "She seeketh wool and flax, and worketh willingly with her hands. She riseth while it is yet night, and giveth meat to her household and a portion to her maidens." She has an eye to business, and does not miss a good chance. "She considereth a field, and buyeth it. With the fruit of her hands she planteth a vineyard." But her special care is of her servants. "She is not afraid of the snow for her household. All her household are clothed in double garments; she looketh well to the ways of her household, and eateth not the bread of idleness. Her children rise up and call her blessed, her husband also, and he praiseth her." We wish we had also a picture of a husband worthy of such a wife; we should like to be told how he dealt with his servants, but we can easily imagine it. How that lady's servants loved their mistress; they adored her, they would have done anything for her. They would not calculate the least they were bound to do, or the exact amount they had contracted to do. All their thoughts would be, what was the most they could do, how they could best requite her care and love, and how they could exceed their obligations, and render some service that would be a free-will offering. Perhaps some of them would be ungrateful. But what did that matter as regards her conduct? She at least had done her duty, and had engendered about her that warmth of affection and love which was her own comfort and reward. I cannot help thinking at this moment of our Queen, and of the loss she has sustained in the lower department of her household. I think we know very well that the regard of Her Majesty was not limited to that one person whom she particularly favoured. He was a single instance, but she observed and watched the conduct of every one about her, and valued them accordingly. Some persons may think that the servant whom she has lately lost, and whose loss I fear may have affected her health and spirits, enjoyed exceptional and even excessive favour. But I never heard that he was unworthy of it, and I know what it is to lose the sight of a familiar face, even though it be the face of an humble dependent, or as some may say a menial. I can only think of the Queen's affection for her faithful servant as an instance of the goodness of her heart, whose sympathies extend to all her servants. And, so far from thinking the relation between them as exceptional, I rather regard it as typical and exemplary, as a type, that is, and instance of the feeling which ought to exist between all masters and all servants, each of course according to the faithfulness of his service and degree.

His regard for dumb animals, noticed in p. 67, appears in the following striking description:—

IV. I would ask here, is there any doubt that animals have thoughts, memories, and feelings, if they have no articulate mode of expressing them? That they have memories is beyond all doubt. Their recollection of places is marvellous, and in respect of permanence and accuracy far exceeds our own. The attachment of the higher order of domestic animals to those who treat them well is a lesson to the ingratitude of man. It has been well observed that the nobility of animals is in exact proportion to their capability of attachment to a being higher than themselves, i.e. to man. And man rises in the scale of being in proportion as he is capable of, and filled with, the love of God. A perfectly independent animal would only deserve to be destroyed; a perfectly independent man, if we can conceive such a one, would be the most degraded of his kind. We are exalted by our dependence on Him who made us, and by our sense of it. I do not know anything more beautiful or more pathetic than the way in which subservient animals submit their own wills to the wills of us their masters and the lords of Creation. They must do many things contrary to their own wishes and impulses, simply because they know we wish them. I will not slander them by saying that it is from fear, it is from a higher motive. A word, a motion, or a touch of the bridle is enough, and they resign themselves. Isaiah compares the brute creation with the very people of God, much to the disadvantage of the latter: "The ox knoweth his owner, and the ass his master's crib, but Israel doth not know, My people doth not consider." Do you suppose that the horse does not remember his long years of faithful service, and that when he is cruelly treated his thoughts are not exactly those which found expression in the mouth of Balaam's ass? There is a pathetic power in his reproach, which is far more telling than if it came from a human creature. He pleads for mercy and justice the more powerfully because he is perfectly helpless. He acknowledges himself to be a slave, "Am not I thine ass, upon which thou hast ridden ever since I was thine unto this day? was I ever wont to do so unto thee?" If dumb creatures could speak would they not frequently have occasion to speak in this way to us? They do virtually say it; they reproach us with their eyes? I have known them do it. They reproach, and they forgive. One word, one touch of kindness is enough, and everything is forgotten. If they are inferior to us in not being able to weigh injuries or unkindness with precision, they are an example to us in forgiving them. Man is, as I said, lord of Creation, and may kill and eat what he likes, but cruelty to dependent creatures seems to me to be like the unpardonable sin.

The following passages bring before the mind's eye pictures of various kinds, the more pleasing from their perfect simplicity.

(a.) *Of the Table in the Wilderness.*

V. The table that was spread in the wilderness was thus sanctified and increased by a marvellous increase. It grew in the Apostles' hands, and multiplied as it was distributed. In their case it was literally true—"There is that scattereth and yet increaseth,"—a visible instance of that law of charity which cannot exhaust herself by giving, but ever finds the blessings which she bestows on others coming back in fuller measure to her own bosom. But when we ask the manner of this increase, or seek to realize it to ourselves, the whole thing eluding the grasp, we cannot follow it even in imagination. There were five loaves to begin with, the material basis of the miracle — they were blessed and broken; but how each of them became the seed of other loaves, increasing in the hands of the Apostles as they passed along the lines of the multitudes, would be an idle enquiry, and it belongs to the wisdom of the sacred narrators to leave unattempted the description of that which cannot be described.

But let not the marvellous character of that which we have never seen make us insensible to the wonders that daily pass before our eyes. Let not God's every-day miracles grow cheap in our sight because we are familiar with them, while we confine our admiration to those special acts by which the Son of Man signalized His Mission among men. Who can tell us how it is that a single grain of corn cast into the earth decomposes, and, as the Scripture says, dies, but in its death gives birth to a new progeny after its kind, first the blade, then the ear, then the full corn in the ear. Take the grain and examine it as you please; analyse and separate its elements; subject it to every kind of scientific skill, and you will search in vain for the principle of life that is called into activity by the genial influence of the sun and rain. It obeys a law of its own, and obeys it under due conditions, with unwavering fidelity; but the process is a hidden mystery to us when we attempt to trace it, and is therefore a fit type of that greater mystery which shall be disclosed when this mortal shall put on immortality, and we shall be changed. If we cannot understand earthly things, how can we expect to understand heavenly? There is need of the same faith in both. "For it is by faith only that we understand that the worlds were framed by the Word of God, so that things which are seen were not made by things which do appear."

(b.) *The ripening Corn in Summer.*

VI. It has always seemed to me that there is no scene in nature more delightful for the eye to rest upon than a bright field of ripening corn. It is so, not only for the ideas of peace and industry, and the promise of comfort and plenty that it suggests, but from its very aspect and appearance. Watch it, as it bends and waves beneath the light winds of summer, or as the clouds and sunshine sweep over it in succession, giving it almost the expression of a smile, and you will have a picture of light and shade, of form and colour, of rest and motion, drawn for you by nature herself, and defying the imitation of art. It may be that all persons have not eye for these things, but those who lack it certainly lack a power of enjoyment which is a source of infinite happiness to its more fortunate possessors. And the aspect of the cornfield seems to me to be invested with other powers besides that of giving pleasure. It teaches us a high moral and religious lesson. It is a visible token and witness of God's Providence and goodness, a memento of our entire dependence upon Him. A heap of corn rising up stage above stage on the terraced hills of Judæa was one of the promised blessings of the reign of Solomon, and the abundance of its increase is ever associated with the bounty of Him who is the Giver of all good things. It appears to me to have a natural tendency, before anything else, to dispose the human heart to goodwill and gratitude, and he must be a worse man than I should like to imagine any man to be, who can walk through the impressive silence or gentle murmur of the cornfield, in an unthankful temper, or harbouring any evil thoughts, either towards God or man. Is not the cornfield more than a moral lesson to us? Is it not a visible parable of life, and death, and resurrection? "Except a corn of wheat fall into the ground and die, it abideth alone, but if it die it bringeth forth much fruit." Who can compare the bare brown fields of the present season with the richness of their summer clothing, without feeling that there is a deep mystery that works this wondrous change. St. Paul at least thought so—"Thou fool, that which thou sowest is not quickened except it die. And that which thou sowest, thou sowest not that body that shall be, but bare grain, it may chance of wheat or of some other grain. But God giveth it a body, as it hath pleased Him, and to every seed his own body."

(c.) *Of Foreign Missions.*

VII. If we wish to strengthen the Church in our own lands, the way to do so is, I am sure, by extending and planting it in other lands. Earthly kingdoms may be weakened by their extension, and a lengthened position may be only a source of weakness; but it is not so with the kingdom of God. We cannot round its borders, or make it neat and compact just for ourselves to dwell in. Extension and progress are the very law of its being, and the necessity of its existence. It is most safe at home, when it is most aggressive and enterprising abroad. To cease to conquer is to cease to live; and what is true of the whole is true of every part. Life at home is sustained and strengthened by life and activity abroad. If we have much to do among our own people, unconverted heathen even at our doors, go more largely and freely into missionary efforts, and the blessing that you carry into other lands may return upon you tenfold here. It is no spirit of faith, but one of mistaken calculation, that would deter us from the fields abroad, because the fields are calling for more labourers here. I do not believe it can be shewn that any Church was ever injured by missionary zeal, or that it lost anything by sending even its best and noblest sons to bear the cross in other lands. And hard pressed as many parishes are to supply their own immediate wants, with schools and churches to build, ministers to support, works of love and charity to establish and maintain, they will derive not weakness but strength, not exhaustion, but a renewal of their vigour, by throwing themselves heartily and zealously into the great work of preaching the Gospel to the heathen. All are not called to be evangelists, it was not so at the beginning, and it is not so now. "He gave some apostles, some prophets, some evangelists, some pastors and teachers." Men's gifts varied, and their calls varied; but the end of all was " the perfecting of the Saints," the work of the ministry, the edifying of the body of Christ. But all are called upon in their degree to promote the kingdom of God, for the coming of which they daily pray in our Lord's own words. We who remain at home, whose lot is cast in the pleasant places of our own land, who minister, or are ministered to, in the churches where our fathers worshipped, and tread daily or weekly the soil that is hallowed by their graves—are one in faith with those who are carrying on the holy warfare in the dark places of the earth. We have one Lord, one faith, one baptism, it will be our own fault if we have not one common interest in the work they have to do. Think you that the memory of all that they have left behind never recurs to those soldiers of the cross, that alone among the heathen, or in the unmeasured wilderness, or primæval forest, they never think of the peaceful homes, and familiar faces, and sacred walls and decent ornaments of public services that they have left; or contrast the meagre congregations—the two or three, perhaps, whom they have gathered together with pains and difficulty to learn the first rudiments of truth — with the overflowing congregations, and united voices, and peals of praise, which they have often heard filling the vast expanse of minster or cathedral; heard it, perhaps, for the last time when they received the Holy Spirit by the laying on of hands, and were commended to their work with prayer. And what greater encouragement for them in their labour and solitude, than to know that our hearts too are with them in their work, that they are not looked upon as men who have thrown themselves away, or separated their interests from ours; but that we are embarked in a common cause, fellow-workers in the same high enterprise, fellow-workers with God; and that they will have a constant share in our prayers, and sympathies, and alms?

VIII. Pearls at random strung.

There is this reason for keeping past sins in remembrance, that we shall be in danger of forgetting the mercy that forgives if we forget the sin that is forgiven.

One vice for a time destroys another, till at last all be-come confluent, and the whole man corrupt in every part.

Out of the fulness of the heart the mouth speaketh, and sometimes out of its emptiness.

Upon Congregational Music:—"In ordinary chanting, I think that those who have no ear or voice may be silent in Church without compromising their rights."

Charity is that affection of the mind whereby we love God for His own sake, and our neighbour for God's sake.

A Proverb is a saying which embodies the wisdom of one man and the experience of many.

Mystery is correlative to Revelation. Revelation is the bright and Mystery the dark side of the same providential scheme.

That Government is best which is least felt.

Though sin is hereditary we can break off the entail.

Of our public dealings with China:—"If we have forced upon the Chinese a drug which we know to be poisonous, we have at least abstained from forcing upon them a religion which we believe to be true."

The existence of evil in any form under the government of an Almighty and all-good Governor of the world is the great insoluble problem; which question those who presume to enter into must be much wiser or much more foolish than myself.

The strength of prayer is feebleness, if we do not *try to be* that which we *pray to be.*

Of field sports:—"I hope that I may be allowed to take delight in wild animals without being under the necessity of killing them."

When certain of the congregation left the church before the administration of the Lord's Supper, their practice was held up to them as *ultra-popish*, because whereas Roman Catholics remained without communicating, they carried their principle a step further and went away altogether: possibly with no greater effect in convincing the seceders of the nature of their fault, than Yorick in maintaining to his astonished host that the vice of the French character was *over-seriousness*.

These extracts may perhaps be most fittingly closed by the expression of a sentiment deeply rooted in the mind of the writer, yet co-existing with absolute loyalty to his own Church.

IX. I thank God that I may allow, not in the niggard spirit of an acknowledgment that has been forced from me, but of a free and grateful confession, that God has raised up many a prophet, and witness, and preacher of righteousness, among those who do not agree with us on matters which we think of great importance, particularly on the subject of an ordained ministry, which traces its commission to the laying on of hands by the Apostles,—and we look forward to the happy time when the schism which now exists shall be closed. Wounds, as I am told, heal in two ways, by first intention as it is called, when the separated parts are brought together at once and immediately unite, and by granulation, where the process is slower and the cure is effected by new flesh forming on both sides, till the chasm is filled up. Believe me that the granulation of charity will fill up the wounds that are now gaping, and when charity has its work, that which is wanting on either side will be felt and supplied. Apostles, prophets, pastors, and teachers, will not be wanting "till we all come in the unity of the faith, and of the knowledge of the Son of God, unto a perfect man, unto the measure of the stature of the fulness of Christ."

APPENDIX I.

—◆—

ORATIO PROCURATORIA CORAM ACADEMIA HABITA TERM. PASCH. INEUNTE M DCCC XLVII.

MIHI hanc concionem pro officii more habituro nihil prius in mentem venit, quam ut semestri tantum honore insignitus, fortunam Universitatis nostræ, quæ hoc anno gravissimi magistratus mutationem sustinuit, commemorem, meam vicem etiam condoleam, qui me in locum viri multo magis idonei subrogatum esse sentio.

Cujus[a] profecto a nobis discessum haud sine causa deploraremus, si eo tantum modo operam Academiæ dedisset, quo civis unusquisque aut alumnus qui in loco aut collegio suo muneribus sibi permissis pro parte virili defungitur, toti adeo civitatis aut Academiæ corpori prodesse censendus est. Verum ille quidem non illorum magis causa qui intra parietes Ædis suæ commorantur, quam alienorum omnium (absit verbo invidia) elaborarat.

Quam bene de Græcis litteris est meritus, testis est in omnium manibus lexicon Græco-Anglicum, quod magna ex parte a Germanico fonte sumptum, magna tamen ex parte denuo recudit, auxit et concinnavit. Cujus duabus editionibus fere exhaustis, tertia jam ante diem postulatur.

Ceterum id jam diu factum est et celebratum, et id opus fortasse, quod ille etiam alter adjutor suus et gloria par absens potuisset absolvere, hoc vero anno ad Archididascali Westmonasteriensis dignitatem evectus, procuratoris simul, moralis philosophiæ professoris, instituti Tayloriani curatoris officia aliis mandanda atque obeunda reliquit. Et in

---

[a] Rev. H. G. Liddell, the present Dean of Christ Church.

philosophia quidem ethica quam vocant, lectiones ejus quamquam rerum multarum turba impediti tanta frequentia audi-
torum celebrabantur ut satis essent documento, nec classem
professoribus nostris, nec adolescentibus audiendi voluntatem
deesse, ubi spes certa fructus percipiendi ostendatur.　Nec
id mihi erat mirum.　Rem enim subtilissimam ita tractabat,
ut cum in veterum philosophorum opinionibus ac disciplinis
illustrandis plurimum versaretur, permulta tamen ad quæs-
tiones et officia nostræ ipsorum ætatis pertinentia inde
deduceret.　Scilicet in eo erat præcipua quædam animi
ejus excellentia, quod veteres philosophos in eadem materia
elaborare, in eosdem errores incidere, in iisdem difficultati-
bus hærere, eadem quærere ac nostri temporis homines vide-
bat.　Itaque lectiones ejus erant non ut de re antiqua et
vetustate exoleta et a nobis aliena, sed ut de hodierna et
maxime ad nos pertinenti, cum non ad reconditas opiniones
explicandas sed ad vitam et mores dirigendos spectarent.
Quo circa (id erat ejus ingenium) nullus equidem dubito, quin
in hoc etiam loco quem extra sortem occupavi, multi vestrum
prudentiam ejus et in rebus agendis sollertiam desidera-
veritis, et fortasse magis desideravissetis nisi me simul et
Vice-Cancellarii benignitas singularis, et collegæ mei opera
atque industria sustinuerat.　Vice-Cancellario quidem maxi-
mas agendas esse gratias sentio, quod bis uno eodemque
anno, quod perraro accidit, novi procuratoris inscitiam
non æquo animo et facillima humanitate tantum pertulit
sed judicio suo et auctoritate compensavit.　Collega vero[b]
meus is fuit in rerum omnium administratione, ut indies
magis sentirem me eum sorte officii juniorem, prudentia
consilio viribus sicut annis aliquanto fortasse seniorem
habere.　Sed in disciplina nostræ civitatis tuenda, mores
et voluntas juvenum ipsorum maximo rerum omnium

---

[b] The late Rev. Thomas Chaffers, B.D., well known as Vice-
Principal of Brasenose College.

adjumento sunt. In nostro enim officio vis imperii parum valet ad utilitatem publicam, nisi animi adsint ad audiendum dociles, ad obedientiam parati, et ad bonos mores amota legum coercitione inclinati. Nec, mehercle, nobis gloriosum esset aut vobis jucundum, compressos tumultus, vindicatam legum majestatem, reos cujuscunque generis comprehensos jactare, si pax et concordia ordinum et boni mores et honestatis amor abessent. Nemo certe nisi qui cum tempestate conflictare, quam in portu navigare mallet, annui magistratus duceret esse, magnum aliquid et inauditum facinus edere, potius quam tuendo innocentes coercendo malitiosos ne quid e corruptione privata res publica detrimenti capiat, curare. Satius est profecto si fieri potest, culpam omnino prohibere quam in noxios animadvertere. Itaque nobis quam maxime gratulamur, quod per totum annum perpauci quidam sive exilio sive majori aliquo supplicio affecti sunt. . . .

In annum magna ex parte quietum incidimus—nihil fere omnino turbæ aut tumultus reminiscor—quod eo magis gratum ferre debemus, quod clamores dissoni usque a Cami ripis auditi illic nobis procuratorias vires non tantum maxima vi oppugnatas, sed debilitatas fractas profligatas nuntiavere. Et nos etiam aliquando perterrefacti sumus, ne ad nostram urbem contagia mali ingravescentis et nondum ut accepimus extincti serperent. . . . . Sed quoniam sororis nostræ ut ita dicam Cantabrigiæ mentionem fecimus, non possumus non recordari luctum illum atque mærorem: quo nuper obruta est Cancellarii[e] morte inopinata, egregii nominis viri, et celeberrimum in antiquissimis regni annalibus locum obtinentis. Nam si ea est hominum inter se necessitudo ut nemo, nisi qui ab humana societate abhorreat, humani aliquid a se alienum putet, si hac conciliatio non homines tantum sed urbes gentes regna inter se constringit,

[e] Hugh, Duke of Northumberland.

quanto arctior inter geminas universitates debet esse amoris
ac studiorum conjunctio. Itaque et audita morte Cancellarii condoluimus, et nunc iidem lætamur, Principem illus-
trissimum, Regium Conjugem afflictam Academiam erigere
ac consolari dignatum esse. Quem nostris etiam adscrip-
tum et honestissimo gradu decoratum grato animo recor-
damur, nec dubitamus quin quicquid dignitatis præsidii
honoris in Regio Cancellario litterarum fautore munificen-
tissimoque artium patrono insit, ejus nos quoque non ut
alienos sed ut suæ etiam tutelæ pro re et parte nostra par-
ticipes fore.

Annum vero cætera prosperum, lugubrem ante omnia
fecit et funestum fames et pestis vi per multa sæcula inau-
dita Hiberniam devastans. Nos etiam nonnihil passi
sumus et patimur, sed nuntii ab extremis ejus insulæ oris
egenæ semper jam vero ope destitutæ indies magis terrifici,
ululatus mortis, salutis desperatio mali quemque sui imme-
morem, ad levandas Hiberniæ miserias accendit. Causa
morbi diu quæsita, sive ex malignitate cœli oriundi sive ex
insectorum multitudine illati, omnes adhuc fefellit. Nunquam vanior fuit philosophorum jactatio, nunquam largior
totius ut ita dicam orbis terrarum misericordia. Ab re-
motissimis imperii fere infiniti oris, a sociis gentibus, a civi-
bus, a coloniis immensa pecuniæ tritici hordei omnis generis
cibi subsidia ad levandam Hiberniæ inopiam confluentia
audivimus. In hac pietatis contentione, testor libens eum
animum juvenum nostrorum fuisse, ut inter primos ultro
miseris succurrere atque opitulari decernerent; neque id
pro facultatibus tantum sed effusiori quadam liberalitate,
ita ut multi voluptatibus, immo necessariis qui perhibentur
sumptibus, modum imponerent, ne quis sive dignus sive in-
dignus, ipsis divitibus, egeret. Ita solatia quidem si non
remedia, morbo quæsivimus, sed ea est mali natura ut spem
salutis non in nostra ipsorum opera sed in Dei Opt. Max.
præsidio ponamus. Idcirco solemnes supplicationes habitæ

sunt ad pacem Dei exorandam, et jejunia cum singulari cleri populique consensu indicta et observata—ecclesiæ ubique maximis iram divinam deprecantium multitudinibus celebratæ, conciones ad caritatem ad pœnitentiam ad bona opera cohortantes habitæ. Et etiam nunc acies ferri hebetari videtur, commeatus ab occidente, annona aliquanto laxior, vis februm in nonnullis locis pigrior, veris scri quidem sed non infausti temperies spem rerum omnium abundantiæ facere.

Restat ut res anno procuratorio gestas breviter recenseam. Inter has semper moris fuit libros a prelo Academico editos enumerare; nec id quidem injuria, quoniam hoc si non præcipuum at domesticum saltem esse videtur opus Academiæ, aut nova in quoque doctrinæ genere proferre, aut antiqua emendatiora, et ad auctoris manum, quantum ex subsidiis superstitibus colligi potest, propius accedentia edere. Hunc annum numero sterilem, dignitate et gravitate operum quæ publici juris facta sunt, haud infecundum habemus. Libri de quibus operæ pretium erit dicere duo sunt. Alter, Demosthenis editio a Dindorfio concinnata et emendata. Alter Reliquiarum Sacrarum a venerabili viro Collegii S. Magdalenæ Præside, editio secunda. Vellem equidem, magnopere novam hanc.eloquentissimi omnium oratorum editionem animos juvenum nostrorum ad perlegendum opera summi dicendi artificis, immo ad imitandam industriam posse excitare. Animadverti enim, non sine admiratione et dolore, quum nomina eorum, qui honestiorem in litteris humanioribus locum ambibant officii mei jure accipiebam, ne unum quidem nisi me memoria mea fefellit Demosthenis aut Ciceronis orationes cognitas habere professum esse. Quod et per se mirum est, et nobis qui in diligenti Græcorum exemplarium studio laudem præcipue quærimus, satis credo, inhonestum. Vereor tamen ne malum hoc et incuria radices altius egerit, quam cui nova libri editione speremus mederi. Vereor ne adolescentes

B b

nostri, aut temporum angustiis, aut exilitate quadam doctrinæ, aut ipsa studiorum ratione a splendidissimis ingenii
atque eloquentiæ monumentis excludantur. Haud inopia
librorum, sed inopia legentium laboratur. Patent omnibus
plures Demosthenis qualescunque orationum editiones, patent
haud ita magno pretio annotationes virorum doctorum a
Gothofredo Shæfero in unum corpus dejectæ, omnigenaque
doctrina refertæ; nemo tamen Demosthenem perlegit,
nemo in historia Demosthenis aut Ciceronis temporum,
uberrima exemplis, ad cognoscendum gratissima versatur.
Sperarem equidem, si fieri posset, hoc dedecus a nobis
amoveri: sed ad alterum librum transeo. Vir[d] omni
laude major, et jam nonagesimo ætatis anno exacto,
alteram reliquiarum sacrarum post triginta annos editionem denuo ornatam emendatamque procudit. In quo
dubito utrum fortunam viri magis debeamus admirari, qui
etiam vivus et superstes famæ honorisque pii præmia, quibus
mortuos prosequimur videtur præcepisse, an indolem atque
industriam, quæ tantos doctrinæ fructus cumulavit, et per
tot annos ab opere instituto nunquam descivit. Quod eo
magis est admirabile, quod cum primum animum sacrarum
litterarum studio intendebat, fere neminem aut laborum
socium aut operæ cohortatorem habuit; jam vero cum
plurimi nostrum iisdem studiis incumbere cœperunt, ipse
se facile omnium principem et ducem viæ paratum obtulit.
Vir vere catholicæ mentis, et qui nos ad mores catholicos
jure quodam et exemplo suo possit revocare. Altera scilicet
manu ecclesiam patrum ab Apostolicis temporibus proxi-
morum, altera Scotorum oppressam spoliatam disjectam
amplectitur; ipse totus noster est. Et mihi quidem præcipue placuit, quod opus suum ultimo limæ labore exor-
natum quasi jam vitæ suæ munere absoluto sacro Scoticæ
ecclesiæ clero constituit dicare. "Aurea hæc," inquit, "pri-

---

[d] Rev. Dr. Routh, late President of Magdalen College.

orum sæculorum scripta misi ad vos, Venerandi Patres, qui laude morum antiquorum, disciplinæ Apostolicæ, fidei Catholicæ floretis. Sunt hæ quidem reliquiæ fragmenta tantum flebilis naufragii, et humilis atque depressæ ecclesiæ monumenta, sed eo magis vobis offerenda quia et ipsi fortuna minus prospera utimini." Quis non amabile illud et dulce fideique plenum viri ingenium admiretur aut omen illud quo ad finem dedicationis meliora tempora præsagire ausus est, nolit accipere? "Faustum omen accipite. Communionem potissimum vestram voluit esse ecclesiæ Novo-Anglicæ matricem, summus ille ecclesiarum pater et dominus, Dominus et Deus noster Jesus Christus. Magnum certe clarumque Divinæ benevolentiæ indicium. Quo etiam provisum est, ut cui genti vos ipsi successionem vestram sacerdotalem debetis, in ejus progenie parem referatis gratiam, et ipsi emineatis nequaquam minimi in principibus Judæ. Valete."

Vereor ne longior sim quam pro norma orationis meæ, et patientiam vestram jam diu defatigaverim. Sed una adhuc res mihi nequaquam est prætereunda. Leges et regulas Instituti Tayloriani plus semel propositas, et a vestra prudentia et voluntate rejectas, unum tandem in corpus redegimus et suffragiis vestris commendavimus. Arduum scilicet erat et perdifficile rem novam et intentatam et a nobis quodam tenus alienam ad opiniones omnium et voluntates accommodare. Nos autem pro viribus nostris in eo tantum elaboravimus, ut quam plurimis vestrum placeremus, et utilitati totius Academiæ quantum in nobis situm est consuleremus. Ea utilitas qualis et quanta sit futura libera omnibus est existimatio. Sunt qui timeant, sunt etiam qui sperent. Equidem nec nimis spero nec magnopere timeo. Dissentio prorsus ab iis, qui neotericorum scripta qualiacunque sive nostra sive aliena in studiorum cursu et formula Examinationis volunt includere; dissentio non minus ab iis, qui animos juvenum a neotericorum scriptis deterrendos et ad antiqua revocandos esse censent. Suo quisque sæculo nascimur, vita cuique quotidiana est vivenda, nostri officii est animos in tutelam nostram permissos in optimis quibusque studiis instituere, sed ad omnia armare, immo etiam pessimis aliquando, sicut milites hosti cum quo dimicaturi sunt, assuefacere. Credo equidem si commercia hominum hodierna, si societatis fœdera indies conjunctiora, si facilitatem huc illuc commeandi admirabilem et patribus nostris ignotam contemplamur, haud nos pœnitebit, linguarum doctrinarumque nostri ipsorum temporis studia in nostram potestatem et moderationem recepisse. Sed de quæstione universa jamdudum judicavit Universitas, magnificæ istius hæreditatis cretione unde tota novi Instituti impensa deprompta est. Nostri fuit in legibus, quibus res nova administranda est, ferendis, voluntati et commodo vestro consulere. Non est cur vos longiori oratione moremur et in publica commoda peccemus.

Itaque, quod bonum felix faustumque sit, officia atque insignia nostra successoribus nostris commendamus.

APPENDIX II.

ORATIO CENSORIA IN REFECTORIO ÆDIS CHRISTI HABITA POST OBITUM THOMÆ GAISFORD S.T.P. ÆDIS CHRISTI DECANI: NECNON REGII GRÆC. LING. PROFESSORIS, TERM. MICH. EXEUNTE MDCCCLV.

PLUS semel mihi accidit exeunte anno orationem lugubrem et funestam habere. Neque temporum vices, aut fortunam meam adhuc conquestus sum, si mihi, tum erga eos qui nobiscum familiariter versati, et mihi ipsi conjunctissimi immatura morte decesserunt, tum eos qui fama rerum gestarum noti ætate remotiores Ædi Nostræ Academiæque universæ decori et præsidio fuere, hoc pietatis officium suscipiendum erat; nisi quod ingenium materia dignum et vires oneri sustentando pares desideravi. Sperabam vero hodiernum munus, quod invito nec tamen dulcedinem ejus abnuenti fungendum est, alii cuivis mandatum fore. Sperabam me, qui usque a tyrocinio primo, unius tantum Decani meminerim, eum a quo tot tantisque beneficiis cumulatus fui, ætate quidem provectiorem, sed viribus animi corporisque florentem, in sua sede relicturum esse. Sperabam quamvis rerum humanarum haud immemor, me saltem sub nullo alio Præside hujusce Ædis administrationis participem fore. Hoc enim in me est præcipuum et singulare. Nonnulli vestrum qui adestis jamdudum hanc ædem domicilio habueratis, antequam ego ad eam accessi. Maxima vero pars, sub eodem Decano, quod de me prædicavi, civitatem nostram nacti estis sub iisdem auspiciis ad hunc fere diem munere quisque suo qualicumque defuncti·

Sed ut ea tenus vestræ conditionis socius fui, ita ad eos ætate proximus accedo, qui alias hujusce Ædis vicissitudines, alienam auctoritatem, alia regna possint recordari. Ex hac frequentia ni fallor primus nostrorum numero manu ejus adscriptus sum, ultimus a latere jam moribundo discessi. Temporis quod interfuit memoria, tam arcta familiaritate viri eximii commendata et consecrata, tanta me recolentem beneficiorum multitudine oppressit, ut qui eum optimo jure in ore et mente habere deberem, nemini non libenter partes hodiernas concederem. Quippe persæpe non magis rerum inopia quam vehementia affectuum impedita hæret mens et laborat oratio, et multo pronius est vanum dicendo fingere quam vero satisfacere desiderio.

Sed ne circa nos nostramque ipsorum ægritudinem diutius commoremur, ab inutili dolore deducendi et avocandi sumus ut vitam et labores ejus quem deflemus commemorare, immo indolem et imaginem aliqua ex parte et pro viribus repræsentare possimus. Unicus erat si quis alius, Academiæ filius, almæ matris alumnus. Nutricem ingenii juvenilis, fautricem virium, singulari quadem fide, ut ita dicam

$$\grave{\epsilon}\kappa\tau\acute{\iota}\nu\omega\nu\ \kappa\alpha\lambda\grave{\alpha}\varsigma\ \tau\rho\phi\acute{\alpha}\varsigma$$

adulti ingenii fructibus nutrivit, et nomine suo tutatus est. In privata schola Wintoniæ sub magistro veteris disciplinæ litterarum elementis imbutus, doctrinam accuratiorem potius quam diffusiorem, dotes animi admirabiles et incredibilem industriam ad nostra studia et exercitationes contulit. Superest adhuc apud nos, et diu supersit, vir venerabilis qui multa de ejus vita quotidiana et moribus possit commemorare. Supersunt pauci, unum et alterum redeuntes anni abstulere, et haud diu erit, quum tyrocinii ejus et adolescentiæ nomen et imago fortasse exoleverit. Itaque pergratum est, amici et sodalis, qui nuper ipse decessit et quem unice diligebat, testimonium proferre et verba

usurpare. "Quinque eramus arctissimis amicitiæ vinclis
conjuncti. Satis erit hæc nomina transcripsisse, ut horas
feliciter actas, festivos sermones, studiorum consortium,
litterarum disceptationes in mentem revocem et jam fere
oblivione evanescentia repræsentem. Hos inter homines,
si quid in me pravi erat emendatum, si quid boni auctum,
si quid infirmi confirmatum testor. Multorum quidem
comitum et jucundæ sed infructuosæ societatis diu me
pœnituit, et tempus in alia quavis consuetudine consumptum
vellem, dies vero cum his sociis et præcipue cum nostro
actos semper lucro apposui." Erant tunc temporis neque
cidem ad honores aditus, neque eadem ingenii præmia et
industriæ incitamentä. Itaque et ipse palmas hodie stu-
diosis propositas, et nos factorum monumenta desideramus.
Sed in eo fortasse id habuit commodi, quod ingenium ejus
libero spatio evagari, et se quocunque vellet convertere,
nullo studiorum curriculo præfinito et nullis impeditum
cancellis potuit. Sed suo ipsius judicio et voluntate, ipsa
natura jubente, ad ea studia quæ tum apud nos in maximo
honore erant ferebatur. Itaque imprimis accuratiori linguæ
Græcæ scientiæ totum se dedit, et hanc sibi provinciam,
quam senior tanta cum laude exornavit, adhuc adolescens
exoptaverat. Primum ingenii specimen et laboris fructum,
perelegantem Electræ Euripidis editionem, quod et con-
sentaneum erat eam vitæ rationem instituenti et modestiam
viri coarguit, in usum puerorum, nisi Westmonasterienses
alumni nomen dedignentur, rogatus ut accepi dedicavit.
Quas deinde per quinquaginta fere annos veterum auctorum
editiones, grammaticorum philosophorum poetarum his-
toricorum exemplaria, quot volumina intermissa nunquam
serie publici juris fecit, contra patientiam vestram peccarem,
et in ignota fortasse nonnullis vestrum materie versarer si
tantum enumerare, nedum aliqua ex facte uniuscujusque
merita examinare instituerem. Neque enim iis tantum auctoribus qui sunt in manibus et quotidiano usu familiares,

quales sunt Græcorum poetarum optimi, Homerus Euripides Sophocles; inter Historicos Herodotus; philosophos Aristoteles, et in quo de provincia sua decessit, Tullius, operam impendebat, sed ex arcanis et pulvere Bibliothecarum tum domi tum foris quæque cognitione dignissima admirabili quadam sagacitate eruebat. In quo, quanquam apud nos qui tritam et usitatam studiorum orbitam sequamur magni merito auctoritas ejus habebatur, multo tamen majori gloria apud exteros et doctissimum quemque judicem florebat. Fama erat apud omnes Europæ universitates præcipua, et ea inter doctos prima cura, ut de Decano nostro sciscitarentur; ita ut mihi ipsi nonnihil aliquando accederet honoris, cum me ejus discipulum et ejusdem Ædis alumnum profiterer. Sed cum utilitati eruditissimorum, potius quam oblectationi vulgi consuleret, reprehendebant harum litterarum rudes, quod in sua etiam provincia perpaucos auctores aut insigni commentariorum copia aut ulla interpretationis novitate illustrasset. Mirabantur virum ea ingenii ubertate, ea doctrinæ copia, iis industriæ quas prima adolescentia compararat subsidiis in mendis et lituris codicum, in litterarum et syllabarum minutiis demersum atque occupatum fuisse. Inceptis et operum labore obstupescebant, sed rem molimine indignam judicabant. Fefellit eos sententia viri deliberata, et lex quam sibi vitæ cursum ineunti præscripserat, alios jamdudum Græcis et Latinis auctoribus, quod ad Commentarios et Annotationes attinet, satisfecisse aut satisfacturos, sibi aliam esse viam neque de Græcis litteris se male meriturum esse si id potissimum curaret, ut veterum scripta quæ in tutamen suum receperat, indies emendatiora, novis subsidiis munita, et ad manum et mentem auctoris quam proxime accedentia exhiberet. His studiis deditum, et hoc sibi fine proposito, jure suo Professoris Regii dignitatem suscepisse nemo non confessus est. Hanc sibi Professor provinciam peculiarem depoposcit, hoc munus vitæ præcipuum promisit. Itaque quamquam nemo minus opinionis hominum studiosus, nemo Professoriam dignitatem, si non vocis laterumque contentione, at oleo et industria, si non coronæ plausibus, at doctorum judicio melius sustentavit. Quas virtutes in scribendo, quantam subtilitatem in corrigendo, quantam modestiam in judicando adhibebat vererer equidem describere nisi alienam laudem in suum præconium convertere liceret. Inter Anglicanos auctores Pearsonum præcipuo honore colebat; haud mirum igitur si e Pearsoni laudatione multa in ipsius honorem convenirent. "Nihil in his Annotationibus ambitiose scriptum est; nulla inest gloriolæ quæ ex doctrinæ ostentatione quæri solet captatio; emendationes simpliciter propositæ sunt, et verba quemadmodum ex nostri sententia legi debent nude proferuntur; virorum doctorum, quorum acumen aut sollertia profuit, emendationes et observata strictim apponuntur, prave aut temere eorum excogitatis leni et modesta animadversione adhibita." Si vestigia aliorum qui iisdem studiis operam dederant sequebatur, ipsum iterum loquentem audiamus; "Laudi potius dandum quam vitio vertendum quod in eadem cum aliis eorundem studiorum cursu valentibus inciderit." Neque frustra hæc in lucem edita quis existimet, nam indignum erat, ut tantus labor totque vigiliarum fructus incassum perirent; deinde memorabili exemplo ostendendum erat quantopere in scriptis veterum auctorum legendis pensitandisque elaborandum sit, si quis litterarum studiosus idem honoris culmen, in quod sudando evasit noster attingere velit.

Sed cuique sua est jactura, suus dolor, et nos in hac æde ubi adhuc adesse et præsidere videtur, Decani propius quam Regii Professoris linguæ Græcæ contingit memoria. Florente ætate integrisque animi corporisque viribus ad gubernaculum hujus ædis accessit: dignitatem et honorem Decanatus si non invitus suscepit, at nulla certe cupiditate exoptaverat, aut mala arte ambiverat Erat enim jamdudum eo loco constitutus, iis fortunæ beneficiis cumulatus, in quibus quivis, nedum vir singularis temperantiæ et modestiæ facile posset quiescere, et cui, ne ab episcopali quidem apice quem oblatum declinavit, aliquid splendoris potuisset accedere. Sed quum longinqua commoratio et diuturna absentia Canonico Dunelmensi necessaria vitæ et studiorum rationes conturbabat, magnificentiam et res opimas ejus ecclesiæ cathedralis cœlo nostro societate doctorum hominum subsidiis Bibliothecæ publicæ, quibus carere non poterat, otio et quiete umbra et lucis peramœnis Academiæ libenter commutavit. Ubicunque esset mente tamen et voluntate ad hanc œdem revertebatur, Decanatus honorem et molestias alii cuivis concessurus si modo in inferiorem locum liceret descendere. Sed ubi nullus huic spei exitus expediri videbatur, multa gravatus in hanc sedem ascendit ubi post administrationem quatuor et viginti annorum e vivis excessit. Et quamquam pristinæ hujus Ædis vix pares fuimus, quamquam unius Decani quem ipse patronum colebat nomen omnium qui eum secuti sunt fulgore quodam suo obscuravit, nemo tamen dubitavit quin Decanum eximiis virtutibus præditum et felicia Decanatus tempora defleamus. Nemo ei ingenii constantiæ justitiæ laudem invidebit; indolem conciliandæ et regendæ juventuti minus aptam et duritiam quandam imperii, sunt qui objectaverint. Profecto si ad opiniones hominum exigendus sit, res lege non arbitrio, ratione certa non voluntate administrandas esse duxit. In quo si quis inerat error, idem erat erga omnes: gratiæ odii favoris simultatis aberat suspicio. Omnia in eo sincera saltem et aperta fuere. Crimina etiam gravissima, in quæ instituenda erat quæstio, delitescere potius quam inhonestis artibus detegi maluit. Testimonia non quorumvis in aurem insusurranda; sed spectatorum hominum palam recitanda esse duxit, si de quo forte judicandum erat, ne dicam animadvertendum. Ab omni delatorum turpitudine, non tantum consilio sed ipsa cogitatione

abhorruit. Qui vero severitatis accusant, veram viri natu-
ram et indolem prorsus ignorant. Paucorum hominum est
et perrarœ felicitatis ita leges et disciplinam vindicare, ut iis,
de quibus cognoscendum sit placeas, neque mirum si ii de
quibus judex constitutus es male de te judicent. Itaque
difficile erat, in necessaria rerum administratione in admo-
nendo coercendo castigando male feriatos et minus obse-
quentes, offensiones omnium evitare, et in multorum animis
fortasse Decani nostri memoria cum quadam tristitiœ et
inclementiœ specie conjuncta erit.

Sed nescio an in alio homine frontem animo, speciem
veritati magis contrariam viderim. Hœ quidem omnibus
patebant ; de illis vero, de humanitate ejus erga omnes, festi-
vitate sermonum, quam leniter de delictis etiam gravioribus
judicabat, quam facilis ad ignoscendum, quam paratus ad
excusandum fuit, quam sœpe defensoris partes agebat, et
festinationem nostram mora interposita, iracundiam aliquanto consilio temperabat, de his ad eos testes provocan-
dum est qui eo familiarissime utebantur.

Sed si quid in ejus indole erat severitatis, id omne ante
mortem exuerat. Et nos qui moribundo fere, et in do-
mestico luctu, nec tamen officii oblito per ultimos illos dies
aderamus, singularem illam indulgentiam et morum dulcedinem memoriis fovebimus. Et illi fortasse, qui ad nos
eo die matriculandi advenerant, quos tam benigne accepit,
tam leniter, si forte verecundia tanti viri et infans pudor
libere profari vetuit, adjuvit et lapsos erexit, famam si quœ
superest severitatis et inclementiœ increduli mirabuntur.
Neque ego qui solus aderam, cum illorum nomina vix a me
ipso adjutus et tremebunda manu nostro numero adscripsit,
placidi illius vultus et lumine quodam caritatis offusi obli-
viscar.

Fama tandem divulgata sedem Decani vacuam esse,
eadem omnium desideria iidem luctus, et non Decanum
modo sed Ædis patrem ferali pompa deducere et sepulcro

condere videbamur. Mortuus est tempore opportuno sibi sed luctuoso nobis, et fortasse discrimina temporum, pericula Universitatis, quæ diu præsagiverat animo, mutata rerum conditio, senescenti ingrata quanquam necessaria aliquid acerbi ægro et adfecto attulerant.

Nec mihi dubium quin Universitate omnibus patefacta, in cæterorum collegiorum æmulatione certamen anceps viribus impares conditionibus iniquis, et optimo quoque milite aliena fortasse castra affectante, inituri simus. Licet saltem dicere, Τῆς ἡμετέρας ἀρχῆς, ἣν καὶ παυθῇ, οὐκ ἀθυμοῦμεν τὴν τελευτήν. Ἡγεμονίαν satis amplam et diu defensam aut digniori concedemus, aut quod equidem non despero, si quid in auctoritate Decani nostri consilio viribus inest præsidii, melioribus auspiciis et exitu opinione lætiori certabimus.

𝕷𝖆𝖚𝖘 𝕯𝖊𝖔.

𝔓𝔯𝔦𝔫𝔱𝔢𝔡 𝔟𝔶 𝔓𝔞𝔯𝔨𝔢𝔯 𝔞𝔫𝔡 ℭ𝔬., ℭ𝔯𝔬𝔴𝔫 𝔜𝔞𝔯𝔡, 𝔒𝔵𝔣𝔬𝔯𝔡.

LaVergne, TN USA
28 October 2009
162337LV00003B/68/A